David Tuffley

# Software Requirements: Closing The User-Developer Gap

David Tuffley

# Software Requirements: Closing The User-Developer Gap

## Technical Writer as Facilitator between User and Developer During the Software Requirements Analysis Phase

VDM Verlag Dr. Müller

## Imprint

Bibliographic information by the German National Library: The German National Library lists this publication at the German National Bibliography; detailed bibliographic information is available on the Internet at http://dnb.d-nb.de.



Cover image: www.purestockx.com

Publisher:
VDM Verlag Dr. Müller Aktiengesellschaft & Co. KG , Dudweiler Landstr. 125 a, 66123 Saarbrücken, Germany,
Phone +49 681 9100-698, Fax +49 681 9100-988,
Email: info@vdm-verlag.de

Zugl.: Brisbane, Griffith University, Research, Diss., 2005



Produced in USA and UK by:
Lightning Source Inc., La Vergne, Tennessee, USA
Lightning Source UK Ltd., Milton Keynes, UK
BookSurge LLC, 5341 Dorchester Road, Suite 16, North Charleston, SC 29418, USA

**ISBN: 978-3-639-00783-1**

This work is dedicated to my second self,
and best earthly companion

Angela

And our beautiful children

John and Nicola

Acknowledgments

Special thanks are due to my wife Angela for her unwavering and unconditional support and encouragement.

Special thanks also to my principle supervisor Sue Nielsen for her guidance and mentoring. Sue has not only provided first-rate academic support throughout my M Phil research, but also sincere friendship and advice about life in general.

I would also like to thank my second supervisor Liisa von Hellens for her ongoing support during the research and preparation of this work.

# Contents

## Figures



## Tables

# 1. Introduction

## *1.1. Overview of work*

This work begins by considering the well documented, but not so well understood problem in Information Systems research that poor system usability is caused, at least in part, by not getting the system requirements right. It will explore the proposition that employing a technical writer as a facilitator in the requirements analysis process may lead to improved system usability, by helping to bridge the cultural gap between users and developers that research has suggested, may be the cause of problems in eliciting user requirements.

It seeks to better understand the nature of the gap that apparently exists between users and developers that prevents the parties from communicating clearly and fully enough during the requirements analysis phase of systems development. With a better understanding of the gap, this work examines whether having a technical writer act as a facilitator of communication might lead to better communication, with the result that a more comprehensive understanding of the user's real needs is derived. The technical writer appears to be well suited to this role because they understand technical issues, and routinely translate technical language into everyday language that non-technical people can understand.

In pursuit of these objectives, an action research project was undertaken at a large Australian energy retail organisation over a 12 month period. The researcher adopts the role of a contract technical writer whose task is to develop a statement of user requirements for an actual development project for which both the risk of failure, and cost of failure was considered unacceptably high. To ensure the efficacy of the research, only the client organisation's senior management were aware of the research project. To the project participants the researcher was a normal technical writer. This avoids the causing the participants to behave differently from a normal development project. This may not be strictly necessary for an action researcher, but it was deemed prudent under these circumstances, to minimise the risk of the participants behaving differently for the researcher.

## *1.2. Statement of the problem*

The problem can be summed up by asking "can IS usability be improved by having a technical writer facilitate stakeholder communication during the development of the requirements specification?"

### 1.2.1. Significance of the problem

The Standish Group's widely circulated 1995 Chaos Report (Standish Group, 1995) cites that the U.S. government and businesses spent $81 billion on cancelled software projects, and another $59 billion for budget overruns. Their survey asserted that in the United States, barely one-sixth of all projects were completed on time and within budget, nearly one third of all projects were cancelled outright, and well over half were considered "challenged." Of the challenged or cancelled projects, the average project was 189 percent over budget, 222 percent behind schedule, and contained only 61 percent of the originally specified features. The Standish Group study identified factors that had the potential to improve a project's chance of success. These include: 1) User Involvement, 2) Executive Management Support, 3) Clear Statement of Requirements, and 4) Proper Planning. The participants in the study identified *Incomplete Requirements* and *Lack Of User Involvement* as two most common factors that cause projects to fail or be cancelled.

While this whole situation has generally improved in subsequent years since the Standish group report (Software Engineering Institute: 1, 2003) there is still considerable cause for concern as the failure rate for projects is still unacceptably high. This SEI report shows that the percentage of failed projects has dropped by 3% between the years 1994 and the year 2000.

Kensing, Simonsen and Bødker (1996), basing their assertion on earlier, widely recognised work by Boehm (1981), and Lyytinen and Hirschheim (1987), come to a similar conclusion, indicating that a large proportion of systems installed into organisations are not used. This does not include systems that were abandoned during development. The distinction is made between the two categories of failed systems to focus on the cause(s) of systems that are not used because in some way they do not meet the requirements of its intended users. 'Failed' in this context does not imply that the system does not conform to its original specification, or that it contains significant defects, only that the system does not meet the user's requirements.

As far back as 1987, Lyytinen and Hirschheim (1987) indicated that the primary reason for the non-implementation of systems is that the developer had not 'got the requirements right' (pg. 6). While it might be self-evident that a system founded on incorrect assumptions is likely to fail, it is not so obvious why developers do not get the requirements right.

More recently, Firesmith (2003) discusses how bad requirements causes failures. He points to requirements problems as the single number one cause of project failure. His research clearly indicates that requirements problems that lead to projects that are significantly over budget, significantly past schedule, significantly reduced scope, produced poor quality applications, and are not significantly used once delivered, or ultimately cancelled.

Given the growing reliance of commerce, industry, government and education on information systems to support mission-critical aspects of their operations, it is a high-magnitude problem that results in the waste of hundreds of person years and possibly billions of dollars each calendar year around the world. The significance of the problem is compounded for the organisations involved through a heightened risk of litigation, payment for damages and lost earnings that accrue through failed systems.

Indeed the system development project that is the subject of the research event described in this work had the potential to cost the client organisation millions of dollars in lost earnings and loss of customer goodwill should the required system fail. The perceived risk of system failure was the primary reason the research event was allowed to take place. Not only is the significance of the problem recognised in academic research; it is also very visible to client organisations.

### 1.2.2. Context of the problem

Baster et al (2001) identify what they call the Technology gap (B-T gap) in which technology specialists lack the domain expertise to react rapidly to changes in the business environment, while business users lack the technology skills to maintain the systems.

This existence of this gap has been recognised at least since the 1990's. Significant differences between IS developers and users have been observed by Feeny, Earl and Edwards (1996). Differences in the way they think and act is likely to make it difficult for these parties to communicate, in the way that people of different socio-economic or cultural backgrounds are likely to have difficulty in establishing common ground and mutual understanding. These differences are likely to result in poor or inhibited communication between the IS developer and the user during the requirements gathering process. A natural consequence of this difficulty in establishing common ground and mutual understanding is likely to be an incomplete or poorly defined statement of user requirements. Systems subsequently developed on such a foundation is therefore unlikely to meet the user's needs and will in all likelihood be abandoned or substantially reworked.

The need for IS developers and users to collaborate was recognised by Lawrance and Lorsch (1967), and later Galbraith (1977) when they suggested a range of integrative processes that can bridge the cultural gap and effectively integrate these different styles in thinking and behaving. According to Feeny, Earl and Edwards (1996), these integrative processes include the ETHICS model for participative systems development (Mumford), Joint Application Development (Raghavan, Zelesnik and Ford) and the use of particular people as integrators, such as the 'hybrid manager' investigated by Earl and Skryme. The literature indicates that where used appropriately, integrative processes are successful in improving the level of collaboration and effective communication between developers and users.

## *1.3. Research objectives*

Based on the academic literature, it appears that many systems development projects fail because the developers did not 'get the requirements right'. As discussed in Context of problem above, one factor contributing to this is a lack of understanding between the developers of the system and those who are to use it. This lack of understanding leads to poor communication between the stakeholders in the same way that people from different cultures might have difficulties communicating with each other. In their widely recognised paper *Four Paradigms of Information Systems Development*, Hirschheim and Klein (1989) recognize the broad paradigms that are employed when developing systems. From these, the paradigm of the Analyst as Systems Expert takes into account these differences. Integrative processes have been developed that work to facilitate communication between stakeholders but these processes are often not used, possibly because they pose a threat to a developer's existing ways of doing things, their entrenched culture. The technical writer can adapt the role of Hirschheim and Klein's (1989) paradigm of the Analyst as Facilitator to bridge the gap between developer and user and to improve the perceived usability of systems.

The situation might be summed by saying, there is a gap between developers and users that can inhibit requirements gathering, traditional methods are not particularly effective at bridging this gap, so a facilitator of communication (in this case a technical writer) might improve the communication between the stakeholders, leading to improved usability.

Given the benefits to stakeholders (Management, IS Developer, and User) of determining ways in which the quality of information systems may be improved, the following research objectives are established:

To better understand the nature of the 'gap' that apparently exists between users and developers of systems, especially in relation to the activity of gathering of user requirements. This objective relates to a key-contributing factor to systems failure in the sense that a substandard statement of user requirements is unlikely to result in a system that meets the user's needs.

To examine the role of the technical writer in relation to Hirschheim and Klein's (1989) paradigms of the Analyst as Systems Expert and Analyst as Facilitator. The remaining two paradigms (Analyst as Labour Partisan, and Social Therapist) will also be discussed but in less detail. Inherent in the Analyst as Systems Expert paradigm is the assumption that the developer knows more about systems development than does the user, therefore spending time, effort and money on liaising with users during requirement gathering is seen as unnecessary, even counterproductive. This objective examines whether the technical writer might function in this context as a facilitator of communication between user and developer, in an attempt to bridge the cultural gap. In effect the technical writer might adopt the role of Analyst as Facilitator.

To examine whether system usability (as defined by the SOLE model, Eriksson and Törn, 1991) can be improved by the technical writer acting as a facilitator between user and developer during requirements gathering. Closely related to the previous objective, this objective builds upon the facilitation activity to examine whether real benefits in terms of improved system usability can be derived by having the technical writer act in this capacity. Or put another way, whether a real solution to the problem of system failure as discussed above can be affected by such means.

**To explore factors which influence the problem of developer and user resistance to previously proposed integrative processes** (Participative Design, User Participation, Joint Application Development etc.) by employing an existing member of the development team. This examines the problem of good ideas being ignored where their perceived threat to developer culture and project budget outweighs their perceived benefits. In developer cultures where the Analyst as Systems Expert (Hirschheim and Klein (1989) is the prevailing paradigm, an inexpensive, non-threatening integrative process might be more readily used than processes like Participative Design et al that involve considerable investments of time and resources.

The objectives enumerated above will be linked to the literature review in the next chapter.

## *1.4. Operable Theory*

The Operable Theory was developed in two stages. The *first stage* was performed during the five-year period prior to the researcher entering academia, when he was engaged in commercial practice as a contract technical writer. This work comprised a series of six to 12 month contracts, some of which involved developing the software requirements specification documentation, for a variety of public and private sector organisations.

Initially this work included developing user documentation and training material, and performing unit testing. It was often the case that usability related issues identified by the technical writer during testing would not be addressed. Only explicit defects would be addressed. The anecdotal reasons given for this was that spending time on addressing usability issues had not been budgeted for.

The technical writer became interested in investigating ways in which usability issues could be incorporated into the requirements specification document. The technical writer observed a recurring theme that users and developers often did not communicate effectively, resulting in an incomplete set of user requirements. The consequence of this was a system that did not fully meet the user's needs. Through a process of observation reflection and trial and error, the technical writer developed a strategy in which he used an IEEE-derived software requirements specification template, and acted as a facilitator of communication between stakeholders. These strategic elements have been operationalised to form the basis of the operable theory. Having applied these two strategic elements to several projects, and learning from the experience, resulted in an operable theory that could be tested with some confidence in the context of a formal research project, as described in this work.

While it is not claimed that this earlier work represents action research, there is a clear pattern of reiteration stretching back from the formal research event, in which theory is tested, the results are evaluated, improvements to the theory made in light of lessons learned, then the theory tested again.

The *second stage* in the development of the operable theory was performed when doing the literature review for this project when it was recognised that given the nature and circumstances of the researcher's usual occupation at that time as a technical writer that an action research project was perhaps the most appropriate method to use.

Accordingly the following three dimensions form the basic structure of the theoretical framework:

Technical writer uses IEEE derived user requirements template (see Appendix) to apply a structured and comprehensive approach to process of requirements gathering.

Technical writer acts as facilitator of communication by applying prescribed facilitation practices (see Appendix) derived from Joint Application Development.

The critical elements of action research conducted in five stages; reflection, plan, action/observation, reflection and write-up conclusions. These are described in detail in the Project Stages section. These activities occur reiteratively in the sense that they may be performed more than once during the entire project.

See section 3.5 Research Strategy for detailed discussion on the operable theory.

While the technical writer is the subject of this investigation, it is not intended to assert that only a technical writer could perform the role outlined. This role could also be performed by a variety of personnel, including a business analyst, hybrid manager, relationship manager, IT-user liaison. By whatever name, this intermediary facilitator can be constructively placed in projects where communication breakdowns occur between users and developers.

The technical writer is tested in this project because it was possible to do so under the circumstances. Having the technical writer as the subject of this investigation also follows on from the earlier non-academic investigation into how the usability of systems could be improved performed by the technical writer as a commercial practitioner. In this sense the entire process has involved multiple reiterations in which reflection, planning, action, followed by further reflection was performed. However only the last iteration is described in this project, due to the constraints discussed above.

Note: when the developing this action research strategy, during and after the literature review, the researcher included material that discusses in detail what constitutes valid action research, and what pitfalls should be avoided when conducting action research. One way is to declare the approach before beginning the research event, then demonstrating how the approach has been applied to produce certain results. Doing this helps to avoid the criticism that action research is merely consultancy by another name (Baskerville, 1999).

## *1.5. Contents of Work*

This section provides guidance as to the contents of each chapter.

### 1.5.1. Literature Review (Chapter 2)

Examines and discusses in terms of the research objectives a range of literature relevant to the problem; namely:

What is meant by "culture",

Cultural differences that are perceived to exist between IS developers and users,

Hirschheim and Klein's, (1989) paradigms of IS development; in particular Analyst as Systems Expert and Analyst as Facilitator.

How is a technical writer defined?

Software and IS quality, including the SOLE model.

Integrative processes, those activities that have been developed over decades to address the perceived problem of cultural differences between developers and users causing requirements to be inadequately recognised,

The nature and process of the activity broadly known as Requirements Engineering,

The nature and role of software project documentation,

### 1.5.2. Research approach and methods (Chapter 3)

The research approach chapter surveys a range of approaches, and then describes in detail the action research approach that is considered most appropriate for this project. This approach will be discussed in relation to a critical review of other possible approaches. This is followed by detailed discussion of the research strategy, and the underlying rationale that informs this strategy.

### 1.5.3. Research project (Chapter 4)

The research project chapter is a detailed description of the site itself, how was it selected, who were the participants, and what happened in the course of the research event.

### 1.5.4. Data analysis (Chapter 5)

The data analysis chapter gives results and analysis of the relevant data collected during the 12 months the researcher was on-site, full-time. The data was collected from a combination of the following activities: questionnaire, interviews with participants, the technical writers views, documentary evidence in the form of email, and observations by the researcher.

### 1.5.5. Findings (Chapter 6)

The findings discuss the how the data can be interpreted in relation to the research objectives. Specifically the findings will examine the:

Cultural gap between IS developers and users,

How the paradigms of Analyst as Systems Expert, and Analyst as Facilitator might be used to interpret the data,

What might be an appropriate model of IS quality,

How the process of requirements gathering was previously undertaken by the developer,

What problems have been recognised with existing integrative processes, and those activities previously developed to address the problem.

### 1.5.6. Conclusions (Chapter 7)

This chapter indicates the contribution made by the work to the body of research knowledge, the significance of the findings in relation to the research question, the limitations and strengths or the project, and possible directions for future research.

### 1.5.7. Appendices

Four appendices detail the (a) exact content and structure of the Statement of User Requirements template used in the project, (b) the elements of Joint Application Development used in the project, (c) a report written by the technical writer six months after the system that was the subject of the research project went live, in which the usability of not just this system, but all of the other modules of the overall system, and (d) the questionnaire used in the project.

## *1.6. Key definitions*

For clarity and ease of use, definitions shall be given for the following key terms.

**Analyst as Systems Expert**. The expert in technology, tools and methods of system design and project management. There is but one reality that is both measurable and essentially the same for everyone. The role of the analyst is to develop a system that models this allegedly objective reality to produce a tool used by management to achieve their organisational goals. (Hirschheim and Klein, 1989)

**Analyst as Facilitator**. Came about partly because of the problems inherent with the systems expert paradigm. It recognises the fundamental complexity and subjectivity of human interaction. There is no objective reality, only individual perceptions and interpretations of 'reality'. System requirements are constructed by a continuing process of an organisation defining its objectives. The developer works from the user's perspective and assists them to determine their preferred view of reality. (Hirschheim and Klein, 1989)

**Culture**. The pattern of basic assumptions that a given group has invented, discovered, or developed in learning to cope with its problems of external adaptation and internal integration, and that have worked well-enough to be considered valid, and, therefore to be taught to new members as the correct way to perceive, think and feel in relation to those problems (Avison and Myers, 1995)

**Requirements Engineering**. The process of determining what a software system must do in order to meet the user's requirements. The process can be broken down into four interrelated steps (Herlea, 1996):

Requirements elicitation -- deriving system requirements through direct (verbal) and indirect (inspection of artefacts) communication.

Requirements analysis -- processing the elicited data.

Requirements specification -- formalising the requirements into a structured specification document.

Requirements validation -- ensuring that the requirements contained in the specification meets the needs of the users.

**SURAC.** Statement of User Requirements and Acceptance Criteria.

**Technical writer**. A technical writer in the context of this project is defined as a person who produces systems documentation such as requirements specifications. Examples of other systems documentation include, but is not limited to, project plans, quality plans, design documents, test plans.

**Use quality**. From the SOLE (SOftware Library Evolution) quality model, originally developed by Eriksson and Törn (1991), use quality, is defined by how well the system does what the user wants it to do.

**Users**. From the SOLE model, users are defined as the people who directly use the system by performing various work practices that prepare data and information for the system.

# 2. Literature review

The sections of the literature review are directly related to the research or objectives, as illustrated in the table below. They can be summed by saying , there is a gap between developers and users that can inhibit requirements gathering, traditional methods are not particularly effective at bridging this gap, so a facilitator of communication (in this case a technical writer) might improve the communication between the stakeholders, leading to improved usability.

| Research Objective | Related section of review |
|---|---|
| To better understand the nature of the 'gap' that apparently exists between users and developers of systems, especially in relation to the activity of gathering of user requirements. | Cultural differences that are perceived to exist between IS developers and users, what is known about them, and what are some of the names that have been used to describe them. |
| To examine the role of the technical writer in relation to Hirschheim and Klein's (1989) paradigms of the Analyst as Systems Expert and Analyst as Facilitator. | The role of Technical Writer in relation to Hirschheim and Klein's paradigms of IS development; in particular Analyst as Systems Expert and Analyst as Facilitator. |
| To evaluate whether a system can be made more usable (as defined by the SOLE model) by the technical writer acting as a facilitator between user and developer during requirements gathering. | Information System Quality and Usability. This will discuss an appropriate definition for usability as it applies in the context of this research project. |
| To explore factors which influence the problem of developer and user resistance to previously proposed integrative processes | Integrative processes as promoters of user-developer communication. Integrative processes are those activities that have been developed over decades to address the perceived problem of cultural differences between developers and users causing requirements to be inadequately recognised, |

**Table 1: Mapping of research objectives to literature review sections**

The formal literature review is comprised of the four sections listed above. These are the core sections of the review. Additional review material has been developed in the topic areas listed below. This material is relevant to this research project, but since they can do not relate directly to the research objectives, they have been included as appendices.

- The role of software project documentation
- The nature and scope of requirements engineering
- What do we mean by software quality and is quality?
- Defining the role of the technical writer
- Culture as two systems
- Summary of Literature Review

Cultural differences that are perceived to exist between IS developers and users, what is known about them, and what are some of the names that have been used to describe them. The existence of cultural differences between users and developers is explored for its relevance to understanding the nature of the interaction between them. It is seen that around half of all IS directors consider this gap as their biggest challenge. This is consistent with the earlier findings of Edstrom (1977), Gingras and McLean (1979), and Zmud and Cox (1979) in their discussion on the distinctive cultural styles of IS professionals.

The role of Technical Writer in relation to Hirschheim and Klein's paradigms of IS development; in particular Analyst as Systems Expert and Analyst as Facilitator. Following on is an examination of Hirschheim and Klein's, (1989) paradigms of IS development, focussing on Analyst as Systems Expert and Analyst as Facilitator revealed that the mindset and outlook of the Analyst as Systems Expert, arguably the dominant IS development paradigm, is significantly different from the mindset and outlook of the user. This is in the sense that the Analyst as Systems Expert is an expert in technology, tools and methods of system design and project management - skills that would require a mindset that the user is unlikely to have. The expert's role seeks to minimise where possible reliance on human intuition, judgement and politics - all of which constitutes the user's world. Indeed it might be concluded from this that in organisational contexts in which Analyst as Systems Expert is the prevailing paradigm, the two groups effectively live in different worlds.

It was then seen that recognition of the problems inherent with the systems expert paradigm brought about the Analyst as Facilitator paradigm. This latter recognises the fundamental and deals with the complexity and subjectivity of human interaction. The role of the technical writer was considered in the context of the Analyst as Facilitator.

**Information System Quality and Usability**. This will discuss an appropriate definition for usability as it applies in the context of this research project. The review examines the broad areas of software and IS quality in order to better understand what constitutes quality and how can it be recognised in relation to the results of the research event. The literature suggests that quality be seen in terms of the user and the organisational context in which they operate. This is at odds with the Analyst as Systems Expert paradigm that minimises the user's importance and maximises the technical aspects of the process. This led to identifying the SOLE model as contributing a definition of system usability that could be used for the purpose evaluating the effectiveness or otherwise of having a technical writer as an Analyst as Facilitator.

**Integrative processes as promoters of user-developer communication.** A review is made of the literature relevant to what methodologies have been developed to mitigate the effects of poor user-developer communication -- the so-called integrative processes. These include the ETHICS model for participative systems development, Mumford, 1983, Joint Application Development, Raghavan, Zelesnik and Ford, 1994 and the use of particular people as integrators, such as the 'hybrid manager' investigated by Earl and Skryme 1992. But while it is recognised that these processes have the potential to work given the right conditions, it is also acknowledged by their advocates that they will only work where there is organisational commitment to making them work. And here is the fundamental problem - they are too often perceived by the Analyst as Systems Expert as a threat to their established ways of performing their work, as well as being perceived as being too expensive in terms of scarce project resources. A viable solution is to devise an integrative process that neutralises these problems. The technical writer acting as Analyst as Facilitator may possibly be the answer.

**Additional indirectly relevant review material in appendices**. The formal literature review is comprised of the four sections listed above. These are the core sections of the review. Additional review material has been developed in the topic areas listed below. This material is relevant to this research project, but since they do not relate directly to the research objectives, they have been included as appendices:

- The role of software project documentation
- The nature and scope of requirements engineering
- What do we mean by software quality and what is quality?
- Defining the role of the technical writer
- Culture as two systems

## *2.1. Cultural differences between developer and user*

### 2.1.1. What is meant by 'culture'

Since the primary objective of this work is to better understand the nature of the cultural gap, and since the concept of culture has been so widely defined, it may be worthwhile to consider just what is meant when we use the word 'culture'. Far from there being a standard, commonly agreed definition of culture, this section will briefly explore the broad range of meanings that have been ascribed to the concept of culture.

A useful starting point is Allaire and Firsirotu (1986) who discuss culture in two broad categories; as an ideational system in which culture and societal realms are distinct but interrelated, and as a sociocultural system in which culture is seen as a component of the larger social system, and that are manifested by certain behaviour and the products of that behaviour.

Extended discussion and exploration of this topic can be found in the appendix.

### 2.1.2. Definition of organisational culture

Johnson and Scholes (1999) propose a model for understanding organisational culture that may be useful in understanding the gap. They suggest that the culture of an organisation can be understood by considering six cultural elements grouped like daisy petals around a central paradigm; organisation structure, stories and myths, symbols, rituals and routines, control systems and power structures.

In Johnson and Scholes (1999) model for understanding organisational culture the paradigm is constituted by the assumptions of how the world works, and which those within the organisation implicitly accept. The paradigm offers a framework for comprehending the complexity of the environment in which the organisation exists.

These six elements are described as follows:

**Formal organisational structure**, or the more informal ways in which the organisation works, reflect power structures and delineate important relationships

**Stories**. The stories related by individuals that embed historical events in the present and highlight important events and personalities.

**Symbols** like logos, offices, cars and titles; or the type of language and terminology commonly used; and which become a short-hand representation of the nature of the organisation.

**Routines and Rituals**. The routine ways that members of the organisation behave towards each other, and that link different parts of the organisation. Rituals include training programmes, promotion and judgments that indicate relative importance in the organisation.

**Control systems**, measurement and reward systems that emphasize what is important in the organisation, and which focus attention and activity.

**Power structures**, the most powerful managerial groupings in the organisation are likely to be ones most associated with core assumptions and beliefs about what is important.

The six elements outlined by Johnson and Scholes (1999) constitutes the set of variables that constitute the gap, and provides a detailed model for analysing the nature of the gap. Such an analysis will occur in chapter 7.

Further discussion of cultural differences will occur in the later section on integrative processes where its effects on their implementation are examined.

### 2.1.3. Cultural differences

IS developers apparently possess characteristics that inhibit their working relationship with other members of the organisation. Grindley (1991) did a survey of IS directors and found that 46% reported that the culture gap between IS professionals and business counterparts was their most important challenge in terms of service delivery. 56% believed that the culture gap inhibits their organisation's ability to achieve strategic advantage using IS. Given that 56% of IS directors, or what might be called today chief information officers, is a revealing figure. CIO's in a unique position to evaluate the effectiveness or otherwise of their department. Subordinates would not necessarily be the position to recognise the scope of the problem that is constituted by the cultural gap inhibiting their organisation's ability to implement strategic information systems development.

Grindley explains that the culture gap is manifested by IS professionals and their business counterparts having differing approaches to motivation, goals, language, and problem-solving. These differences brought about not only difficulties in communication, which is an overt manifestation of the gap, but also reveals that the mind set is likely to be different. Mind set can be said to be a covert manifestation of the cultural gap. Having different notions of goal-setting and problem-solving are indicative of these differences. Grindley's findings are consistent with the earlier findings of researchers such as Edstrom (1977), Gingras and McLean (1979), and Zmud and Cox (1979) when they reported on the distinctive ways of thinking and acting of IS professionals. Given the relatively oldage of these studies it is worthwhile to note that despite a comprehensive search of the academic literature, relatively little has been done in recent years that explores this apparently persistent problem.

Taylor-Cummings and Feeny (1997) also highlight the existence of what they call the 'cultural gap' between IS developers and users, a factor which has been blamed for the failure of IT projects since IT projects first began in the 1950s. This cultural gap is widely acknowledged but poorly defined. Definitions of the culture gap are descriptions of the symptoms, rather than the culture gap itself. While it is not well defined, its existence is causing rising alarm among IS management. Taylor-Cummings and Feeny (1997) mention a 1991 Price Waterhouse survey of IT directors in the UK, in which 47% of respondents said this culture gap is their biggest problem. 56% thought the gap was seriously hampering their organisation's efforts to gain strategic advantage.

Taylor-Cummings and Feeny (1997) attempt to define the culture gap between IS developers and users in terms of two metaphors - organisations as cultural systems, and organisations as political systems (Morgan 1986). Taylor-Cummings' and Feeny's (1997) definition is based on concepts of cultures and sub-cultures, diverse interests, conflict and power. This is a useful definition in the sense that it frames the problem in terms of culture. Other definitions discussed in this section have focused on differences in the thought processes of participants, those cognitive elements that comprise differing mind sets. Taylor-Cummings and Feeny recognise the explicit existence of organisational culture, with sub-cultural elements within the broader organisational culture who have competing priorities and interests that then lead to conflict as each subculture attempts to realise their own particular goals and priorities. Power is sought after as a necessary way of achieving goals.

Wang (1994, p1) defines the culture gap as 'a conflict, pervasive yet unnatural, that has mis-aligned the objectives of executive managers and technologists and that impairs or prevents organisations from obtaining a cost-effective return from their investment in information technology'. This statement highlights the nature of the gap in terms of a misalignment of objectives. This is in agreement with Grindley's earlier study that discussed the problem in terms of different approaches to goal setting, problem solving and language. This misalignment of objectives causes impairment of an organisation's achievement of cost-effective systems development because the two categories of stakeholder pulling in different directions.

In recent times this misalignment of strategic objectives, or the differences in language, approaches to goals and problem-solving, has been recognised and discussed in terms of the Business-Technology gap. Baster et al (2001) refer to Business-Technology gap (B-T gap) in terms of technology specialists lacking the domain expertise to react rapidly to changes in the business environment, while business users lack the technology skills to maintain the systems. This is discussing a gap in which the two categories of stakeholder are unable to adequately recognise, understand and accommodate the needs and wishes of the other. Technology specialists are identified as having well-developed skills at implementing technology, but do not have sufficient understanding of the way in which the domain or industry operates at commercial level. Domain specialists on the other hand have well-developed understandings of the commercial realities of their industry, but have only a sketchy understanding of how technology can be applied strategically to believe organisational objectives.

Hornik et al, (2003) highlight that good communication between IS professionals, IS staff and IS users is critical to the successful completion of an IS development project. They point out that the ability to interact with all potential stakeholders in an organisation, to clearly document requirements, and to effectively express ideas has long been recognised by researchers and practitioners as critical success factors.

Mann (2002) notes that there is little literature on the gap between end-users and the IT department. It has been observed that IT personnel have different personality traits than the general population, going some way towards explaining why there is a gap. Martinsons & Chong (1998), and Shore (1998) discusses the important skills required for working in and IT environment, particularly those needed for effective collaboration with end-users.

While there is relatively little academic literature in dealing with the IT user gap, recent practitioner literature is increasingly vocal on the subject. It is recognized in this practitioner literature that a serious gap exists, and that organizations are using a variety of approaches to close it. It is an acknowledged and understood in this literature review that practitioner literature is not strictly admissible, however given the relative scarcity of academic literature on a topic that is of some considerable interest to the practitioner community helps to strengthen the claim that the gap between users and developers is a significant one and worthy of further investigation in an academic sense.

The gap has been characterised in no less than nine ways in the academic and practitioner literature (Mann, 2002). These include:

**Perspective Gap**: when the point-of-view of one stakeholder group is incomplete or ill-conceived. Developers may lose sight of the necessity for Systems to provide value to the business by meeting evolving business goals and that the IT department is not the centre of the universe (Scalet, 2000/2001). Users sometimes lose sight of technology as being a tool, and not an end in itself (Pender, 2000/2001).

**Ownership Gap**: where developers feels a sense of proprietary ownership over the infrastructure, while users feel ownership over the business processes, leading to the demarcation disputes and territorial conflict that strain the relationship and create misunderstandings and misconceptions (Lin & Conford, 2000; Avital & Vandenbosch, 2000). Users can get the impression that developers are technical elitists and developers come to see users as reactionary detractors.

**Cultural Gap**: when the stakeholder groups display different traits, values, working behaviours, and/or priorities due to each group attracting certain kinds of person, or acculturates members in the group. Developers tend to be more introverted, analytical, using rational persuasion to influence others. Business users are usually more extroverted, intuitive and use more sophisticated influence strategies (Shah, et al., 1994; Champy, 1997). Both users and developers tend to adopt the culture of their respective professions.

**Foresight Gap**: where one stakeholder group has greater insight into how the future might unfold, but is unable to communicate that vision convincingly to the other stakeholder group. Developers may be well placed to foresee that a user proposed solution cannot work from a technical point-of-view. Alternately users may be better at determining that a developer proposed solution will not be acceptable to them, or will have a negative impact on some aspect of their operations (Fisher, 1999).

**Communication Gap**: where one stakeholder group simply fails to understand what the other is saying. It is often said by users that Developers have an impenetrable jargon, yet it is also observed that the users may well have their own well-developed jargon. Developers find it difficult to translate the user needs of business units into useful productive systems because they do not understand the business processes and underlying rationale for them. (New Group Will Bridge, 1999; Shah, et al., 1994; McCann, 1995).

**Expectation Gap**: where users have unrealistic expectations about what developers are feasibly able to do. Users have come to expect more from systems because they have generally become more computer literate, or because they have become accustomed to the sometimes heroic efforts of developers to deliver the goods. (Whiting, 1998; Melymuka, 1998). At the same time, developers are sometimes known to make overblown claims as to what they can deliver, expecting all users to be technologically naïve.

**Credibility Gap**: where the past performance of developers has been substandard. This is often attributable to failed development projects, or poor customer service such as a not very helpful helpdesk. (New Group Will Bridge, 1999). From the developer's perspective, they may have found users to be overly demanding and/or resistant to change.

**Appreciation Gap**: where one stakeholder group implicitly feels unappreciated by the other. Developers may form a view that their hard work, long hours and contributions to the organization go unappreciated except when something goes wrong (Mottl, 1999; Ouellette, 1999; Wallace, 1998). There is some suggestion that developers, in some cases, wish to be more involved in business planning, but are not invited to do so (Hayes, 1998).

**Relationship Gap**: where the stakeholder groups do not interact with sufficient frequency to be able to form a viable, constructive relationship as the basis for ongoing work. This might be reinforced by entrenched preconceptions about the other group. (Shah, et al., 1994; Scalet, 2000/2001).

From the literature discussed in this section, it would seem that communication is of fundamental importance, both as an enabler of successful project outcomes, and as an indicator of a gap. Poor communication is cited as one manifestation of a cultural gap between stakeholders (differing approaches to motivation, goals, language, and problem-solving, Grindley, 1991). Taylor-Cummings' and Feeny (1997) discusses the nature of the gap in terms of cultures and sub-cultures, diverse interests, conflict and power. Communication is a consistent factor in each of these elements. Good communication enables the reconciliation of diversion and interests, poor communication makes the problem worse. Wang (1994) discusses the nature of the culture gap in terms of a misalignment of the stake holder's objectives. The communication process necessarily mediates the formulation of objectives and strategic plans.

### 2.1.4. The user-developer communication process

The Information Systems literature has long recognised that user participation during development projects is desirable. (Gallivan and Keil, 2003) Users who are more involved during the requirements determination process are more likely to feel they have a stake in the system, and therefore are more likely to be satisfied with the system. It has been implicitly assumed that any user participation is beneficial, yet this is not necessarily the case. Gallivan and Keil (2003) suggest that project managers and software developers must look beyond the information content that users provide. They should also investigate what information users may not be readily volunteering, and try to create an environment in which users feel free to openly discuss their concerns, regardless of whether these concerns are positive or negative in character.

Gallivan and Keil (2003) acknowledge that user participation in system development is critical to the successful design and implementation of systems, but that it is dangerous to assume that user participation necessarily leads to successful project outcomes. They discuss the concept of power asymmetry between developers and users. Where developers had sanctionary power over users, users would be less inclined to adopt a system that they had jointly designed developers, even when the users had explicitly agreed to use the said system. Ineffective communication occurs when developers have this sanctionary power over users. It makes it more likely that they (the user) will not use a conjointly designed system (Gallivan and Keil 2003).

## 2.2. Role of Technical Writer re Hirschheim and Klein's paradigms

Hirschheim and Klein's, (1989) paradigms of IS development; Analyst as Systems Expert and Analyst as Facilitator is considered in detail. The former in relation to it being a commonly used approach, and the latter in terms of it embodying the necessary facilitation activities to address some of the problems inherent in the former. Hirschheim and Klein explicitly recognise that the facilitator paradigm can be an effective remedy to some of the problems inherent in the expert paradigm.

### 2.2.1. Defining the Technical Writer

Before discussing the possible role of the technical writer in relation to Hirschheim and Klein's paradigms, it will be useful to define what is meant by a technical writer. (See Appendix for additional discussion).

Since the role of the 'technical writer' is central to the whole research project, it is important to clearly define what a technical writer is and does. In the context of this project, a technical writer is defined by the researcher (refer Houp et al below) as a person who produces software development project documentation such as requirements specifications. Examples of other software development project documentation include, but is not limited to, project plans, quality plans, design documents, test plans.
Houp, Pearsall and Tebeaux (2001:6) offer this widely recognized definition that is a more generalized statement of a technical writer's activities that is consistent with the more specific definition offered above: *Technical writers may be viewed as the "funnel" for an organization. We take the technical information of the organization and convert it into everyday language that the average reader may comprehend. The persona or role we adopt when writing, must relate, be on the same level of knowledge, and maintain a relationship with the readers throughout the length of the document.*

Good technical writing entails for the writer to always:

- Know the reader
- Know the objective
- Be simple, direct, and concise

Dobrin (1989) argues against definitions of technical writing that focus only on identifying specific formats, scientific or technical content, or an "objective" style, or those definitions that assume a universal theory of language. Instead of technical writing as information transfer or the simple imparting of facts, Dobrin uses the philosophies of Wittgenstein and Quine as well as the speech act theory of John Searle and Hubert Dreyfus to define technical writing as *writing that accommodates technology to the user* (p. 54). Dobrin (1989) suggests that the role of the technical writer should extend beyond both the act of writing and the written product itself to include *the practices of groups the writer is writing to, writing for, and writing from, as well as the practices of groups in which the writer* is located (p. 58).

Technical writers are often called upon to write software user documentation. In her survey of Australian technical writers, Fisher (1998a) found that in their role as developer of user documentation, the technical writer contributes to the usability of the end product. Fisher (1998a) found that the technical writers' role has been extended beyond their traditional role of simply writing the user manual. These extended activities include producing training material, acting as a user advocate, writing on-line help, error messages, and by helping to design user interfaces. Such extended documentation activities, with the exception of user advocacy, might nonetheless still be considered 'user documentation' in the sense that Torkzadeh and Doll (1993) discuss. To define the user manual as the only form of user documentation is too narrow a definition.

Fisher (1998a) investigated the importance of involving technical writer is early in a software development project. Fisher (1998a) investigated when respondents became involved in the development process. The findings indicate that where the technical writer is involved at or before the design stage they were firstly more likely to be producing on-line help system and error messages, and secondly more likely to be asked by developers to contribute to interface design. A third finding was that the technical writer was more likely to be acting in the role of user advocate.

Miller (1989) observes that technical writing, with its focus on *the rhetoric of the 'world of work,' of commerce and production* is often viewed as a "practical" discipline, with the term "practical" often intended to suggest that technical communication is merely an applied, vocational field rather than one defined through a body of theoretical knowledge (p. 15). Miller argues against this view, saying that while technical writing has a practical side but that it is a field characterized by the prudent application of theoretical knowledge, doing so in specific situations with the wider aim of enhancing the well-being of the organization.

Slack et al (1993) comment that technical communicators (including writers) are viewed by many as simply transmitters of messages or translators of meaning instead of being thought of as *authors* who are instrumental in articulating meaning. They explain that in each of these views *the place of the technical communicator—and of the technical discourse itself—shifts in different relations of power* (p. 14). They suggest that it would be appropriate to *give up the faith that the goal of communication is always clarity and brevity* by claiming that technical communicators need to be sent out *armed* and prepared to take full responsibility for their work (p. 33). Technical communicators can empowered by understanding their roles as articulators of meaning; resulting in *technical communicator as author and [ ... ] technical communication as a discourse that produces an author* (p. 12).

### 2.2.2. Analyst as Systems Expert

Hirschheim and Klein propose that IS developers and users have different assumptions about the nature of the IS development process, and the relationship between users and developers (1989, p1203-1204). These assumptions are based on different views of the world, and are called paradigms.

Reacting to the widespread assumption that IS development is about technical systems with social implications, Hirschheim, Klein and Lyytinen (1995) comment that this is an assumption that sees problems in terms of technical complexity and solutions in terms of ever more sophisticated technical solutions. It has been recognized for some time that human involvement in IS development cannot be reduced to technical issues only. IS development should more properly be viewed as being about social systems, technically implemented. Information technology is a social technology because its existence depends on social institutions like language and various forms of social influence.

In an earlier related work, Hirschheim and Klein (1989, p1203-1210) classify four main IS development paradigms; Analyst as Systems Expert, Analyst as Facilitator, Labour Partisan, and Emancipator. These paradigms are referred to as "generalised story types" which represents possible ways that the role information systems analyst can be conceptualized in their work context (von Hellens, 2001). Beyond this conceptualization, Hirschheim and Klein (1989) describe "classes of behaviour'" that the analyst will exhibit at different stages of IS development. The approach taken by Hirschheim and Klein (1989) is useful in that it allows us to consistently analyze the role of the analyst and the outcomes of software development (von Hellens, 2001).

Critics of Hirschheim and Klein's (1989) do not accept this paradigmatic approach (Chua, 1986). There are emerging ISD paradigms, leading to the development of new methodologies. Some existing methodologies are not able to be related to any of Hirschheim and Klein's paradigms because they span several paradigms (von Hellens, 2001). An additional limitation of Hirschheim and Klein's paradigms is that the contents are imbalanced. The functionalist paradigm has traditional approaches towards ISD, while the other three are rather relatively empty (von Hellens, 2001). Nurminen (1997) proposed an alternative interpretation of the four paradigms and this has brought about a different distributions of the existing ISDs and Information Systems Research (ISR) directions (von Hellens, 2001).

These criticisms notwithstanding, Hirschheim and Klein's (1989) paradigms of system development offer a useful vehicle for the analysis proposed by this research project.

**Analyst as Systems Expert**. Such a role is that of the expert in technology, tools and methods of system design and project management. But while their role aims to make systems development more formal and rational, minimising where possible reliance on human intuition, judgement and politics, these human factors are in practice virtually impossible to dispense with. At some point in the requirements gathering process, the users and management need to articulate their needs to the developers in a mutually intelligible form. Human intuition, judgement and politics form an inherent part of the communication between the users and the developers. Structured analysis approaches seek to minimise the effects of these human factors by making the analysis more formal. The approach taken in this research project is to recognise the reality of these human factors and the need to deal effectively with them, but to also recognise the value in taking a structured systematic approach in the sense of using the IEEE-derived SURAC template.

For the Analyst as Systems Expert there is but one reality that is both measurable and essentially the same for all everyone. Were it otherwise, it would be very difficult to derive the true requirements of the system. The role of the analyst is to develop a system that models this allegedly objective reality to produce a tool used by management to achieve their organisational goals.

**Analyst as Facilitator** came about partly because of the problems inherent with the systems expert paradigm. It recognises the fundamental complexity and subjectivity of human interaction. There is no objective reality, only individual perceptions and interpretations of 'reality'. In particular, system requirements are constructed by a continuing process of an organisation defining its objectives. In this sense, the developer's role is to analyse with management what kind of system will achieve these objectives. The developer in this paradigm works from the user's perspective and assists them to determine their preferred view of reality. But to achieve this consensus, it is essential that continuous interaction between developer and user take place. And here lies the inherent problem with this paradigm in that given the widely recognised existence of a culture gap, continuous interaction is unlikely to occur. While this paradigm has merit in that it addresses the problems outlined in the literature, and recognises the fundamental subjectivity of human interaction, it is also impractical for the reasons discussed earlier. That is, while integrative processes are acknowledged to have merit, and will work when correctly performed, in the so-called 'real world' of software development, they are very often not implemented, possibly because they are seen as too costly in terms of time, effort and staff resources. They might also be perceived by the developer as a threat to their culture.

**Analyst as Labour Partisan** postulates that there is a fundamental conflict between the owners of the means of production and labour in the sense that labour is exploited by the owners who place their own interests ahead of labour's and do so to the detriment of labour. The developer must side with one or the other, to develop a system that meets the needs of the organisation. There may be some truth to the assertion that the owners of the means of production are exploiting labour, however improvements in recent years in industrial relations have seen a growing move towards enterprise bargaining agreements in which owners and labour negotiate mutually agreeable terms – the so-called 'win-win' deal.

**Analyst as Emancipator**, like the Labour Partisan paradigm is essentially a theoretic position although some work has been done in Scandinavia in this area. The Analyst as Emancipator paradigm sees systems development occurring through a process of rational discourse that results in the emancipation of the organisation. Hirschheim and Klein characterise this as a hypothetical paradigm in that it cannot be observed in practice, whereas the previous three can be observed. In the 'real world' of software development however, there are very few instances of any paradigm other than Analyst as Systems Expert.

Hirschheim, Klein and Lyytinen (1995) later elaborate the four development paradigms described above into Functionalist, Social Relativist, Radical Structuralist, and Neohumanist accordingly.

### 2.2.3. Technical writer as Analyst as Facilitator

Hirschheim and Klein (1989) suggest that this paradigm developed as a reaction to the perceived shortcomings of the expert paradigm. While not explicitly named, a technical writer might indeed play the facilitator role. The author has performed the role successfully on at least three development projects where the Analyst as Expert was the prevailing paradigm. The technical writer as facilitator was able to facilitate communication between developers and users during the requirements stage, which may lead to a complete set of requirements upon which to base design.

Added to the role of facilitator as defined by Hirschheim and Klein (1989) is recognition of the merits of the various integrative processes like Participative Design and JAD. The Facilitator fits comfortably with the processes outlined by PD, JAD and other integrative processes in that they all recognise the requirement for effective communication as a pre-condition of successful collaborative outcomes.

Having the technical writer act as Analyst as Facilitator also recognises that budgetary pressure and established organisational culture work against the adoption of integrative processes. The technical writer is already a member of the project team, and so is more likely to be accepted by the project team as a facilitator, than an external person might be. The technical writer's involvement is also less likely cause budgetary problems than an external person.

## *2.3. Information System Quality and Usability*

There is more than one definition of usability, indeed the term usability has been used interchangeably with software quality, and even Information Systems quality when looking broadly at the academic and practitioner literature. The purpose of this research project, the definition of usability (IS Quality as it is called in this model) will be defined by the SOLE (SOftware Library Evolution) quality model, originally developed by Eriksson and Törn (1991)

While there might be more recent definitions of usability, the SOLE model is used in the context of this research because it allows usability to be evaluated by asking three simple questions; how easy is the system to use?, how easy is the system to learn?, and how well does it allows you to do your work?. Improvements to the usability of the system that is the subject of this project can be evaluated by asking users to give their rating on a five point ordinal scale.

The SOLE quality model creates divisions of quality classes that are consistent with the decisions made by key decision-makers during the software life-cycle. SOLE identifies three divisions; business quality, use quality, and IS work quality. At each level the listed quality factors relate to individuals who are primarily interested in the quality of the respective quality factor.

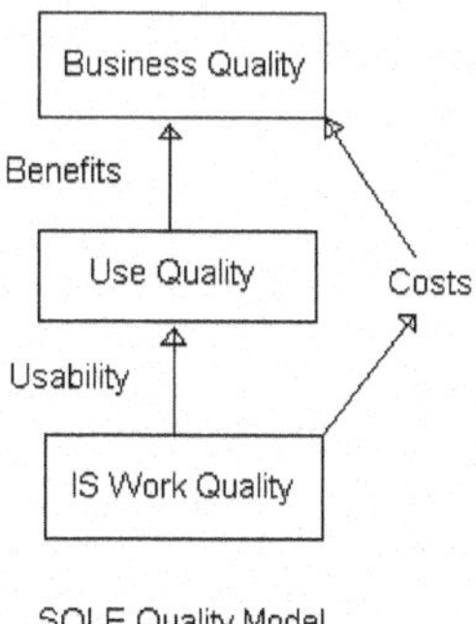


**Figure 1: SOLE Quality Model (Eriksson & Törn, 1991)**

The first division, business quality, is the domain of senior and departmental management. It is seen in terms of costs and benefits. If benefits outweigh cost, then quality is good. Business quality refers to the quality of the activities that control the IS work throughout the entire lifecycle. The success criteria include whether deadlines and schedules are met on budget. It is the province of the Chief Information Officer (CIO). The CIO is responsible for the efficient deployment of all types of resources, towards meeting the organisation's defined information needs/goals. The

Project Manager must keep on-going projects running smoothly with no surprises. Success criteria is the approval and acceptance of the deliverables.

The second division of the SOLE model, use quality, is defined by how well the system does what the user wants it to do. Users are defined as the people who directly use the system by performing various work practices that prepare data and information for the system.

The third and final division, IS work quality, is defined by the level of the performance of management, development, maintenance and operation of the Information System, and the final products of software and documentation. ISWQ considers the management functions required to assure evolution quality (assessed in terms of process quality and product quality) and user support quality (quality of guidance, training, and operations provided). Lindroos (1997) discusses ISWQ as being concerned with all aspects of the way an IS serves the user. The two main features of use quality in the SOLE model is what does the system do for the user, and how the interface is designed, otherwise called requirement quality and interface quality. The requirement dimension includes such factors as does the artefact meet the user's needs, is it secure and is it easy to change according to new needs. The user interface dimension is concerned with how easy the artefact is to use, whether effective help is available and that the artefact does not control the user's work performance.

## *2.4. Integrative processes as promoters of user-developer communication*

The term “Integrative Process” has been coined in the context of this work to refer to that range of activities and techniques developed over time by academia and practitioners to solve the problem of poor communication between stakeholders. Integrative processes include Participative Design, ETHICS, Joint Application Development, Soft Systems Methodology, and User Participation. References to these and discussion are found later in this section.

In the context of requirements engineering (RE) as discussed in an earlier section, integrative processes are relevant to all four stages of the RE process (requirements elicitation, analysis, specification and validation), though the first two stages are likely to involve a greater degree of interaction between the stakeholders.

According to Koltzblatt and Beyer (1995), successful requirements definition is contingent on effective communication between the parties. Those partys' ability to collaborate and negotiate an agreed set of requirements is seen as a critical success factor, and this is precisely the purpose of integrative processes. Where communication difficulties exist between the parties, the requirements engineering process will not be performed effectively.

The existence of a cultural gap between user and developer has long been recognised, both in the academic and practitioner literature. Finding ways of addressing the problem has been an ongoing search, with a variety of solutions, as discussed below, having been proposed. These solutions that shall be termed 'integrative processes' in that they seek to integrate the differing cultural styles of developers and users. This section of the literature review shall examine what integrative processes have been developed to counter the differences, and how effective they have been.

As discussed by Feeny, Earl and Edwards (1996), the culture gap problem is evidently significant to many IS directors because the literature of information management emphasises the need for IS stakeholders to be involved with each other, to have commitment to desired outcomes and collaborative effort. Arising from this need, Lawrance and Lorsch (1967), and later Galbraith (1977) suggested a range of integrating processes that can bridge the cultural gap and integrate these different styles. According to Feeny, Earl and Edwards (1996), these integrative processes include the ETHICS model for participative systems development (Mumford, 1983), Joint Application Development (Raghavan, Zelesnik and Ford, 1994) and the use of particular people as integrators, such as the 'hybrid manager' investigated by Earl and Skryme (1992). Checkland and Scholes (1990) developed Soft Systems Methodology (SSM) to deal with situations where there is a high social component, including political interaction. This integrative process distinguishes those situations that can be described as having "soft" problems from those that display "hard" problems that might have a well-defined technological solution.

McKeen et al (1994) studied User Participation from the point of view of the effect of user participation on satisfaction with Information Systems. They looked at four contingency factors; task complexity, system complexity, user influence, and user-developer communication, and how these factors affected the relationship between user participation and user satisfaction. They analysed 151 independent system development projects in eight different organisations and found that user participation has a direct relationship with user satisfaction. In projects where the level of task difficulty was high, the relationship between user participation and user satisfaction was significantly stronger than in projects where task complexity or system complexity was low. McKeen et al (1994) concluded that user influence and user-developer communication were independent predictors of user satisfaction.

Participatory Design is sharply distinguished from traditional design methods in which designers have an Analyst as Systems Expert (as discussed by Hirschheim and Klein 1989) mindset. PD began in 1970s Norway, though it came to be practised widely Scandinavia (Stiemerling, Kahler, and Wulf, 1997). For the first time, software developers worked directly with trade unionists (Winograd, 1996). Its purpose and rationale was to allow the workers to have more influence on the design and introduction of computer systems into the workplace. Kristen Nygaard, who was a well known developer of object-oriented languages, worked with union leaders and members to create a national codetermination agreement that codified the rights of unions to participate in the design and deployment of workplace systems (Winograd, 1996). But the right to participate in design is frequently ignored and even when it is accepted, obstacles including perceived pragmatic/economic deficiencies and organisational concerns, inhibit the participation process (Reich et al, 1996).

PD is distinguished from JAD (discussed below) by placing more emphasis on greater user involvement. This involvement is meant to foster a mutual learning process between users and designers, and to synworke joint experiences into a simulated use case.

Checkland (1981) observes that it is direct action not indirect reflection upon earlier actions that constitutes our fundamental way of being. Developers and users are not subject to the same experiences that have the consequence that they cannot easily understand each other's experience. PD focuses on lower-level end users who are introduced to the developer's workplace and who learn about technical possibilities through 'joint applications'. In the same way, during requirements analysis the developers try to collaborate with users in their place of work and both have the potential to be transformed by learning from one another. The developer in PD act both as facilitators and technical advisors to the user, and this can encourage creativity and free thinking among the participants. Not having a clearly defined structure that must be adhered to, as in JAD, allows PD to have greater flexibility. Users and developers have a shared responsibility for the quality of the requirements.

Williams and Begg (1993) in their study of Participative Design (PD) point to the need for someone to act as a translator between the IS developer and the user. They remark that when IS developers are asked how they design a system for an unfamiliar domain, the reply is typically ‘Either I have to learn enough about what the users do to be able to tell them what they want, or they have to learn enough about computers to tell me’ (p102). The IS developer makes at least two assumptions here; that software design takes place in isolation from the workplace context in which the software is used, and that either the developer or the user has the time and inclination to learn substantial amounts about the other’s domain so as to engage in useful dialogue. Williams and Begg (1993) performed PD case studies using such diverse types as physicists, English teachers, psychiatric nurses and CAD engineers.

Joint Application Design (JAD) was developed by the IBM Corporation beginning in 1977. JAD is a collaborative approach to system design that became widely practised in North America since the 1970's. The impetus to use JAD derived in part from the recognition by organisations that a high degree of user involvement during development would often lead to higher quality systems (Carmel, 1993).

The JAD methodology involves a structured, controlled session led by a facilitator. In it purest form JAD is intended to support the entire System Development Life Cycle (SDLC), however in practice it appears that it is largely confined to the requirements definition process. JAD sessions tend to be highly structured, supporting involvement by all interested parties. The JAD venue is set up with whiteboards, overhead projectors and flip charts, and participants are encouraged by the facilitator to write their ideas on the various media in the room to stimulate discussion.

In the 2000's, JAD sessions are conducted using Computer Aided Software Engineering (CASE) tools to easily facilitate the production of dataflow diagrams, entity-relationship diagrams, state transitions as well as other diagramming techniques and screen painters. Another technology in the JAD community is Groupware (Mumford, 1979). JAD was conceived as collaborative practice whose object is to enhance the viability of given technical goals (Carmel et al 1993).

### 2.4.1. The role of documentation in participative design

Shackel (1991) in discussing the PD process explicitly points to the high potential value to be derived from writing those parts of the operating manual that describe the user interface and how to use it. While Shackel (1991) acknowledges that this process is not easy, it is still worth doing because the draft manual then allows the user to test the interface and reveal potential usability problems before they are embedded in the design.

Reich et al (1996), indicate how PD can be used to construct a social reality based on the multiple perspectives that can be incorporated into the design of a new system. In their survey of participation projects, Reich et al (1996) identified four principle factors that influence the success of a PD project. These are (1) the recording of historical data on participation activities; (2) the availability of instructional material; (3) the articulation of informal knowledge; and (4) support for asynchronous communication among participants. This first factor, the need to accurately record information can perhaps be linked to Iivari's (1991) conclusion that information is seen as descriptive facts, which by inference must be documented effectively.

The collaborative work of designers and users in engineering projects is made complex by the differences in technical skills, technical jargon, skills in the use of computational and other tools (Reich et al 1996). They discuss the broad stages involved in the PD process. Each stage involves communication on some level, for example oral leading to written communication. The stages are, (1) capture the user's requirements; (2) reconcile the terminological differences between the designers and the users; (3) admit continuous revisions of the message being passed back and forth, and (4) communicate back to the user the implications of the requirements. While documentation is not specifically mentioned, it could nonetheless be asserted that effective documentation is important to the success of the PD project.

Mumford & Henshall (1991) suggest that the dual, related objectives of PD are to increase user satisfaction while increasing their work efficiency. They indicate three levels of participation; (1) consultative participation which leaves the bulk of the design decisions with the traditional systems design group; (2) representative participation which calls for a higher level of involvement from the staff of a user department; and (3) consensus participation which attempts to involve all staff in the user department continuously throughout the system design process. Without the support of high quality documentation, it is possible that the outcomes of each of these three levels of participation would be adversely affected.

The importance of communication in PD, and the inherent need to document that communication is further illustrated by Sackman (1983). Designers are required to communicate more (both in writing and verbally) with project stakeholders than in traditional design approaches. The designer's role is as a relatively neutral technical facilitator among conflicting parties of system hardware, software and communications. The designer has an expanded role that includes the technical responsibilities of the traditional approach, plus new psychological, political, educational, and co-ordination skills.

### 2.4.2. Problems with integrative processes

Williams and Begg (1993) in their study of Participative Design (PD) point to the need for someone to act as a translator between the IS developer and the user. They remark that when IS developers are asked how they design a system for an unfamiliar domain, the reply is typically 'Either I have to learn enough about what the users do to be able to tell them what they want, or they have to learn enough about computers to tell me' (p102). The IS developer makes at least two assumptions here; that software design takes place in isolation from the workplace context in which the software is used, and that either the developer or the user has the time and inclination to learn substantial amounts about the other's domain so as to engage in useful dialogue. Williams and Begg (1993) performed PD case studies using such diverse types as physicists, English teachers, psychiatric nurses and CAD engineers.

Reich et al (1996), indicate how PD can be used to construct a social reality based on the multiple perspectives that can be incorporated into the design of a new system. In their survey of participation projects, Reich et al (1996) identified four principle factors that influence the success of a PD project. These are (1) the recording of historical data on participation activities; (2) the availability of instructional material; (3) the articulation of informal knowledge; and (4) support for asynchronous communication among participants.

A problem arises when IS project management is encouraged to use integrative processes. IS developers are reluctant to do participative systems development because it is seen to be expensive and time-consuming (Feeny, Earl and Edwards, 1996) and such approaches may also challenge the organisational culture, leading to avoidance and sometimes the subversion of the integrative process. From the literature it would appear that while such processes are useful, in practical terms it is necessary to develop a process which poses the least perceived threat to the IS developer's established method of conducting projects. It is suggested that only then is the integrative process likely to win acceptance from both IS developer and user.

Lockett (1989) found that successful projects managed to bridge this gap within the development team. Based on the 29 projects studies, the most critical area identified by Lockett are the conversion of business needs into IS requirements. A 'project champion' appears to perform this most effectively. In the absence of a champion, the gap is best bridged by either someone moving from the user side to the technical side as a mid-career change, or else by an IS developer with a long working relationship with the users. This pattern appears to fit generally with Hirschheim and Klein's Analyst as Facilitator (1989).

The basic skills shared by Hirschheim and Klein's Analyst as Facilitator and Lockett's project champion who bridges the cultural gap is the ability to understand both the technical and the general perspectives. It is possible, even likely that the ability to understand that technical and the general perspectives is a skill possessed by the technical writer. It is necessary to be able to understand the technical language used by developers, and be able to translate that technical language into a form that can be readily understood by the user (and vice versa). In practical terms this is one way, perhaps the principle way, that a cultural gap might be bridged.

To assist with the complexities experienced by the design group, Mumford (1983 p31) suggests that a neutral 'facilitator', who could be either internal or external, can help the designers and the users to reconcile their differences and analyse the task at hand with a view to achieving solutions. This research project suggests that the technical writer with the ability to interpret technical information to a general audience might be well placed to act is this facilitator.

## 2.5. Conclusion

To provide a foundation upon which the research project's objectives might be reached, this literature review has explored the following conceptual areas and seeks answers to the questions listed below:

### 2.5.1. What cultural differences are perceived to exist between IS developers and users?

The existence of cultural differences between users and developers is explored for its relevance to understanding the nature of the interaction between them. It is seen that around half of all IS directors consider this gap as their biggest challenge. This is consistent with the earlier findings of Edstrom (1977), Gingras and McLean (1979), and Zmud and Cox (1979) in their discussion on the distinctive cultural styles of IS professionals.

### 2.5.2. What are Hirschheim and Klein's, (1989) paradigms of IS development; in particular Analyst as Systems Expert and Analyst as Facilitator?

Following on is an examination of Hirschheim and Klein's, (1989) paradigms of IS development, focussing on Analyst as Systems Expert and Analyst as Facilitator revealed that the mindset and outlook of the Analyst as Systems Expert, arguably the dominant IS development paradigm, is significantly different from the mindset and outlook of the user. This is in the sense that the Analyst as Systems Expert is an expert in technology, tools and methods of system design and project management - skills that would require a mindset that the user is unlikely to have. The expert's role seeks to minimise where possible reliance on human intuition, judgement and politics - all of which constitutes the user's world. Indeed it might be concluded from this that in organisational contexts in which Analyst as Systems Expert is the prevailing paradigm, the two groups effectively live in different worlds.

It was then seen that recognition of the problems inherent with the systems expert paradigm brought about the Analyst as Facilitator paradigm. This latter recognises the fundamental and deals with the complexity and subjectivity of human interaction. The role of the technical writer was considered in the context of the Analyst as Facilitator.

### 2.5.3. Information System Quality and Usability

The review examines the broad areas of software and IS quality in order to better understand what constitutes quality and how can it be recognised in relation to the results of the research event. The literature suggests that quality be seen in terms of the user and the organisational context in which they operate. This is at odds with the Analyst as Systems Expert paradigm that minimises the user's importance and maximises the technical aspects of the process. This led to identifying the SOLE model as contributing a definition of system usability that could be used for the purpose evaluating the effectiveness or otherwise of having a technical writer as a Analyst as Facilitator.

### 2.5.4. What are some of the Integrative Processes developed to bridge the cultural differences?

A review is made of the literature relevant to what methodologies have been developed to mitigate the effects of poor user-developer communication -- the so-called integrative processes. These include the ETHICS model for participative systems development, Mumford, 1983, Joint Application Development, Raghavan, Zelesnik and Ford, 1994 and the use of particular people as integrators, such as the 'hybrid manager' investigated by Earl and Skryme 1992. But while it is recognised that these processes have the potential to work given the right conditions, it is also acknowledged by their advocates that they will only work where there is organisational commitment. And here is the fundamental problem - they are too often perceived by the Analyst as Systems Expert as a threat to their established ways of performing their work, as well as being perceived as being too expensive in terms of scarce project resources. A viable solution is to devise an integrative process that neutralises these problems. The technical writer acting as Analyst as Facilitator may possibly be the answer.

### 2.5.5. Additional indirectly relevant review material in appendices

The formal literature review is comprised of the four sections listed above. These are the core sections of the review that relate directly to the research objectives. Review material (see topic list below) that is relevant to this work, though not directly relevant to the research objectives, has been moved to the appendix, where it may be readily referenced. This was done also to meet the constraints of the prescribed work word limit.

- The role of software project documentation
- The nature and scope of requirements engineering
- What do we mean by software quality and is quality?
- Defining the role of the technical writer
- Culture as two systems

# 3. Research Approach & Methods

## *3.1. Introduction*

This chapter details the research approach and methods adopted for this research project. It begins by identifying the constraints, and how a satisfactory resolution of those constraints were negotiated with the client.

For completeness, a detailed discussion of two other qualitative research approaches, positivist and critical research is conducted as a way of validating action research as the appropriate methodology. This can be found in Appendix K.

Relevance and rigour issues are examined in relation to the particular problems with maintaining rigour in relation to action research projects in general, and this project in particular.

The research strategy is outlined in detail, which basically focuses on the following three elements:

Action research typically consist of five stages; reflection, planning, action/observation, reflection and write-up conclusions. These are described in detail in section 3.6 Project Stages.

Technical writer uses IEEE derived user requirements template (Appendix A) to apply a structured and comprehensive approach to process of requirements gathering. See discussion in section 3.5.3.

Technical writer acting as a facilitator of communication by applying prescribed facilitation practices (Appendix B) derived from Joint application Development (See discussion in section 3.5.1-3.5.2), and

A discussion of the previously mentioned five stages of action research will focus on providing a detailed task description for each stage.

Chapter 3 will conclude with a description of the proposed data collected methods, which in summary include; questionnaire, interviews with participants and stakeholders, documentary evidence in the form of email, and observation over a 12 month period.

Chapter 3 seeks to clearly define before moving into the research event itself, the approach and methods to be used. It is followed in later chapters with how the approach and methods were subsequently implemented.

It is important to clearly define before the research event what approach is to be used, as it helps to defend the project against allegations that action research projects are little more than standard consultancy work with elements of soap opera included when writing it up. Some critics have suggested that the researcher might be tempted to retro-fit the approach and methods after the research event in light of the unforeseen events that occurred.

## *3.2. Constraints influencing choice of preferred approach*

It must be noted that a constraint upon the choice of research approach was the researcher needing to remain in on-going full-time employment.

Over a three month period before the research event, the researcher made use of established contacts within the IT contractor employment agencies to obtain a commercial contract that would fit the requirements of the research approach and methods. Good relationships with the agencies, and a good reputation as a technical writer enabled a suitable contract to be located.

A suitable contract to perform technical writing/user requirements development services presented itself in the form of EnergyCorp (discussed in detail in Chapter 4). The researcher was commercially qualified and an acceptable to EnergyCorp in this regard and was subsequently contracted for an initial six months to perform this work. It is as Baskerville (1999) suggested, that the researcher is also a consultant who is engaged to perform commercial consulting work.

During the initial interview with James, the EnergyCorp executive responsible for the software development project, permission was sought and given to perform an action research project concurrently with the software development. At this interview, it was decided that the research project would not be discussed with the other participants, as it might detract from their primary task of completing the M&M software upgrade. James was of the view that ComTech did not "need to know".

Chapter 4 is a detailed description of the research site and how the research strategy was implemented.

## *3.3. Preferred research approach*

For the purposes of this project, Johnson and Scholes (1999) model of organisational culture is used. The model is comprised of six elements, clustered (it may be recalled from the literature review) like daisy petals around a central paradigm: organisation structure, stories and myths, symbols, rituals and routines, control systems and power structures.

Given the unpredictable nature of the research site and the individuals that interact with each other during the research event, this model offers a useful vehicle for the exploration of the nature of the cultural gap in general, and how communication between IS developer and user might be better understood in relation to the development of user requirements.

The research approach is interpretivist. It is how reality is perceived that is important to the research (Burrell & Morgan, 1979; Orlikowski & Baroudi, 1991). It is concerned with the communication occurring between two categories of person (developer and user) with differing perspectives on organisational 'reality'. It is an assumption of the research that these differences exist.

Seen in the context of social science research, the approach can be placed in column 2 of Mumford, Hirschheim, Fitzgerald and Wood-Harper's (1984) approaches to social science research. Mumford et al's matrix illustrates the continuum of research approaches, from the most subjective to the most objective. It provides useful perspective with which to place the proposed research approach in context.

| | **Subjective approaches to social science** | | | **Objective approaches to social science** | | |
|---|---|---|---|---|---|---|
| | 1 | 2 | 3 | 4 | 5 | 6 |
| **Core ontological assumptions** | Reality as a projection of human imagination | Reality as a social construction (relativist) | Reality as a realm of symbolic discourse | Reality as a contextual field of information | Reality as a concrete process | Reality as a concrete structure |
| **Assumption about human nature** | Human as a pure, spiritual consciousness | Human as a social constructor, symbol-creator | Human as actor, symbol user | Human as information processor | Human as an adaptor | Human as a responder |
| **Basic epistomological stance** | To obtain phenome nological insight | To understand how social reality is created ` | To understand problems and patterns of symbolic discourse | To map contexts | To study system process changes | To construct positivist science |
| **Some favoured metaphor** | Transcendental | Language game, understanding text | Theatre culture | Cybernetic | Organism | Machine |
| **Examples of research methods** | Exploration of pure subjective | Hermenuetics | Symbolic Analysis | Contextual analysis of gestalten | Historic analysis | Lab experiments, surveys |

**Table 2: Continuum of social science research approaches (Mumford, Hirschheim, Fitzgerald and Wood-Harper, 1984)**

The ontology of the proposed research is based on social construction (Mumford, Hirschheim, Fitzgerald and Wood-Harper, 1984) or what is sometimes called social relativist. The 'reality' in which the research takes place cannot be said to be objective since it is exploring the transient communication between people with differing views. The proposed research will explore the viewpoints of individuals whose perception of 'reality' is built upon their world-view, so the epistemology is anti-positivist.

Social relativist, anti-positivist assumptions lead to an ideographic research methodology. The ideographic approach seeks to represent and conceptualise complex social phenomenon in symbolic terms (Burrell & Morgan, 1979). The social world can be interpreted through direct observation to gain first hand knowledge. Subjective impressions or knowledge about a situation that have been directly gained are valid forms of observation when using an ideographic approach. The phenomena observed during the later stages of the action research might emerge and cumulatively build upon earlier phenomena to produce a set of results from which conclusions might reasonably be drawn.

### 3.3.1. Action research

Given the context and timeframe allowable for this exploration, it is proposed to adopt action research as the research method.

Historically, Action Research (AR) grew out of Kurt Lewin's view of the limitations of studying complex social interactions in a laboratory setting (Checkland, 1996). AR involves the researcher becoming proactively involved in a real problem situation, working collaboratively with participants towards a solution, and then retrospectively seeking to gain practical and theoretical insights from the experience.

The critical elements of action research include there being collaborative problem-solving interaction between researcher and the other people in the situation. It is a process of critical enquiry in which problems are actively searched for and identified, followed by the formulation of a possible solution or set of solutions, the implementation of the solution(s) then an evaluation of the effectiveness of the solution(s) in the context of reflective learning.

There is a focus on social practice, upon how individuals interact in the research situation. (Argyris, Putnam and McLain-Smith, 1982). Action research is distinguished from case study research by their essentially active / passive natures.

Seeking to explore a research question using action research will meet the requirements of an interpretivist research approach, because the research will try to understand phenomena through the meanings ascribed to them by the participants. As Walsham (1993) indicates, interpretive methods of IS research aim to produce an understanding of the context of the information system, and the way in which the system influences and is influenced by the context.

Järvinen (1991) places action research into the second 'family' or category of research approaches. Also included in this category are case study, hermeneutics and phenomenology. This is the category of sensitive exploratory approaches catching a current reality.

Perhaps one of the greatest challenges facing IS action researchers is to maintain a clear distinction between the various roles played by the participants. As Baskerville (1999) indicates the researcher is also likely to be a consultant who is expected to do commercial consulting work. In the sometimes pressurised environments in which many consultants work, it is sometimes a challenge for him or her to be sufficiently objective to maintain a clear distinction in their own minds between the role of the consultant and that of the researcher. A technical writer with particular skills might be substituted for a consultant in this regard.

Acknowledging this challenge, it is clearly stated in the description of the research site and event (Chapter 4), the term technical writer applies when the actions contain little or no researcher component. Researcher applies when the actions contain little or no technical writer component.

The challenge was met in this project by consciously asking oneself before any action, either interpersonal or reflection, who exactly is doing this? This was achieved by inwardly asking 'would I be doing this if this was only a consultancy job?' Since the role and actions performed by the technical writer are similar in nature to those performed in previous projects, and since this is the first action research project performed by the researcher, it is therefore possible to obtain a clear answer to this question as an on-going method of maintaining a clear mental distinction between the technical writer and the researcher.

Lau (1999) discussing earlier work by Checkland discusses the necessary structure of any action research project for it to be accepted as a legitimate alternative to positivistic hypothesis testing. These criteria are:

- There is a real-world problem relevant to research themes of interest to the researcher.
- Respective roles of the researcher and participants defined in the problem situation.
- Inclusion of an intellectual framework by means of which the nature of research lessons can be defined and the method in which the framework is embodied.
- Researcher involvement in unfolding the situation with a view to help bring about changes deemed improvements.

- Rethinking of earlier stages by making sense of the accumulating experience through the declared framework and method, and revising changes.

- Point of exit for the researcher in order to review the experience and to extract lessons for learning in relation to the research themes and/or definition of new themes.

To help enhance the validity of the findings, the research design follows this structure.

Baskerville (1999) distinguishes action research from consultancy in the following ways (quoted in full):

**Motivation**. Action research is motivated by its scientific prospects, perhaps epitomised in scientific publications. Consulting is motivated by commercial benefits, including profits and additional stocks of proprietary knowledge about solutions to organisational problems.

**Commitment**. Action research makes a commitment to the research community for the production of scientific knowledge, as well as to the client. In a consulting situation, the commitment is to the client alone.

**Approach**. Collaboration is essential in action research because of its idiographic assumptions. Consulting typically values its 'outsider's,' unbiased viewpoint, providing an objective perspective on the organisational problems.

**Foundation for recommendations**. In action research, this foundation is a theoretical framework. Consultants are expected to suggest solutions that, in their experience, proved successful in similar situations.

**Essence of the organisational understanding**. In action research, organisational understanding is founded on practical success from iterative experimental changes in the organisation. Typical consultation teams develop an understanding through their independent critical analysis of the problem situation.

### 3.3.2. Action research and action learning

Action Research, though related to Action Learning, is distinguished from it a several ways. According to Dick (1997) Action Learning occurs when a group of people meet regularly, as a mutual support group, to learn from their experiences. Participants can be drawn from a diverse background, often from different organizations. Current practice focuses more on setting up such a program within an organization, usually without a facilitator. An example of an application of action Learning might be to undertake a software process improvement program.

Dick (1997) makes this distinction;  in action learning, each participant derives unique learning from their experience. In action research a team of people drew collective learning from a collective experience. In the sense that the technical writer is collaborating with his project participants only at a project level, not at a research level, there is an element of action learning to this project.

Action research and action learning are comparable with Experiential Learning, a process of learning from experience. The experience can be something which is occurring, or is contrived for the occasion by a facilitator (Dick 1997). Obviously, both action research and action learning are essentially to do with learning from experience. All three are cyclic, involving action and then reflection on the action. All have learning as one of their goals. Experiential learning is the basis for the learning component of both action learning and action research (Dick 1997).

Both action learning and action research are aimed at improving practice. Action research aims to make changes, whereas action learning uses a planned change as a way of learning through reflection. In action research, the learners draw their learning from the same change activity. In action learning, the learning and the activity used to be unique to each learner (Dick 1997).

## *3.4. Comparison between action research and positivist science*

When making a comparison between action research and positivist science, von Hellens (Seminar notes, 1999) outlines the matrix represented by the table below. It can be seen that positivist research seeks to remove contextual information in order to objectify the researched phenomena to the point where they might be used to deduce predictive instruments. Anti-positivist research in contrast regards context as the dynamically changing vehicle by which the researcher both achieves constructive negotiated outcomes and a degree of insight into the process by which the outcomes were achieved.

| | **Positivist** | **Anti-Positivist (Action Research)** |
|---|---|---|
| Scope | Context-free ∴ static | Context-based ∴ dynamic |
| Methods | Cause/effect relations | Insights/observations may not be quantifiable |
| Role of Re-searcher | Detached observer | Actively involved |
| Goals | Set by researcher and selected participants | Negotiated with whole group |
| Outcomes | Laws, generalisations | Context-dependent insights |

**Table 3: Positivism vs. Anti-Positivism (von Hellens 1999, Seminar notes)**

In further contrasting action research and positivist science, Wood-Harper (1991) observes that on the dimension of time, positivist science makes observations of present, while action research observes the present, while also interpreting the present from knowledge of the past, and conceptualising more desirable futures. This iterative approach to finding solutions to existing social/organisational problems is well suited to the research site. Action research enables the actively involved researcher who is there as a change agent to do their work, rather than be a detached observer who regards the client system members as objects of study.

The problem of developers and users not communicating well enough during requirements collection indicates the need to recognise the language being used by both sides as connotative and metaphorical, (Wood-Harper, 1991) which action research can be said to do. This contrasts with the denotative view of language favoured by positivists.

Epistemologically, the positivist approach seeks to predict events based on hierarchically arranged propositions (Wood-Harper, 1991), while action research aims to develop an understanding that may be used to guide future endeavours.

### 3.4.1. Relevance & rigour of the research

The central issues of relevance and rigor in IS research is summed up by Galliers (1994) "In an applied discipline such as Information Systems, I would argue that it is important that we undertake research that is seen to be relevant by our colleagues in [IS Practice], as well as sufficiently scholarly by our colleagues in academia. This is the challenge associated with the term 'academic' in the field of Information Systems. While we wish to be scholarly, we do not wish to be labelled "unpractical," which is one of the meanings of the term 'academic.'"

The lack of consensus in the IS research community as to what constitutes valid measures of research maturity inevitably raises questions of relevance and rigour in relation to specific research projects. The lack of consensus derives from disagreement between those who regard the multiplicity of paradigms and methodologies as a sign of immaturity, therefore a weakness, and those who regard this diversity as offering a wide choice, therefore a strength.

The IS research literature broadly categorise research as being either interpretivist or positivist. There is a perception that positivist research is more rigorous than interpretivist since it deals with objective, quantifiable data. Rigour in this sense is being able to make mathematical proof. As a result, a lack of objectivity casts doubt on the ability of interpretivist research to produce valid outcomes.

To achieve relevance, the research needs to relate directly to an issue that has been identified and generally agreed by the IS research community. Such an issue is the problem of systems project failure as discussed by Kensing, Simonsen and Bødker (1996), Boehm (1981), and Lyytinen and Hirschheim (1987), as outlined in Chapter 1.

Having identified a significant problem, a researcher seeking to be rigorous and relevant would use a conceptual framework derived from the literature and from experience in the industry to identify a major problem for which a possible solution has been identified. One that might be subsequently tested by a research project.

Keen (1991) maintains that IS research should be purposive, indicating that relevance should be the prime determinant of IS research. Keen further argues that relevance must precede rigour. In terms of this research project, Keen's position is interpreted to mean that the correct sequence of events is to identify a suitably relevant research topic, determine and design a research strategy that is appropriate to the question, then rigorously apply the predetermined research approach, using appropriate means to record the results.

## *3.5. Research Strategy*

While the primary concern remained that the research strategy had to be academically rigorous, as discussed in the previous section, the strategy was nonetheless constrained by the researcher needing to be in full-time employment, as discussed in Section 3.2. But given that the nature of the researcher's usual full-time work was to, in part, engage in collaborative problem-solving in real situations by applying structured methodologies, the foundations for an action research project already existed.

But this close fit presents the problem of how to avoid the criticism that action research is consultancy by another name. The research strategy needs to effectively deal with this potential problem by making a clear distinction between those activities that would normally be performed by a technical writer, and those of the researcher only, as discussed in Section 3.3.

Another way to make a clear distinction is to structure the action research project to maximise the validity and usefulness of the results (Checkland, 1991). By declaring the approach before beginning the research event, then demonstrating how the approach has been applied to produce certain results, the criticism that action research is merely consultancy by another name can be avoided (Baskerville, 1999).

Accordingly the following three dimensions form the basic structure of the theoretical framework:

- The critical elements of action research conducted in five stages; reflection, plan, action/observation, reflection and write-up conclusions. These are described in detail in the Project Stages section.

These activities occur re-iteratively in the sense that they may be performed more than once during the entire project.

- Technical writer uses IEEE derived user requirements template (see Appendix) to apply a structured and comprehensive approach to process of requirements gathering.
- Technical writer acts as facilitator of communication by applying prescribed facilitation practices (see Appendix) derived from Joint Application Development.

The methods used to test the research question are a combination of questionnaire, interview, documentary evidence and observation. By using a formal questionnaire as the basis, the results can be compared with those of the other three methods, thereby improving the chances of identifying consistencies and inconsistencies in the results.

It should be noted that the second and third elements of this research strategy (use of IEEE template and technical writer as facilitator) were developed by the researcher over the ten years prior to becoming an RHD student, while working as a technical writer/business analyst in public and private sector organizations. The research project allowed these pre-existing theories to be tested for validity in a commercial software development project.

### 3.5.1. Technical writer as facilitator

Using the facilitation techniques outlined in JAD (in the next section) (Wood and Silver, 1995), a technical writer attempts to bridge the developer/user cultural gap. See Section 4.6 for detail of the nature of the collaborative relationship.

The Figure below illustrates Hirschheim and Klein's (1989) traditional Analyst as Systems Expert approach to developing the statement of user requirements. The developer is central to the process with the user having little or no direct access to the statement of user requirements due to communication difficulties with the developer, and perhaps a reluctance on the part of the developer to allow the user to enter what is perceived to be their expert domain.

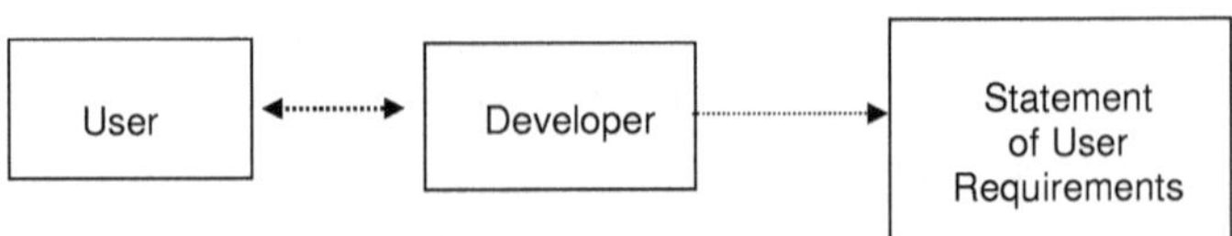


**Figure 2. Developer (Systems Expert) liaises directly with user to produce the statement of user requirements (Tuffley, 1999).**

With the technical writer as facilitator, the process changes to one in which there is a multi-directional communication between the developer and the technical writer, the user and the technical writer and to some extent between the user and the developer taking advantage of the ongoing facilitated communication.

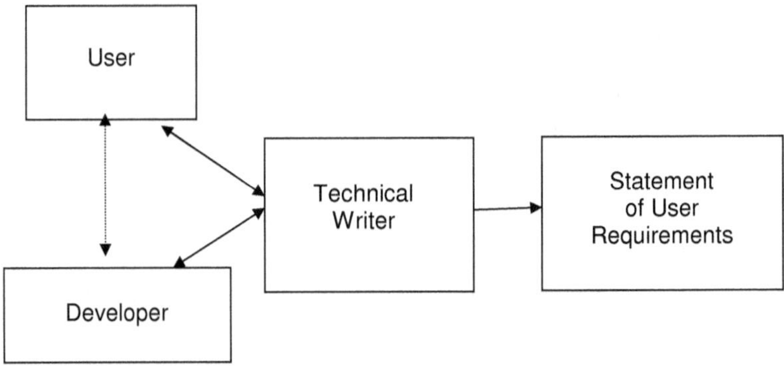


**Figure 3:Technical writer as facilitator (Tuffley, 1999).**

It may be recalled from the literature review that the culture gap between developers and users leads to poor communication between the parties that in turn leads to an incomplete statement of user requirements (Taylor-Cummings and Feeny, 1997). Hirschheim and Klein recognise recognises the existence of the culture gap in their discussion of Analyst as Facilitator, describing its existence as a direct consequence of the communication difficulties experienced between Analyst as Systems Expert and users. The Analyst as Systems Expert paradigm was consistently the case. No examples of Analyst as Facilitator, Labour Partisan, or Emancipator could be found. The relevance of such rarely encountered categories may perhaps be questionable.

The developer in this sense indicated in Figure 3 therefore equates to Hirschheim and Klein's (1989) Analyst as Systems Expert. Such a role is that of the expert in technology, tools and methods of system design and project management. But while their role aims to make systems development more formal and rational, minimising where possible reliance on human intuition, judgement and politics, these human factors are in practice virtually impossible to dispense with. At some point in the requirements gathering process, the users and management need to articulate their needs to the developers in a mutually intelligible form. Human intuition, judgement and politics form an inherent part of the communication between the users and the developers. Structured analysis approaches seek to minimise the effects of these human factors by making the analysis more formal. The approach taken in this research project is to recognise the reality of these human factors and the need to deal effectively with them, but to also recognise the value in taking a structured systematic approach in the sense of using the IEEE-derived Statement of User Requirements template.

For Hirschheim and Klein's (1989) Analyst as Systems Expert there is but one reality that is both measurable and essentially the same for all everyone. Were it otherwise, it would be very difficult to derive the true requirements of the system. The role of the analyst is to develop a system that models this allegedly objective reality to produce a tool used by management to achieve their organisational goals.

Hirschheim and Klein's (1989) second development paradigm Analyst as Facilitator came about partly because of the problems inherent with the systems expert paradigm. It recognises the fundamental complexity and subjectivity of human interaction. There is no objective reality, only individual perceptions and interpretations of 'reality'. In particular, system requirements are constructed by a continuing process of an organisation defining its objectives. In this sense, the developer's role is to analyse with management what kind of system will achieve these objectives. Hirschheim and Klein (1989) indicate that the developer in this paradigm works from the user's perspective and assists them to determine their preferred view of reality. But to achieve this consensus, it is essential that continuous interaction between developer and user take place.

And here lies the inherent problem with this paradigm in that given the widely recognised existence of a culture gap, continuous interaction is unlikely to occur. While this paradigm has merit in the sense that it addresses the problems outlined in the literature, and recognises the fundamental subjectivity of human interaction, rather than seeking to reduce reality to a single objective entity, as the Analyst as Systems Expert does, it is also impractical for the reasons discussed earlier in the literature review. That is, while integrative processes are acknowledged to have merit, and will work when correctly performed, in practice, in the so-called 'real world' of software development, they are very often not implemented, possibly because they are seen as too costly in terms of time, effort and staff resources. They might also be perceived by the developer as a threat to their culture.

The approach suggested in this research project can be seen as an adaptation of Hirschheim and Klein's (1989) Analyst as Facilitator. It recognises the merit of integrative processes as discussed by Lawrance and Lorsch (1967) and later Galbraith (1977), but it also recognises the existence of and applies a strategy for the minimisation of the risk factors that work against their implementation. These risk factors include reducing the perceived cost of implementation, in terms of time and effort, and the threat to developer culture by employing an existing member of the development team, someone who is an existing participant of the developer culture. The suggested approach also implicitly recognises that projects are funded by a process of management decision-making. From observation and experience project funding decisions are made somewhat consistently throughout the commercial environments of the United Kingdom and Australia in the sense that budgetary considerations are paramount. So cost minimisation is the key benefit from the management point-of-view, and the one that probably stands the best chance of resulting in sufficient funds being allocated to employ a technical writer earlier in the project. The usability benefits that are the real objective of the suggested approach are not management's over-riding concern. Usability improvements have been described by several managers in the course of this research project as being 'nice to have'.

The remaining two paradigms, Analyst as Labour Partisan and Analyst as Emancipator are rarely seen, and are discussed in some detail in Chapter 2.

### 3.5.2. Joint Application Development - role of Facilitator

The collaborative development approach Joint Application Development recognises and defines the role of Facilitator (Wood, Silver 1995). Originally developed by IBM to address the problem of developer/user cultural differences, Joint Application Development (JAD) uses a structured, systematic approach to the development of system requirements. There may be considerable value in this structured approach in the sense that stating it explicitly at the outset of the project, and applying it consistently during the project, the results may be made more useful and valid, as emphasised by Checkland (1991).

Other integrative processes like Participative Design, are not seen as inferior to JAD. The selection of JAD was made on the basis that it offered a defined role for a facilitator. In seeking to maximise the validity of the results, such a structured approach offers an advantage. The other perceived advantage of JAD in this context is that had been developed by an organisation that embodied the orthodoxy of the system development world of the 1970's and 80's, and as such are least likely to be criticised for being marginal or untested. As with the selection of the IEEE-derived template, discussed in the next section, the selection of JAD was made in an attempt to 'stay on safe ground'.

JAD also implicitly recognises and attempts to deal with the problem of developer/user cultural differences. One of its stated basic objectives is to achieve consensus from all parties that the project requirements are correct and complete. Consensus implies that some means of bridging the cultural gap is an essential feature of the process.

JAD is conducted in five phases; project definition, research, preparation, the session and the final documents. The facilitator role is enacted during the fourth phase - the session. Compared with the five stages of the action research (AR) project (reflection, plan, action/observation, reflection, write-up conclusions) it can be seen that they are not dissimilar. Facilitation occurs during the action/observation stage of the research project.

JAD has research and preparation as two distinct phases, while the AR project combines the two into a single planning stage. JAD combines AR's reflection and write-up into a single final documents phase. AR places more emphasis on reflection than does JAD.

Since the researcher would not be authorised to conduct formal JAD sessions as defined by the process, it is the essential JAD facilitation techniques seen below that are applied by the researcher. While hired to be proactive, the researcher is also expected to fit in with the client organisation's existing methods of scheduling and conducting meetings and conducting sessions. The client has an expectation that the researcher will perform certain actions by way of collecting requirements, but that the specific way these actions are performed are at the discretion of the researcher. The appropriateness of these actions was carefully evaluated by the client at the job interview. That the researcher was appointed to the job constitutes a mandate to perform those actions, as described.

Under these circumstances, the formal procedure of JAD would not be performed, yet the essential actions of the facilitator are to be applied, as defined, in a way that is appropriate under the meeting circumstances. The facilitation techniques are condensed into the following six, general purpose guidelines. These can be applied in specific situations, without knowing in advance the exact nature of those meeting situations.

- Keep to the point, stay focussed.
- Listen actively to the other person/people, asking questions to clarify.
- Treat ideas impartially, not evaluated on basis of whose ideas they are.
- Remain in control of the meeting but do so discretely, not overtly.
- Be aware of the organisational context. Recognise and make the connection between the matter at hand and the organisation context in which they are discussed.
- Focus on solving business, not technical problems.

(Wood and Silver, 1995)

### 3.5.3. IEEE Std 830 - Guide to Software Requirements Specifications

As discussed earlier, it is important that a theoretical framework for an action research project be clearly stated at the outset, and for that framework to be consistently applied during the project so that the results may be viewed as valid and useful. It is also recognised that for the results to be seen as valid, their chances might be improved by using a commonly accepted, orthodox theoretical framework. This might help to avoid criticisms based on the theory being marginal and untested.

In his previous work in the commercial systems development industry, the researcher was exposed to a range of development methodologies that had varying degrees of acceptance and rigour. It became clear over time that practitioners with any interest in development methodologies regarded the IEEE Software Engineering Standards as a sound basis upon which to model the software development lifecycle. Notwithstanding the acceptance by practitioners of other methodologies, IEEE represents the consensus view.

If there are criticisms among practitioners of the IEEE standards, it is their complexity and the difficulties surrounding the use of highly detailed procedures suitable for large, safety critical projects, to small to medium sized, non-safety critical development projects. In the literature review it was recognised that any approach to IS quality must acknowledge the fundamental importance of the organisational context of systems use rather than focus exclusively on prescriptive approaches. While organisational context is acknowledged as being of over-arching importance when defining IS quality, there is nonetheless room in the context of this research project to use certain prescriptive processes if they help to establish the basis of more valid and useful results. Prescriptive processes therefore have value when testing research objectives that seek fundamentally to address an organisational problem.

So IEEE Standard 830-1984 - Guide to Software Requirements Specifications, and IEEE Standard P1233 - 1992 - Guide for Developing System Requirements Specification offer the comprehensive structure and content to enable all relevant user requirement issues to be addressed. The problem of their relative complexity in relation to the small to medium size of the development project that is the subject of the research had been previously solved by the researcher by having developed a plain-English, simplified version of these two IEEE standards (see Appendix A). The size and scope of this scaled-down version of the IEEE standards was appropriate to the projects that the researcher had commonly worked on in the past, and of the kind that was likely to the subject of the research. Its appropriateness had been determined by refinement over the previous five years, where it had been used on a number of medium sized commercial development projects. Feedback from others who have used the template have indicated that they are considered useful and appropriate for the purpose of developing a statement of user requirements (SUR).

The orthodoxy of the IEEE derived SURAC template was seen as an advantage in this research project because it is seen to be important to the success of any integrative process that it not be perceived as radical or a threat to the developer culture. It is hoped that developers will accept the value and orthodoxy of the IEEE-derived SURAC template and to perceive it as no threat. While the facilitation techniques defined by JAD can be applied with some transparency since the participants see only the technical writer, a formal template is likely to pose more of a problem to the development of an acceptable integrative process in the sense that because it has an objective existence that may or may not fit with a developer's culture. So the selection of the most commonly accepted methodology might increase its chances of acceptance.

Facilitation techniques can be described as transparent in that if they are applied correctly and consistently they probably won't call attention to themselves. The participants won't notice them in their own right because the participants are actively engaged in gathering requirements rather than analysing the way in which the facilitator is conducting the meeting. In other words people are less likely to think 'I notice the technical writer is listening actively and is treating people's ideas impartially' unless they are actively engaging in discourse analysis instead of requirements gathering. The participants are more likely to think 'this is a productive meeting'.

## 3.6. Project stages

The research project assesses whether Information Systems Quality (in terms of usability as defined by the SOLE model) can be significantly enhanced by the facilitation of the technical writer between the IS developer and the user during the development of the statement of user requirements by using the role of facilitator as outlined by JAD and using IEEE Stds 830 and P1233 during the facilitation process. The assessment is done through a combination of a questionnaire (see Appendix D), interviews, observation and review of documentation.

The project is performed in five stages:

| Stage | Task | Task Description |
|---|---|---|
| 1 | Reflection | The research question is identified through previous observation, reflection and discussion with academic colleagues and practitioners. It is recognised that requirements gathering is often problematic and that the proposed approach might be helpful in bringing about improvement. |
| 2 | Plan | The research proposal and plan to address the question whether IS Quality can be influenced by the technical writer as facilitator is developed, reviewed, discussed and submitted. |

| | | |
|---|---|---|
| | | A focussed literature review is performed.<br>An appropriate action research framework and methodology are proposed.<br>The aims of the research are harmonised with the aims of the client organisation, so that both research and consultancy goals are achieved. |
| 3 | Action, and Observation | The plan is put into action by the researcher who is hired as a technical writer who is to develop the statement of user requirements for a project whose success is critical for the client organisation.<br>The researcher records observations for later consideration and analysis. |
| 4 | Reflection | Researcher reflects on the results of the implemented plan. |
| 5 | Write up Conclusions | The researcher draws conclusions based on consideration of the results and presents the findings in a research report. |

**Table 4: Action research project stages (Baskerville and Pries-Heje, 1995)**

## *3.7. Data collection method(s)*

To help maximise the usefulness of the results, four different data collection methods were used. By a process of triangulation (Jick, 1979) the results of any one of these data collection methods might be validated or invalidated.

**Questionnaire**. Asks the operational user how well, on a scale of 1 to 5, did the V1.0 (original) bulk data load module and the V2.0 (upgraded) module rate on the following three usability characteristics, as defined by the SOLE model; ease-of-use, ease-of-learning, and how well the system meets the user's needs.

**Interviews**. Formal and informal discussions with users, management and developer in which they are asked to evaluate, from their perspective what effect, if any, using the formal Statement of User Requirements had on the completeness of the requirements gathering process. The users have used the old system intensively for several months, and is in the position to competently rate it on the three characteristics. The users used the upgraded system for a month and then asked to rank the system on the three usability characteristics. This month is an intensive time, due to rising volumes and backlogs of customer data needing to be processed.

**Documentary evidence**. Review and evaluate the documentation generated by the developer as a result of using the formal Statement of User Requirements.

**Observation**. Observe, make notes and interpret the verbal and non-verbal behaviour of users, management and developer during the requirements collection process.

## *3.8. Basis of collaboration*

The basis of the collaborative relationship was that only one other person at the research site was aware of the research project. That person was James, the EnergyCorp manager who hired the technical writer. The researcher and James held detailed discussions at the very beginning of the research event in which the research strategy was discussed, the underlying theory outlined, and desired outcomes identified. James felt that to involve the other project participants directly in this discussion would be a distraction that might impact negatively on this critical project for EnergyCorp. Therefore all other participants perceived the event as a more or less normal software development project.

This was desirable from the researcher's point of view. It meant that the other participants would act normally, thus strengthening the validity of the results. It was a concern that should the technical writer be perceived as a researcher the other participants would behave differently. They might possibly feel threatened, that they were under unusual scrutiny, or that they would tell the researcher what they think he wanted to hear, rather than what they actually thought or felt.

During these early discussions with James regarding the nature and scope of the research project, it was made clear to him that the research strategy derived directly from the technical writer's earlier work. Indeed it is likely that it was on this basis that the technical writer had been successful at the initial job interview. The technical writer had a successful track record at performing the process tested in this research project. This track record met the needs that James had for this particular contract. James had a very specific need to fulfil, he needed somebody to develop the software requirements specification for a critical upgrade project. Hiring the technical writer was a risk management measure. The technical writer was able to satisfy James that his earlier work in optimising requirements development would meet his need.

It may therefore be seen that this action research project was theory driven. It is based on strategies developed by the technical writer during the previous five years of commercial practice, combined with the theory of action research as outlined in academic literature. While it is not claimed that this earlier work represents action research, there is a clear pattern of reiteration stretching back from the formal research event, in which theory is tested, the results evaluated, improvements to the theory made in light of lessons learned, then the theory tested again.

# 4. The research project

## *4.1. Introduction*

Chapter 4 focuses on the details comprising the active part of the research project. It does not discuss the larger, end-to-end project.

As such this chapter is a detailed description of the:

- way in which the research site was selected
- project participants
- research site itself, and
- research event chronology

## *4.2. Selection of research site*

As discussed in detail in the previous chapter, the choice of research site was constrained to include not only suitability in relation to the research objectives, but also its ability to provide the researcher's normal income. To enable this, the research was designed to allow the researcher to act in his normal capacity as a contract technical writer. Hence the research site could have been any organisation wanting a technical writer to develop the user requirements for a software development project.

The first constraint was nonetheless the prime determinant in the sense that the research site had to provide the scope of opportunity to meet the research objectives, as follows.

To better understand the nature of the 'gap' that apparently exists between users and developers of systems, especially in relation to the activity of gathering of user requirements. The EnergyCorp work environment housed both EnergyCorp and ComTech development staff, so 'the gap' was likely to be present in some form.

Examine the role of the technical writer in relation to Hirschheim and Klein's (1989) paradigms of the Analyst as Systems Expert and Analyst as Facilitator. As discussed in the literature review, Hirschheim and Klein comment that Analyst as Systems Expert appears to be the dominant development paradigm. So the technical writer employed in a typical software development environment such as this one would be in a good position to observe and consider his role in relation to Analyst as Systems Experts.

Evaluate whether a system can be made more usable (as defined by the SOLE model) by the technical writer acting as a facilitator between user and developer during requirements gathering. It had been discussed at the initial contract application interview whether EnergyCorp would be interested in improving the usability of their systems. The EnergyCorp executive conducting the interview, James, had been in favour of the idea, saying that poor usability was an on-going issue. He was in favour of using suitable means, in the form of a questionnaire to evaluate the current level of usability of the module to be upgraded, then the new level of usability after the upgrade.

Explore factors that influence the problem of developer and user resistance to previously proposed integrative processes (Participative Design, User Participation, Joint Application Development etc.) After reviewing the literature, the hypothesis is advanced that resistance to integrative processes is in part due to their being seen as costly and time-consuming, plus a threat to traditional ways of developing software. Being employed to develop the requirements specification for a particular software upgrade project placed the technical writer in an ideal position to explore the role of facilitator. It also places the writer in a good position to assess the resistance, if any, by the developer to having a technical writer develop the specification when traditionally it is the developer who performs this process.

## *4.3. The participants*

The participants are comprised of the following people. A short biographical note is provided for reference. All names are aliases, yet they retain something of the real person's character.

| Name | Role |
|---|---|
| James | *EnergyCorp Data & Applications Manager.* James is an ambitious, middle-level executive, in his 30's. An electrical engineer with a recently completed MBA. James explicitly recognized that the research project had the potential to manage a major risk and impediment to his advancement in the organisation. |
| Brian | *EnergyCorp IT Manager.* Brian is whom James reports to. He is an experienced executive in his 40's who had acted in a Chief Information Officer role since EnergyCorp was formed. Brian had negotiated the original partnership with ComTech |
| Donald | *EnergyCorp User (user #1).* Donald is an experienced electrical engineer in his 40's who had been with EnergyCorp and its precursor organisation since he left the Queensland Institute of Technology 25 years earlier. His competence is highly regarded by the many people in EnergyCorp who know him. He was the pivot around which the upgrade project revolved in the |

| | |
|---|---|
| | sense that he was the sole possessor of the knowledge needed to process the meter data, and while Francis was being trained to do the job also. |
| Francis | *Second EnergyCorp User (user #2).* Francis is in his late 20's and has an IT development project background, with an emphasis on database management. He had been with EnergyCorp for a year or so before the commencement of the project under discussion here. His previous employer had been with the IT department of a household white goods manufacturer. Francis could be described as an exacting, reserved person. |
| George | *ComTech Project Manager.* George is a senior IT project manager in his 50's with thirty-plus years of IT development experience, having originally come from an electrical engineering background. Independent of this project, the researcher knew of advanced project management work that George had performed at Prime Computer's Canberra Research & Development Centre in the 1980's. George was now a freelance contractor, working for ComTech. |
| Larry | *Principal ComTech Analyst / Programmer.* A self-assured analyst programmer in his 20's with three years post-university project experience. Larry was responsible for some of the design and most of the coding and testing involved with the project. |
| Carl | *Second ComTech Analyst / Programmer.* Carl has a similar background to Larry. He substituted for Larry on the project when Larry was allocated other project work by George. |
| Arthur | *ComTech Managing Director / Owner.* Arthur, in his 50's is the co-director of ComTech whose principal activities were business development, sales and marketing. He had a sales background. |
| William | *ComTech Technical Director / Owner.* William, also in his 50's is the co-director of ComTech who is the technical expert. It is principally William's domain knowledge that is the foundation for ComTech's software development activities in this market niche. |

**Table 5: Research event participants**

## 4.4. The research site

The information contained in the section was derived largely from briefing sessions with James. Additional information was gathered during informal interviews and publicly accessible documents (web-site) and emails. It contains no commercial-in-secret information and breaches no non-disclosure agreement.

### 4.4.1. EnergyCorp

The research site was the Energy Trading Department of EnergyCorp (fictitious name), a leading retailer of electricity and gas in Australia. EnergyCorp had been formed some two years earlier to capitalise on newly deregulated markets. The organisation's annual sales at the time were in the region of A$1.5 Billion.

Being a newly restructured industry, EnergyCorp and its competitors faced a particular challenge -- there was relatively little organisational knowledge about the industry they were in, compared with organisations in industries that had operated for decades. Prior to deregulation, they were government-run monopolies that had little commercial focus. After deregulation, they needed to acquire commercial know-how and compete with each other for business.

In the rush to obtain knowledgeable IT staff during the previous three years, EnergyCorp and its competitors found there to be a shortage of such staff. The supply of Australian candidates was limited, while international candidates were limited to the United Kingdom, New Zealand and South Africa, countries with similar regulatory environments. In practice, EnergyCorp perceived that there were insufficient suitably qualified people available.

EnergyCorp needed to rely on consultants with industry-specific expertise to help them run their business and be competitive. One critical area in which EnergyCorp turned to outside help was in the development of suitable information systems to meet their expanding business needs. Certain customisable off-the-shelf software packages had been evaluated, but these were deemed by EnergyCorp management to be unsuitable.

### 4.4.2. Alliance with ComTech

An alliance had been formed between EnergyCorp and a software developer, who shall be called ComTech (fictitious name). From the researcher's discussions, observations and readings of pre-contract documentation, ComTech marketed itself as being the pre-eminent software developer in the state for the retail energy market. EnergyCorp in turn perceived ComTech to have the appropriate domain knowledge to help EnergyCorp be competitive. Furthermore, ComTech perceived itself as having this expertise, which would tend to place their development approach in the Analyst as Systems Expert (Hirschheim & Klein, 1989) paradigm of systems development.

The basis of the alliance was that ComTech, using their domain knowledge, would design and develop an integrated suite of systems (called TASS – Trading and Settlements System). This system received meter data and processed it into a form that could be used for demand forecasting (Trading), accounts receivable (Billing) and accounts payable (Settlements). Given that the outputs from TASS were required to perform these three vital activities, it was perceived by EnergyCorp as being of vital importance.

The ComTech-EnergyCorp alliance had been formed some two and a half years before the beginning of the research event. TASS would be developed using a combination of modules that they had earlier developed for EnergyCorp, and new modules (developed from scratch). ComTech's overall development activity was characterised by a series of ongoing functional upgrades, implemented sequentially.

### 4.4.3. EnergyCorp's dissatisfaction with alliance

EnergyCorp was well acquainted with ComTech's earlier work, and so was in a position to evaluate how well ComTech did their work, in terms of meeting EnergyCorp's needs. From early discussions with EnergyCorp's James, Donald and Francis, it was clear that a growing dissatisfaction with ComTech was developing. This dissatisfaction was a major contributing reason to the hiring of the technical writer. One cause of this dissatisfaction was that the ComTech was also producing TASS as their own customisable off-the-shelf package (COTS), which they intended to sell to other retailers in the same market -- EnergyCorp's competitors.

Based on meeting proceedings with ComTech's proprietors and senior management, it became clear that ComTech simply wanted EnergyCorp to leave the details to them, and they, using their domain knowledge, would develop a system that would meet EnergyCorp's needs. ComTech did not want to enter into extended discussions about what EnergyCorp wanted. They simply wanted EnergyCorp to pay the bills while ComTech used them to fund the development of their flagship product.

This being the case ComTech was perhaps less inclined to include those user requirements that were unique to the EnergyCorp's particular way of doing business, and which wouldn't necessarily fit with the ComTech's product marketing strategy.

Another cause of EnergyCorp's dissatisfaction, according to James, Donald and Francis, was poor software usability. TASS did not meet EnergyCorp's expectations in terms of being fault-free, user-friendly, and equipped with adequate documentation and training. James, Donald and Francis indicated that the factors appearing to contribute to this poor usability were ComTech having ad hoc development processes, sketchy project documentation, and lack of suitably trained and experienced staff to meet production deadlines.

From a review of earlier project documentation and discussions with EnergyCorp's James, Donald and Francis, and ComTech's George, Larry and Carl, it was determined that ComTech's usual approach to the development of a new module was to produce a relatively brief, high-level requirements list, based on their product development strategy and discussions with the user. Then they would produce a software design document, omitting the intermediate step of a formal statement of user requirements and a software requirements specification.

It was in this context that EnergyCorp hired a new Data & Applications Manager, James, in December 1998 (the research project commenced the following March) to take responsibility for TASS development. As James later said to the technical writer, he had performed a risk analysis and developed an action plan to manage the risk. He recognised that neither the users nor the EnergyCorp's business's needs were being met, so he hired the technical writer, who also had previous experience developing statements of user requirements, in March 1999 to manage the risk that the requirements for this particular upgrade project would be inadequately gathered.

### 4.4.4. Impetus to hire technical writer

The impetus to hire the technical writer (the researcher) was that the electricity retail market was in the process of becoming ‘contestable’ in four stages, or tranches as they are called. Contestable is the term used for open retail contestability where suppliers (such as EnergyCorp) make competing bids to customers for their business, as opposed to the former 'franchise' system where a supplier had a monopoly in their designated franchise area.

Tranche 1 included the highest volume consumers of electricity. These were such organisations such as Alcoa's aluminium smelter in Gladstone, Mount Isa Mines, Queensland Rail and other large industrial sites whose consumption of electricity is enormous, measured in millions of megawatts. At the other end of the scale, Tranche 4 included domestic consumers. A sliding consumption scale thus segmented the market into four grades of consumers. At the time the research project began (March 1999), only Tranche 1 and 2 were contestable, that is, able to be competed for by the various retailers.

However in four months, on July 1st 1999, Tranche 3 would become contestable. As this would then include all small to medium enterprises, from restaurants to every kind of small to medium commercial and industrial organisations, EnergyCorp anticipated a sharp rise in the volume of meter data that would need to be processed. An inability to process the new volume of data, would both lose EnergyCorp profits and customers, but would also seriously embarrass them.

The regulatory environment in which EnergyCorp operates is controlled by the National Electricity Market Management Company Limited (NEMMCO). NEMMCO describes itself as the body corporate responsible for the administration and operation of the wholesale national electricity market in accordance with the National Electricity Code. NEMMCO introduced a regulatory amendment in June 1999 that was to have a very significant effect on the TASS upgrade (and therefore research) project. The amendment basically staged, rather than released all at once,

Tranche 3 contestability (retailers may bid for business from customers), which meant that retailers such as EnergyCorp would not be swamped with high processing loads. As he later said, James was unaware of this regulatory amendment until it was made public. So up until only a month before the proposed 1st July deadline James was proceeding on the assumption that July 1999 would see a dramatic rather than a modest rise in processing volume.

As a consequence, this extra 'breathing space' meant the deadline for the TASS upgrade project could be extended from June 30, 1999, all the way to December 11, 1999. Almost all of the work done by the technical writer in relation to the research project had been done before news of the postponement had been received.

ComTech, the producers of TASS, had some 8 developers working on a number of projects at EnergyCorp's premises. ComTech staff relevant to the TASS upgrade project (the research project) was George, the Project Manager, Larry, the Team Leader, and Carl, programmer. The remaining ComTech staff was involved in developing other modules of TASS.

## 4.5. Research event

The description of the research event is based on information gained during interaction with the technical writer's co-participants as well as other EnergyCorp and ComTech staff who were indirectly related to the event. A record was kept in a research journal.

The subject of the research project was an upgrade to the TASS system, as previously described, to automate a semi-manual process, the Bulk Data Load V1.0 module. This original module performed some processes automatically, but required substantial user intervention. The V1.0 module took raw consumption data, and processed it into a usable form and then placed in a common data store that was then used by accounts receivable and accounts payable for billing and settlements purposes.

As discussed in the previous section, the upgrade of the Bulk Data Load V1.0 module is of critical importance to EnergyCorp because they expected their customer numbers to double within four months, due to previously inaccessible customers becoming accessible. Within 18 months, customer numbers are expected to increase by a power of 10. After that customer numbers were expected to rise exponentially during the medium term.

The existing system, while currently able to process 500 customers would be overwhelmed by 1000, much less 5000. Since the system processes data that is necessary for the production of customer invoices EnergyCorp saw the V2.0 upgrade as being critically important to their business.

The upgraded Bulk Data Load V2.0 module had to automatically be able to process up to 5000 customers per hour with minimal operator involvement. The processed data is the core data that is used by other functional areas (i.e. accounts payable/receivable, forecasting, and service delivery).

Given EnergyCorp's dissatisfaction with the ComTech performance, and the importance of the project, the EnergyCorp Manager implemented a risk management plan, the key element of which was to have the technical writer manage the collection of the user requirements, plus several other related tasks not included in the research.

### 4.5.1. Detailed chronology of the research event

The chronology outlined below is based on the perceptions of the technical writer as the project unfolded. The information is drawn principally from detailed diary notes that were updated on a daily basis by the technical writer and researcher. The diary served as both a work diary chronicling the events of the days, and as a research diary. These two aspects are kept clearly separate as can be seen in the examples in Appendix E.

Keeping a detailed diary of events was likely to be seen as a mark of professionalism by the participants, given the climate of mistrust between EnergyCorp and ComTech that existed for much of the research event. A detailed diary of meeting notes was useful for clarifying matters agreed to, and matters in dispute.

| Wk | Events / Milestones |
|---|---|
| 1 | Week 1 (week beginning Monday 22nd March 1999) was spent learning the technical and business background of the Bulk Data Load V2.0 module project, and how it fitted within the larger context of TASS, the larger suite of modules that was being developed by ComTech. Much of this information came from James during formal daily meetings lasting an hour, plus a series of informal meetings with James, Donald and Francis and various TASS users.<br><br>During these discussions, it became apparent to the technical writer that all but one TASS user were dissatisfied with TASS. As the users said to the technical writer, the source of their dissatisfaction was due to the factors listed below. These four points were the cumulative perceptions of the users:<br><br>• the system having so many 'bugs' that it kept 'falling over'<br>• minimal user documentation,<br>• virtually no training,<br>• unannounced, undocumented changes were made to functionality without informing the users, who would subsequently discover the changes at the cost of the work |

| Wk | Events / Milestones |
| --- | --- |
| | they had just performed.<br><br>EnergyCorp management was unhappy with TASS because they were paying commercial rates for a custom-built system, but after 18 months they had a generic system that did not meet their perceived needs, and which they knew would be sold to their commercial competitors. |
| 2 | In week 2 (week beginning Monday 29th March), through investigation and discussion, the technical writer and James the EnergyCorp Data & Applications Manager decided that greater control needed to be taken by them over the TASS development process. This was seen as a necessary first stage in the process of moving out of a position of dependency to a single supplier of development services.<br><br>A meeting with ComTech was arranged at which the IEEE-derived Statement of User Requirements template was tabled. ComTech were requested to demonstrate that they comprehensively understood the user requirements for the Bulk Data Load V2.0 module by addressing each of the points outlined in template (see Appendix). George, the ComTech project manager, dismissed the tabled Statement of User Requirements as 'irrelevant' to a project of this nature. The technical writer suggested that it was not unreasonable to ask for assurances, particularly in view of past 'misunderstandings' resulting in required functionality not being present in TASS. ComTech agreed to 'consider' the request.<br><br>Arthur and William, the two partners who owned ComTech, were also present at this meeting. They quickly reassured James and the technical writer that they did indeed have a well documented quality management system and that their projects do use equivalent-standard templates as the Statement of User Requirements template tabled by the researcher-technical writer. As the technical writer discovered seven months later, ComTech had no formal quality management system (QMS). This came about during discussions with ComTech in which they expressed an interest in acquiring a QMS in order to satisfy a requirement for a Tender bid that they were making. The technical writer was in a position to provide this. |
| 3 | In week 3 (week beginning Monday 5th April), no progress had been made by ComTech on the Statement of User Requirements. When pressed by the technical writer, the situation escalated to the next higher level of management; it now involved Brian the EnergyCorp IT Manager and ComTech directors, principally Arthur. Arthur complained to Brian that it was 'unreasonable' to request that a formal statement of user requirements be prepared. It had not been necessary in the past, and should not be now.<br><br>James, who was directly responsible for the project was pressured by Brian (his manager) into relaxing the requirement to provide the technical writer's formal statement of user requirements. He, James, told the technical writer that while it was desirable, a |

| Wk | Events / Milestones |
| --- | --- |
| | Statement of User Requirements was in the 'nice to have' category but that 'in the real world' of this project the practical necessities of time and money ruled it out. It appeared that ComTech had successfully managed to avoid the developing a statement of user requirements, despite low EnergyCorp user/management satisfaction with TASS. This presented an obvious crisis for the research project.<br><br>To confirm that it really was necessary for a Statement of User Requirements to be produced, and that it was not a bias of the technical writer, or a self-serving end for the researcher, several senior academic colleagues who had a background in commercial software engineering were consulted. The question was put, 'in a commercial development project such as this, was it reasonable to expect an Statement of User Requirements to be developed?'. The replies all indicated that it would not be unreasonable in the normal course of a project, but given ComTech's poor performance with requirements gathering and poor system usability, it was a prudent risk management measure. |
| 4 | In week 4 (week beginning Monday 12th April), after the events of the previous week, a decision had to be made whether to abandon the project, since it appeared ComTech were unlikely to develop the Statement of User Requirements according to the IEEE-derived template. To proceed, it would be necessary to force them to produce the Statement of User Requirements, which raised the question, was it feasible and appropriate to do so? While it might not be ethical for the researcher to force ComTech, it would be ethical for the technical writer to do so since it formed part of the necessary course of action that EnergyCorp had hired the technical writer to perform.<br><br>The critical question was, if this was consultancy only, would the technical writer be forcing compliance? The answer was yes. It was necessary for a systematic Statement of User Requirements be developed, given the developer's past performance of omitting requirements.<br><br>After reflection, the technical writer advanced the proposition to James, the EnergyCorp Data & Applications Manager, that while a formal Statement of User Requirements might delay the release of the Bulk Data Load V2.0 upgrade, if all of the necessary requirements were not included now, they would still have to be included later which would delay the project even more. 'Do it right first time'. Also if ComTech did understand all of the necessary requirements, and be in a position to proceed as they maintained, then a Statement of User Requirements based on the technical writer's template should not reasonably take ComTech more than a few days to complete. If the developer didn't know all requirements, then it is better to know now and take corrective action. In either case, it was worthwhile to develop the Statement of User Requirements. James accepted the proposition and agreed to support the technical writer in renewed efforts to have ComTech |

| Wk | Events / Milestones |
|---|---|
| | provide the document based on the template. |
| 5 | (week beginning Monday 19th April) At a subsequent meeting between the technical writer and ComTech at the beginning of week 5, it was put to George and Larry that the Statement of User Requirements would have to be produced for this and subsequent projects. George had not been aware that James had reversed his position on the matter, and was disappointed to learn of it.<br><br>ComTech's George resumed his earlier strategy of referring the matter to the ComTech directors who tried to persuade James's manager, Brian, to direct James to put aside the requirement to produce a formal SURAC. James managed to persuade Brian to support the technical writer, presumably by using the same argument. |
| 6 | By week 6 (week beginning Monday 26th April), ComTech reluctantly agreed to the technical writer's request to supply the Statement of User Requirements, the target for completion of which was by the end of week 7. |
| 7&8 | The research project went "on hold" during weeks 7 and 8 due to the need for the technical writer to attend to another EnergyCorp matter that was not related to the research project. The technical writer however contacted the developer every two or three working days during this period to inquire after progress. George or Larry replied each time that the Statement of User Requirements had not been completed, saying that they were too busy, it was too time-consuming and they were unclear about what was required. The technical writer's offer of direct help was declined. The situation was tense. In week 8, George and Larry finally, reluctantly agree to produce the SURAC, as requested. |
| 9 | By week 9 (week beginning Monday 17th May), the Statement of User Requirements had still not been completed. The technical writer, after gaining James' support, said to George that in the interests of making progress, and given continuing delays and staff-shortages, the technical writer would develop the Statement of User Requirements.<br><br>The technical writer also suggested that the users, developer and technical writer meet at a convenient time to walkthrough the Statement of User Requirements in order to confirm that all important requirements were present, that the acceptance criteria were agreed and that the developer could assess whether they could deliver a system that contained those requirements.<br><br>George indicated that Larry had begun work on the IEEE-derived Statement of User Requirements and suggested that Larry be allowed to complete it. But because Larry was absent due to illness, a completed Statement of User Requirements would not be available until the end of the following week (week 10 Friday 28th May) at the earliest. The technical writer indicated that too many delays had already occurred. He asked George that in the interests of |

| Wk | Events / Milestones |
|---|---|
| | progressing matters, would they please let the technical writer have their Statement of User Requirements work-in-progress.<br><br>Somewhat surprisingly given their reluctance to date, the document was forwarded as an email attachment. It had been based on the template given to them by the technical writer and they had made reasonable efforts to address the points. It was perhaps 50% completed before work was stopped on it. The 50% that had been done is likely to have represented the balance of what Larry and George knew collectively about the requirements. The remaining 50% included areas of significant functionality that could not be omitted, given EnergyCorp's stated need to have a system that met all of their requirements. Some of the content was not relevant. The content that *was* relevant was subsequently integrated into the technical writer's Statement of User Requirements and Acceptance Criteria.<br><br>The technical writer finished the Statement of User Requirements in three days, working at a steady pace, alternating between writing and talking to people to gather information. The relevant content from ComTech's template-based version was integrated into the final document. The resulting Statement of User Requirements was therefore the result of collaboration between the technical writer, Larry, George, Donald and Francis (users), in accordance with the research design.<br><br>The technical writer employed the Statement of User Requirements template and the facilitation techniques in the process of having the users, EnergyCorp management and the developer contribute content and later review the document for accuracy and completeness. As a result of this process, the technical writer captured ***six new requirements*** that the developer did not know about and had not included in their original version of the requirements document that was to have formed the basis of their development effort. The technical writer added these to the Statement of User Requirements, and the users and management did a final review. |
| 10 | When all EnergyCorp staff were satisfied, an electronic copy was forwarded to the developers several hours ahead of the review meeting on Tuesday of week 10 (week beginning Monday 24$^{th}$ May). Due to unforeseen circumstances (an off-site staff development day), no EnergyCorp staff were present at the walk-through meeting. Only the ComTech's George and Larry plus the technical writer were present. The technical writer facilitated the meeting using the JAD techniques. Given the resistance to the technical writer's efforts and the resulting tension that this created, it was necessary to begin with pleasantries that served to reduce tension and to indicate good-will on the part of the technical writer towards George and Larry. The absence of the EnergyCorp staff assisted in this process in the sense that the meeting would have been more formal with little time allowed for apparently unproductive activities. James had a highly formalised ap- |

| Wk | Events / Milestones |
|---|---|
| | proach to conducting meetings.<br><br>The technical writer, using empathy and open-ended questions reduced the tension after around 10 minutes to the point where he thought ComTech's George and Larry were ready to collaborate. By keeping the discussion to the point, actively listening, and remaining aware of the organisational context in which the discussion was occurring, the technical writer facilitated a walkthrough of the Statement of User Requirements and Acceptance Criteria (SURAC).<br><br>The requirements that ComTech already knew about caused little or no comment. The six new requirements were the basis of lengthy constructive discussion that were characterised by a 'yes we can do these for you' attitude. George and Larry's attitude had changed from very unco-operative to quite co-operative. The technical writer was surprised at the degree to which George and Larry's attitude had become positive and co-operative. Possible factors noted at the time include:<br><br>the absence of EnergyCorp people (with whom a high degree of antagonism had developed)<br><br>the facilitation techniques employed by the technical writer, and how much was attributable to unknown factors,<br><br>ComTech recognising that the work of the technical writer had brought about a benefit for them (the preparation of the SURAC) and had saved them time.<br><br>With the absence of James, Donald and Francis at the staff development event, it was not possible to finalise the SURAC at this meeting. The technical writer arranged a meeting for the following week at which all interested parties could be present. |
| 11 | In week 11 (week beginning Monday 31st May), the full SURAC walkthrough meeting was held. As before, the known requirements received minimal attention. Extensive technical discussions were held concerning the feasibility and importance of including the additional six requirements. The discussions were held in the same co-operative manner as the previous meeting. This was in contrast with earlier meetings, a situation that was noted by James, Donald and Francis. These earlier meetings had been tenser.<br><br>The presence of the six extra requirements highlighted the usefulness of producing a comprehensive and systematic SURAC. For reasons that were unclear at the time, ComTech's attitude had become significantly more amenable to EnergyCorp's wishes. For example, whereas before, a request for one of the five new requirements was met by the reply 'Well I'm not sure we're prepared to give that to you. It doesn't fit with our product development strategy'. At the week 11 meeting, a request for the same requirement, now framed in the Statement of User Requirements, |

| Wk | Events / Milestones |
|---|---|
| | received the 'yes we can do that for you'. |
| 12 | In week 12 (week beginning Monday 7th June), it became apparent that the V2.0 Bulk Data Load module would not be complete by the July 1st (week 14) target release date. The pressing need for the bulk data load module had eased considerably due to a change in the regulatory environment (NEMMCO) that governed this industry sector. Essentially, while the same number of potential customers as expected still existed, regulatory changes had removed the incentive for many of these new potential customers to move from their current supplier, to EnergyCorp. The V1.0 data load module could continue to be used at least until the beginning of the following year (2000). This was welcome news to ComTech.<br><br>However this information was with-held from ComTech by James who believed ComTech would proceed even more slowly if they knew.<br><br>Discussions were held with ComTech about a feasible new release date. ComTech explained that 'unforeseen' circumstances had robbed resources from the project at hand. Resource shortages had been a characteristic of the entire development project, however it was becoming more acute. A tentative completion date was set down for six weeks (week 18, week beginning 19th July). |
| 13 | In week 13 (week beginning Monday 14th June), the requirements had reached a level of stability that all parties agreed were sufficient to use as the basis for development. It was now a matter of waiting until the developers completed the project, and the usability of the finished product could be assessed. The technical writer was not involved in the development work, however he remained involved in the development project by means of weekly progress meetings with EnergyCorp and ComTech staff. |
| 14 to 27 | Development continued until week 27 (second last week of September) when testing began. The reason for the extended delay in completing the design and implementation stages was unclear. Apparent excuses were made, but the reasons given did not appear to be truthful, or at least the whole truth. From the apparent absences, it was clear that ComTech staff had been re-deployed, possibly as a result of ComTech learning of the change in the NEMMCO regulations referred to in week 12. |
| 28 | Unit testing continued until the end of week 28. |
| 29 to 31 | The first round of acceptance testing and "bug fixes" continued until the end of week 31 (last week of October). The acceptance testing, which was performed by the technical writer and the principal user Donald, revealed numerous technical and usability problems. It became increasingly apparent that the system would not be ready for release by the end of October. This created a complication because EnergyCorp had imposed an October 31 freeze on all systems development and release in order to stabi- |

| Wk | Events / Milestones |
|---|---|
| | lise systems ahead of the December 31 transition to the new millennium. James negotiated an exemption to the freeze with higher management to enable the technical and usability problems with M&M to be resolved. |
| 32 to 35 | Progress during weeks 32 to 35 (month of November) was slow and frustrating. ComTech management had apparently redeployed their people elsewhere, which meant at EnergyCorp they now lacked the resources and possibly the technical expertise to complete the work satisfactorily. The frequency of the weekly project review meetings was increased to daily or three times a week in an effort by James to exercise more control over the process. George, the ComTech Project Manager was at pains to re-assure James and the technical writer that all was under control, and that the project could be brought to a successful conclusion.<br><br>The absence of completed, defect-free, usable deliverables suggested otherwise. Specific action Items that were agreed at the review meetings were consistently ignored to the point where the meetings were becoming pointless. While George was an experienced project manager, skilled at explaining problems away, Larry was less experienced. Review meetings where he was the principal ComTech representative degenerated almost into farce, despite James' efforts to keep the meeting business-like. For example, James would ask, "And item 14, I suppose I know the answer, but has it been done?" Larry replied with a shrug. |
| 36 | Week 36 (first week of December) was the week before the scheduled release date. It was characterised by last minute fixes of various functional or usability-related problems. |
| 37 | M&M V2.0 finally went live on Saturday 11 December 1999 (Week 37). The first two days of processing went moderately well with no major problems. |
| 38 to 40 | In weeks 38 to 40 the technical writer was on holidays. However progress was monitored via email. The period was characterised by on-going use of M&M V2.0, with problems being identified by Donald and fixed by Larry as they occurred. |
| 41 to 52 | The same pattern was repeated over the subsequent 11 weeks. Most of the interviews described in the Data Analysis chapter occurred during this period. In the period from week 37 to 52 a total of 103 issues relating to the operation of M&M V2.0 were raised and resolved. When the technical writer exited EnergyCorp on the 10 March 2000, M&M V2.0 had been effectively bedded down and was functioning correctly in the opinion of EnergyCorp management, on advice from the users. |

**Table 6: Detailed research event chronology**

### 4.5.2. Timeline summary

Timeline of events at EnergyCorp that set the context for the research project.

| When | Events/Milestones |
|---|---|
| 1996 | EnergyCorp established as a commercial enterprise. |
| 1997 | Alliance between EnergyCorp and ComTech established |
| 12 / 99 | James (Data & Applications Manager) hired. |
| 22 / 3 / 99 | Technical writer / research hired on six month contract, subsequently extended a further six months) |
| 22 / 3 / 99 | Research project begins |
| 29 / 3 / 99 | Bulk Data Load V1.0 module upgrade project begins (as part of larger TASS upgrade project |

**Table 7: Summary of EnergyCorp milestones relevant to the research project.**

## *4.6. Conclusion*

### 4.6.1. Summary of significant research event chronology

This table presents an overview of the significant events that occurred during the research event. A detailed week by week chronology follows after this summary.

| Wk | Events/Milestones |
|---|---|
| **1** 22 / 3 / 99 | Orientation of technical writer |
| 2 | Initiate meetings, discussions with ComTech's Arthur, William and George, in company with EnergyCorp's James, Donald and Francis. |
| 3 | ComTech's Arthur persuades EnergyCorp's Brian (CIO) that SURAC is not necessary. Brian instructs James to not require the SURAC that the technical writer was to use. |
| 4 | Technical writer persuades EnergyCorp that SURAC is necessary. |
| 5 | ComTech openly refuse to produce SURAC by means of upper level EnergyCorp management politicking. |
| 6 | ComTech verbally agree to produce SURAC, no follow-up action. |
| 9 | Technical writer assumes responsibility for producing the SURAC. ComTech hand over work-in-progress. |

| Wk | Events/Milestones |
|---|---|
| | The technical writer produces the SURAC in 3 days. |
| 10 | ComTech and technical writer walk through the completed SURAC. New atmosphere of co-operation. |
| 11 | EnergyCorp, ComTech and technical writer walk through the completed SURAC. Technical issues resolved. |
| 12 to 27 | ComTech continue with development based on agreed SURAC. |
| 27 to 28 | Unit testing |
| 29 to 31 | Acceptance testing |
| 32 to 36 | Defect fixing |
| 37 | M&M V2.0 released on Saturday 11 December 1999 |
| 38 to 51 | Ongoing problem resolution |
| 52 | Technical writer exits research site. |

**Table 8: Summary of significant research event chronology**

In relation to the potential problem alluded to by Baskerville (1992) and others that the roles of the consultant (technical writer in this case) and that of the researcher becomes blurred, it is important to emphasise that during this action research project it was almost exclusively the technical writer who is the active participant. It is the technical writer who has the authority to act and make things happen. The researcher had no authority at all. The researcher's role was limited to the phases before and after the research event, and during quiet periods either at the client's site or elsewhere when no interaction with participants could occur. This deliberate strategy was to avoid the kind of criticisms alluded to by Baskerville (1992).

The researcher therefore devised a research strategy in consultation with EnergyCorp manager, James, that allowed the technical writer to function as a normal technical writer, albeit with an extended role. James agreed that it would be simplest and probably best if the research component were not relevant to the technical writer's primary responsibility, to coordinate the development of the SURAC. The actions performed during the research event, and the interaction with the other participants, were in the persona of the technical writer. Clearly some of the technical writer's actions were prescribed by the researcher in the earlier planning of the research project. This included such matters as using the SURAC template and employing JAD facilitation techniques. Having been prescribed, they could then be performed by the technical writer as a normal and expected part of his job to develop the SURAC.

The researcher's role, as distinct from the technical writer's role during the research event was limited to making careful observations and either recording them immediately into the diary, or later if it would appear unusual to the participants. The diary is an A4-sized standard office diary that people would expect to see. Such detailed observations would not usually be performed in a normal software development project, although it did not look out of place since it is simply good commercial practice to keep detailed notes to refer back to in the event of a dispute about how events had occurred.

The technical writer made sure that his co-participants were not reminded of his research role. Those that needed to know were made aware that the project formed the basis of a Master's level project, but this was not dwelled upon as it might have influenced the way they perceived and related to the technical writer. This further helped to make a clear distinction between the actions of the researcher and those of the technical writer.

During the final four months of the 12 month research event, the technical writer gradually spent more time with the ComTech staff, assisting with such activities as testing. The technical writer found them agreeable to work with, similar in many ways to other developers he had worked with in the past. Over this period, ComTech gave the technical writer their perspective on the whole situation with EnergyCorp. It was startling to realise the degree to which EnergyCorp and ComTech perceived events differently.

# 5. Data analysis

## 5.1. Introduction

This chapter presents the results of the analysis of the data from the sources described at the end of Chapter 4. The technical writer had collected the data from 18 March 1999 to 10 March 2000 while on-site at EnergyCorp's premises. A period of four years had elapsed between when the data was collected and when it was analyzed. This was due to a combination of delaying factors; these included ill-health, family commitments, and a heavy workload. The analysis was performed on the raw data as collected, using the analysis techniques outlined in the research strategy, which had already been written. Reference may be made to the research journal to view the raw data.

In order to strengthen the validity of the results, four different sources of data are used. Using data triangulation (Jick, 1979), the results of any one of these data collection methods are evaluated against the others in the Conclusion section of this chapter.

It was considered important during the design stage of the research project to have multiple sources of data, given the inherent problems with action research projects, as discussed in detail earlier (loss of objectivity by the researcher).

It is shown how each data collection method relates to the research objects, whether a particular instrument supports a specific objective(s). For reference, the research objectives are reiterated below.

- To better understand the nature of the 'gap' that apparently exists between users and developers of systems, especially in relation to the activity of gathering of user requirements.
- To examine the role of the technical writer in relation to Hirschheim and Klein's (1989) paradigms of the Analyst as Systems Expert and Analyst as Facilitator.
- To examine whether system usability (as defined by the SOLE model, Eriksson and Törn, 1991) can be improved by the technical writer acting as a facilitator between user and developer during requirements gathering.
- To explore factors which influence the problem of developer and user resistance to previously proposed integrative processes

## *5.2. Data collection*

This section describes the data collection instruments and shows how each instrument is applied to achieve the research objectives. The data had been collected during the twelve months that the technical writer was at the EnergyCorp site.

As seen from the table below, the questionnaire is a vital element of the results, but it serves only one objective, to evaluate the user's perceptions of the changes in usability. The remaining collection methods cover the remaining research objectives.
It is indicated for each data collection method whether they support the achievement of the research objectives. How they support the objectives are discussed in detail in the next Chapter. For reference purposes, the objectives are numbered and summarised below.

### 5.2.1. Relating the data collection methods to the research objectives

The table below indicates whether a specific data collection method assists with achieving a specific objective. Detailed discussion of how this happens is given in Chapter 5.

| | **Questionnaire** | **Interviews** | **Doc. Evid.** | **Observations** |
|---|---|---|---|---|
| **Understanding the 'Gap'** | No | Yes | Yes | Yes |
| **Tech Writer / Hirschheim et al** | No | Yes | Yes | Yes |
| **Improve Usability** | Yes | Partially | Partially | Partially |
| **Resist to Integ. Processes** | No | Yes | Yes | Yes |

**Table 9: Summary of relation of data collection methods to research objectives**

### 5.2.2. Data collection methods

**Questionnaire**. Asks the operational user how well, on a scale of 1 to 5, did the V1.0 (original) bulk data load module and the V2.0 (upgraded) module rate on the three usability characteristics, as defined by the SOLE model. This collection method supports the third research objective, to assess usability before and after applying the facilitated requirements gathering techniques. The results of the questionnaire do *not* constitute quantitative data, given the small size of the sample. These results are therefore qualitative.

**Interviews.** Mostly informal discussions with users, management and developer. The interviews were approached using a relaxed conversational style in which the respondents were encouraged to feel at ease and to discuss their opinions to questions relevant to the research objectives. The technical writer was aware of the danger that he would be told what the respondent thought he wanted to hear, rather than what they actually thought. By asking the same question two or three times using a different angle of approach each time, the degree of consistency could be evaluated as an indication of how truthful the responses were. The respondents were asked to evaluate, from their perspective what effect, if any, using the formal Statement of User Requirements had on the completeness of the requirements gathering process. Interviews were an integral part in contributing to the achievement of all four objectives, though to a lesser extent for objective number three.

**Documentary evidence**. Review and evaluate the documentation generated by the developer as a result of using the formal Statement of User Requirements. These documents are shown in the appendix. Documentary evidence also includes email between project participants. As with interviews, documentary evidence contributed significantly to achieve all four objectives, though again to a lesser extent for objective number three.

**Observation**. Observe, make notes and interpret the verbal and non-verbal behaviour of users, management and developer during the requirements collection process. These observations were made as the technical writer went about his work interacting with the other project participants to developing the statement of user requirements document. These observations, made over a twelve-month period were made as an 'insider' rather than as an external researcher.

## *5.3. Questionnaire*

The questionnaire supports the third objective; Improving usability. It does not directly support the remaining three objectives.

The results of the questionnaire completed by the two users, Donald and Francis form the basis of the questionnaire results.

While not specifically part of the original research design, since the opportunity was not foreseeable, an opportunity to administer the same questionnaire to all TASS users presented itself during February 2000. This was around two months after the first questionnaire was administered. While performing a second, organisation-wide questionnaire was not specifically part of the original research design, it was recognised in the research design that windfall opportunities might occur and could be used that was directly related to the research objectives. This constitutes returning to a data collection instrument, particularly one with such a limited sample, in order to collect a greater sample. The report is included in the appendix.

The second set of questionnaire results help to strengthen the validity of the first set in that it provides data on how Donald and Francis's perceptions of V2.0 usability might have changed after three months of use, plus it gives an insight into how the users of other TASS modules regard its usability.

### 5.3.1. Usability of Bulk Data Load module (a component of TASS)

Once V2.0 had been running live for a month, the users, Donald and Francis were asked to compare the usability (as defined below) of V1.0 with that of V2.0. The technical writer expressed no opinion one way or the other so as to avoid indicating what the technical writer wanted to hear. There was little chance of that happening in any event; the users were both experienced electrical engineers who were forthright in expressing their opinions.

Donald and Francis were asked to rate usability of V1.0 and V2.0 as defined by Eriksson & Törn's (1991) SOLE model. Specifically, they were given a written questionnaire that asked the following three questions:

How easy was the module to use?,

How easy to learn was the module?, and

Does it do what you need it to do (in terms of doing your job)?

Note that V2.0 is the subject of the research project. Version 1.0 was the existing module. ComTech had developed both versions.

A numerical value is assigned by applying a five point scale, with Very Easy/Well at 1, through to Very Difficult/Badly at 5. A higher cumulative score indicates poor usability. Again it must be emphasised that the use of an ordinal scale in this instance produces qualitative not quantitative results in the sense that a sample of two is insufficient for quantitative purposes. It does however provide a reliable indication of the user's perceptions.

**Results**

| **Donald** | Q 1 max 5 | Q 2 max 5 | Q 3 max 5 | Total max 15 |
|---|---|---|---|---|
| **V 1.0** | 5 | 4 | 4 | 13 |
| **V 2.0** | 3 | 3 | 2 | 8 |
| **Francis** | Q 1 | Q 2 | Q 3 | |
| **V 1.0** | 5 | 5 | 4 | 14 |

| | | | | |
|---|---|---|---|---|
| **V 2.0** | 4 | 3 | 2 | 9 |
| **Average** | Q 1 | Q 2 | Q 3 | Av. Tot |
| **V 1.0** | 5 | 4.5 | 4 | 13.5 |
| **V 2.0** | 3.5 | 3 | 2 | 8.5 |

**Table 10: Donald and Francis's responses**

In terms of the usability criteria established above, both users appear to find V 2.0 more usable than V 1.0.

## 5.3.2. Technical Report into TASS provides further data

As discussed in the previous section, the technical writer was later to prepare a technical report for use by EnergyCorp as part of contract renewal negotiations with ComTech. This was not part of the research project; rather it was a report to be used by EnergyCorp to determine how much and how well ComTech had delivered on the existing contract. The results are expressed in percentage delivered.

This specific opportunity was not foreseeable, and so was not part of the original research design. However, the occurrence of these windfall opportunities sometime during the course of the 12 months that the technical writer was on-site was foreseeable, if not likely.

EnergyCorp had initially required a straightforward 'percentage delivered' for each of the modules included within the scope of the contract. The technical writer suggested that while he was interviewing the various users of the overall system, he might also ask them to complete the same questionnaire as Donald and Francis in order to get an additional indicator that might be useful during contract negotiations. This involved talking to around 35 individuals within various departments of EnergyCorp. These 35 represent the entire TASS user group. The questionnaire was administered either verbally by the technical writer, or via email. The response rate to the questionnaire was good; only three did not respond.

Detailed results can be found in Appendix C Technical Report into TASS'. A summary of results is shown below, indicating the usability rating for all six TASS modules. A higher cumulative score indicates poor usability.

- Forecasting: 6/15
- Whole Sale Portfolio Management: 0/15 (no result)*
- Energy Trading: 15/15
- Wholesale Pricing: 0/15 (no result)

- Meter Data: 9/15
- Wholesale Hedge Contract Settlements: 6.25/15

* No results indicated that the module did not exist or was not in a condition to be used therefore there were no users to survey.

A period of eight weeks separated the two surveys, and it can be seen that in that time Donald and Francis grew slightly less satisfied with the meter data module as indicated by their average rating changing from 8.5 to 9.

## *5.4. Interviews*

Interviews were central to the achievement of all four of the research objectives. Objective number three (evaluate whether a system can be made more usable, as defined by the SOLE model, by the technical writer acting as a facilitator between user and developer during requirements gathering) was partially supported by interviews. Interviews took place when the timing was appropriate for the technical writer as collaborator, and this could not in practical terms be fitted into an interview schedule such as someone explicitly perceived as a researcher might devise.

The interviews were conducted as an 'insider', that is an existing member of the project team who was perceived to have no special status beyond the authority to co-ordinate some of the activities of the users and developers. This approach was carefully cultivated so as not to contaminate the data by people saying what they think the interviewer wants to hear, or otherwise not express their real opinions.

Hence an informal, relaxed approach was adopted in which people were likely to be unaware that they were actually being interviewed. The exception here is the interview with James, seen below. This was a formal debriefing session of the research project.

Each interviewee is introduced with some biographical information that might help the reader understand what kind of person they are.

Formal interviews are constituted by making prior arrangement to meet, using a meeting room, and proceedings being typical of a meeting in a commercial environment. Informal interviews are constituted by seemingly spontaneous, usually one-to-one encounters with participants in places such as their work cubicle, lunchroom, elevator, and even in the designated smoking area outside of the building. The value of this latter meeting place should not be undervalued. Donald was a smoker, and a key participant. He was more inclined to speak frankly under these circumstances than at his desk within earshot of his co-workers. Indeed much interesting information and insight into the workings of EnergyCorp were derived from informal chats with Donald.

It should be noted that the technical writer informal day-to-day contact was with James, Donald, Francis, George, Larry and Carl. Much of the interview information was derived from the hundreds of interactions typical of co-workers operating in a project environment over an extended period of 12 months, and as such the informal interviews are too numerous to list individually. The consolidated results of the informal interviews are found in the sections following.

No interviews were conducted with Brian, Carl, Arthur and William. The researcher basically had no access or opportunity to do so. Brian was senior management whom the researcher had no direct access. William and Arthur were directors of ComTech, who were not present at the EnergyCorp site. Carl was an occasional participant in the project whose involvement was peripheral. He had been redeployed to another site by the time the interviews described below were conducted.

### 5.4.1. EnergyCorp's view

#### *5.4.1.1. EnergyCorp Data & Application's Manager (James)*

About James: an ambitious, middle-level executive, an electrical engineer with a recently completed MBA. James had the insight to realise that the research project had the potential to manage a major risk and impediment to his advancement in the organisation.

James had been aware of the research project from the start. He was the sponsor in that it was his decision to hire the technical writer/researcher.

Private debrief interview (in week 27, Friday 24 September 1999)

In a private one-to-one formal debrief interview (in week 27, Friday 24 September, lasting 45 minutes, held in level 6 meeting room 2) at the researcher's request, he was asked whether in his view, the application of the Statement of User Requirements and the facilitation of the technical writer had improved the usability of the Bulk Data Load V2.0 module. He gave the qualified reply that in his opinion it had *'undoubtedly improved the outcome'* by forcing the developers to listen to what the users and management wanted, to formally document the requirements, then to feedback what they thought the client wanted in order to confirm their understanding was correct.

James commented that for the process to work, several prerequisites had to be present:

*a clearly understood and agreed contract must exist between the developer and the client, that creates a legally binding contract as the 'basis in law', the contract notwithstanding, all parties should nonetheless be willing to 'negotiate around reasonable commercial outcomes', in other words, to use the contract as a lever rather than a club, being flexible when required.*

From his perspective, James summed up the process of developing the Bulk Data Load V2.0 module as being 'a negotiated rather than a fixed outcome'. It was a process in which the 'top down' movement of the developer, met and negotiated with the 'bottom up' (sic).movement of the user.

James said that by forcing the application of the Statement of User Requirements, the basis of the developer client relationship had shifted from 'Expert Consultancy' to 'Process Consultancy'. The term 'Expert' used by James resonates to some extent with Hirschheim and Klein's Analyst as Systems Expert. The term 'Process Consultancy' refers to the shift to the client having influence over the process used by the ComTech in producing V2.0.

In James' view, a pre-requisite of this 'process consultancy' is to have good communication between the stakeholders. When asked about the need for a facilitator, James agreed that when communication is not good, as it had become in the case at hand, then a facilitator is needed. The facilitator role as defined by Hirschheim and Klein's Analyst as Facilitator might therefore be a key agent in the improvement of communication between stakeholders.

When asked about usability, and how it may have been improved or otherwise as a result of the technical writer performing the process, James commented that it is naturally follows that the overall level of usability would improve when sufficient effort was made to clarify the user's needs and ensure that they are incorporated in the requirements. Given that ComTech's initial statement of user requirements did not contain the six additional requirements subsequently identified by the technical writer was evidence of this. James had mentioned in previous discussions, as had many of the system users within EnergyCorp, that the overall level of usability of the systems developed by ComTech was extremely poor. The M&M version 2 module was distinctly more user-friendly, according to Donald and Francis, in their discussions with James.

James concluded by saying that the exercise had resulted in the developer shifting from 'we're the experts with world's best practice' to 'how can we help you do what you need to do?'. Expert in this context is analogous to Hirschheim & Klein's (1989) Analyst as Systems Expert. As indicated by James during weeks 1 and 2, this was what EnergyCorp had wanted the technical writer to achieve, if possible, in addition to the basic task of obtaining a more complete set of user requirements for V2.0.

#### *5.4.1.2. EnergyCorp Users (Donald & Francis)*

About Donald and Francis. Donald is an electrical engineer who had been with EnergyCorp and its precursor organisation since he left the Queensland Institute of Technology 25 years earlier. His competence is highly regarded by the many people in EnergyCorp who know him. He was the pivot around which the upgrade project revolved in the sense that he was the sole possessor of the knowledge needed to process the meter data, and while Francis was being trained to do the job also, Francis had quite some distance to go before being a fully competent replacement for Donald.

Francis has an IT development project background, with an emphasis on database management. He had been with EnergyCorp for a year or so before the commencement of the project under discussion here. His previous employment was in a commercial IT development environment. Francis could be described as an exacting, humourless, reserved person.

Donald, private debrief interview (in week 27, Thursday 23 September)

In a private one-to-one informal debrief interview (in week 27, Thursday 23 September, lasting 10 minutes, held on balcony overlooking Anzac Square) Donald was asked whether in their view using the Statement of User Requirements and having a facilitator mediate in the requirements collection had resulted in a more complete set of requirements.

Donald replied laconically *'Yeah, it probably did help'* (using the SURAC template.) His subsequent comments included that ComTech seemed reluctant to take the time to develop a structured statement of user requirements. Donald felt that it had been worthwhile to have someone systematically facilitate communication between the developer and the client organisation. Donald observed that though it was worthwhile, project personnel were usually too busy to do this in an organised way.

When asked about the usability of M&M version 2, Donald replied that it was a distinct improvement over previous efforts by ComTech. Donald was a resourceful user and had invented numerous workarounds when using earlier ComTech modules. He took this in his stride, though the extra effort and time overhead was somewhat resented. M&M version 2 did not require him to perform these overheads.

Francis, Private debrief interview (in week 27, Thursday 23 September)

In a private one-to-one formal debrief interview (in week 27, Thursday 23 September, lasting 20 minutes, held in level 6 meeting room 2) Francis was asked whether in their view using the Statement of User Requirements and having a facilitator mediate in the requirements collection had resulted in a more complete set of requirements.

Francis replied *'Yes, I'd say so'*. He was highly critical of ComTech's software development approach in general. Francis's perception of Com-

Tech was that they continually cut corners, omitted important steps, including the development of the full range of development documentation (project plan, quality plan, configuration management plan, software requirements specification, software design description etc.). He appeared to derive considerable satisfaction that ComTech had been forced to produce at least some of this development documentation.

In terms of usability, Francis commented that M&M version 2 did appear to be easier to use than version 1. Francis was in the position of understudy to Donald. He needed to learn what it was that Donald did so that EnergyCorp would not be so dependent upon Donald. Francis had clearly struggled to use version 1, not having Donald's experience. There was the impression that Francis were somewhat anxious about his ability to learn Donald's job. M&M version 2 appeared to come as a relief to him in that it simplified the process in such a way that he could understand readily. While Francis did not specifically use the word usability, he was describing improved usability leading to a reduction of anxiety. If anything, the improved usability increased his hostility towards ComTech, possibly because he had been blaming himself for what he came to see as ComTech's shortcomings.

### 5.4.2. ComTech's view

#### *5.4.2.1. ComTech project manager (George)*

About George. A senior IT project manager with thirty-plus years experience, having originally come from an electrical engineering background. Independent of this project, the researcher knew of advanced project management work that George had performed at Prime Computer's Canberra Research & Development Centre in the 1980's. George was now a freelance contractor, working for ComTech.

Private debrief interview (in week 28, Tuesday 29 September)

In a private interview (in week 28 Tuesday 28 September, lasting 15 minutes, held in ComTech work area, level 2), when the tension that had existed in the SURAC development stage had largely dissipated, George was asked first to discuss his perceptions of ComTech's role at EnergyCorp. He commented that their ongoing role at EnergyCorp had often involved their (ComTech) being a 'facilitator' between different functional areas within EnergyCorp. This was necessary in order to resolve issues relevant to projects but which EnergyCorp seemed reluctant to resolve themselves, despite being 'internal issues'.

According to George, ComTech adopted the facilitator role because 'someone had to get people talking to each other'. He described EnergyCorp as having 'a silo mentality' in which knowledge is hoarded and not willingly shared with those within the organisation that need it for upstream or downstream processing. This "silo mentality" had contributed to their difficulties in obtaining, amongst other things, complete user requirements because in some cases users and management either did not know or would not say what their requirements were. George said that as the relationship between stakeholders degenerated, ComTech were finding it increasingly difficult to perform the facilitator role.

George commented that they had been forced through circumstance to adapt their expert approach to include elements of facilitation. They did so reluctantly because it added time and effort to fixed price projects, thus reducing profitability. Here is a strong indication as to why existing integrative processes are not used on development projects, plus an acknowledgement of the need for someone to facilitate, though preferably not them.

While George did not explicitly say so, it appeared that ComTech continued in the facilitator role until the relationship between EnergyCorp and ComTech had reached a low point where ComTech were no longer able to perform their adapted facilitator role. The precise reason for this is not clear. It is interesting to note that from the developer's point of view communication was difficult not just between themselves and EnergyCorp, but also between the various departments comprising EnergyCorp, a 'house divided'.

As discussed earlier, George regarded integrative processes as a worthwhile practice, but that they are usually not performed because 'getting the client to pay for it' is usually a problem. Best practice is often sacrificed for expediency. George's comment about 'getting the client to pay' for something that will ensure success appears to reduce the problem to its most basic.

#### *5.4.2.2. ComTech analyst programmer (Larry)*

About Larry. A 20-something, self-assured analyst programmer with three years post-university project experience. Larry was responsible for some of the design and most of the coding and testing involved with the project.

Private debrief interview (in week 28, Tuesday 29 September)

Also in week 28 (Tuesday 28 September, lasting 5 minutes, held at Larry's cubicle in ComTech work area, level 2), Larry was asked what his perceptions of the Bulk Data Load upgrade project had been. Perhaps understandably Larry was reluctant to speak freely, remaining highly guarded in his responses. Essentially he did not see practical value in the development of a formal SURAC because it took time that he felt was better spent on actual software design and development.

When asked whether the extra six functional requirements suggested that the formal SURAC approach might indeed have some value, Larry conceded that it (the SURAC) might be alright, provided someone else performed the process.

### 5.4.3. The technical writer's view (David Tuffley)

In the early stages of the project, ComTech regarded the technical writer with suspicion. They apparently saw him as a threat and resisted all efforts by him to have them change their development approach in accordance with EnergyCorp's wishes. In the early stages, the technical writer was getting only EnergyCorp's version of reality and this led to a biased view during the early stages. Once ComTech came to view the technical writer as a technical writer performing a facilitator role, the relationship became collaborative. This occurred during and after the SUARC development stage when their former adversary became helpful and collaborative in the role of technical writer.

At the beginning of the project, the communication between developer, management and user had been confined to formal, somewhat tense meetings. Someone was required to facilitate frequently in order for the discussion to remain constructive. By the end of the project, less facilitation was necessary due to the developers, management and users having apparently learned to communicate constructively with each other. The opinion of each party was again sought in private, and while opinions differed on why it had changed, it was universally agreed that the relationship had become significantly more constructive and collaborative, relative to the early stages of the project.

By about week 27, the technical writer became a de facto member of the development team. ComTech's own staff shortages facilitated their acceptance of the technical writer, particularly since EnergyCorp were paying the technical writer. Another reason for this acceptance was that the researcher was comfortable in the role of technical writer and was able to use his well-practised software project team skills to establish good, collaborative relationships with other (ComTech) team members.

## *5.5. Documentary evidence*

As with interviews, documentary evidence was important to the achievement of all four of the research objectives. Objective number three (evaluate whether a system can be made more usable, as defined by the SOLE model, by the technical writer acting as a facilitator between user and developer during requirements gathering) was only partially supported by interviews.

Documentary evidence is in the form of ComTech's original SUR and the technical writer's enhanced SURAC (both are provided in the Appendix). The remaining documentary evidence takes the form of email. Indeed email is an effective data collection tool in the sense that it was the primary way that the development project participants communicated with each other. Project members see email as a convenient way of communicating in that it is asynchronous in the way formal letters are, yet the mode of communication in email tends to be less formal, more conversational. Permission was not granted to quote e-mails verbatim in their entirety, therefore they have been paraphrased.

### 5.5.1. ComTech had no intention of producing a Statement of User Requirements

ComTech developers had not intended to produce an Statement of User Requirements for the Bulk Data Load V2.0 Module upgrade project, as indicated by the following verbatim extract from George, the ComTech project manager to James, the EnergyCorp Data & Applications Manager in week 3 (CCed technical writer):

From (the technical writer's) email, ... *it's clear that you want something different from what had been planned in the costing for the investigation phase and from what we had scoped. ... the Statement of User Requirements wasn't in the original scope at all, but we had concluded we could fit in the statement of business requirements (already produced), and rely on existing documentation / industry standards / known behaviour of the current system as a base.*

### 5.5.2. Negotiating the production of the Statement of User Requirements

In week 9, when it became clear that ComTech were unlikely to produce the Statement of User Requirements themselves without further prompting, the technical writer progressed the matter by volunteering to develop the Statement of User Requirements himself. The following is a verbatim email extract from the technical writer to George, the ComTech project manager concerning the matter:

*... you recall at our last meeting you indicated that progress had not been made on the Statement of User Requirements due to not being clear what was required, and you requested an example of the Statement of User Requirements that EnergyCorp want ...*

*... in the interests of moving things along, I will write it myself. When its done and checked, I'll organise a meeting with you, (everyone concerned, developers, users, management) say on Friday or Monday next week when we can go over it and confirm that what is being planned has everything EnergyCorp wants/needs within the practical scope of the project.*

George, the ComTech project manager responded with the following email extract in which he made a further attempt to discourage the technical writer from developing the Statement of User Requirements himself:

*... my gut feeling is that if you tried to produce SUR from ground zero, it would be counterproductive, given that it needs a lot of info about the new module set which is being used as a base ... and it's likely to lead to a fairly heavy review/rework cycle ...*

The technical writer, with James' backing did nonetheless produce the Statement of User Requirements. Having conceded this point, the ComTech project manager sent this email to the technical writer the following day:

*... the earlier we have a draft the better, since this isn't green fields work, and consequently there are many dependencies that we will need time to consider. William (ComTech Managing Director) will also need to be involved because of the potential implications on ComTech's product (development) strategy.*

This paragraph is packed with implications. Specifically, three points emerge:

When he (George) says 'there are many dependencies which we will need time to consider' the project manager implies that rather than being a check to ensure all requirements are present and the context of the development is well-enough understood prior to proceeding, the Statement of User Requirements was perceived as an instrument which would cause significant disruption to the system they planned to develop. This is despite the technical writer and the EnergyCorp Data & Applications Manager repeatedly characterising the Statement of User Requirements as a means of confirming ComTech's readiness to proceed.

By involving one of the two owners of ComTech indicates that it was likely a further attempt would be made to subvert the process undertaken by the technical writer and the EnergyCorp Data & Applications Manager. The owner had already made several attempts to persuade senior EnergyCorp management to abandon the idea.

Mention of potential implications on ComTech's product strategies clearly indicates that ComTech were in the business of producing an off-the-shelf package for sale to EnergyCorp's competitors, and was using EnergyCorp to finance its development.

### 5.5.3. Comparison of initial SUR as developed by ComTech with SURAC as developed by the technical writer

Following on from the previous two sections, the actual SURAC developed by the technical writer can be compared with the SUR (there were no acceptance criteria) developed by ComTech's Larry after prolonged efforts to get him to do so. These can be seen in the Appendix.

The only editing to have been done to either of these documents is to change people's names and the names of the organisations involved to be consistent with the rest of the work.

Once George had agreed to make it available to the technical writer, ComTech's SUR (there was no Acceptance Criteria) was used as input into the technical writer's SURAC. ComTech's SUR was disassembled and the components slotted into the technical writer's SURAC template, serving as a starting point. The technical writer then completed the blank sections of the SURAC over a three-day period to form the full SURAC.

A review of the two documents reveal that the SUR has less detail, less structure, and a narrower breadth that resulted in a document that did not list all known user requirements, nor did it list acceptance criteria that could form the basis if constructive discussion between the parties. ComTech indicated that this SUR was typical of their approach to user requirements.

### 5.5.4. EnergyCorp Data & Applications Manager (James) sees usefulness

Later in week 9, James, who had overall responsibility for the upgrade project, sent this email to his superior, Brian, EnergyCorp's IT Manager, after the Statement of User Requirements had been developed and the extra requirements identified:

... please note that in the absence of documentation and quality processes by ComTech, the IEEE approach that (the technical writer) has expertise in has been very useful with regards the V2.0 development."

The manager takes the view that a major contributing factor to poor systems quality was ComTech's lack of documentation and quality processes, and that the application of the IEEE-derived Statement of User Requirements has brought about a discernible improvement in Bulk Data Load V2.0 (the subject of the research project)

### 5.5.5. Documentation often an early casualty

That project documentation can be an early casualty in projects with tight schedules is indicated by this verbatim extract from an email sent to the EnergyCorp Data & Applications Manager by the ComTech project manager, outlining the revised estimates for completing the project:

... we also looked at what we could delay until after there was a running system, and although it is tight even with a couple of people working on it, it looks as though it is possible to have a beta in place by June 30 provided acceptance and doco (sic) are delayed or at least taken out of the main project line.

## *5.6. Observations*

As with interviews and documentary evidence, observations played an important role in the achievement of all four of the research objectives. And as was the case with interviews and documentary evidence, observations only partially supported objective three (evaluate whether a system can be made more usable, as defined by the SOLE model, by the technical writer acting as a facilitator between user and developer during requirements gathering).

Observations are woven throughout the description of the research event (see Chapter 4.5 Research Event).

The observations were made from the point of view of an EnergyCorp insider over a 12 month period. It might be analogous to the point of view of the ethnographer who fully immerses himself in the culture he is studying and is accepted as 'one of us'. In this sense, the point of view of the observations is different from that of a researcher who comes into an organisation to perform a case study, and who is introduced to people as such. This 'one of us' perception was carefully cultivated so that the potential problem could be avoided of people speaking and acting in uncharacteristic ways due to the presence of an outsider who may or may not pose a threat. In these times of job insecurity, the issue is a real one.

The technical writer as a EnergyCorp contractor was treated as a de facto '9 to 5' employee of EnergyCorp. Indeed a significant proportion of the staff, including some management of the Energy Trading Department was employed on fixed term contracts. No day-to-day distinction was made between permanent employees and contractors. There was no sense of the contractors being here today, gone tomorrow.

Observations included events witnessed during formal and informal project meetings, during departmental and organisation-wide briefings, conversations in the coffee room, in someone's cubicle, in the corridors and in the lifts. Conversations overheard and events witnessed in the open-plan office environment.

One place where some significant observations and informal interviews were conducted was in the open-air place where EnergyCorp smokers went to have a cigarette. Donald, the principle user of M&M, was a smoker who frequently went to a nearby park to take a break and have a cigarette. He was a friendly, down-to-earth person who enjoyed 'a yarn' and was easy to talk to. If one was prepared to tolerate a certain amount of passive smoke, it was a place where useful data could be collected, possibly because it was out of earshot of other staff, and probably also because of the satisfaction he derived from the cigarette. Donald would frequently be joined by other EnergyCorp staff who smoked, and who might be called 'smoking buddies'. They would usually be quite happy to discuss their opinions and perceptions of TASS (the collection of modules of which M&M was one). Without validating smoking, it was certainly the case that people were often at their most candid in this context.

So the observations were based on hundreds of hours of contact with staff from all but the highest level of management down to junior clerks. As mentioned in the Research Event, the consensus was that TASS in its then form was an extremely unsatisfactory system, because it lacked much of the functionality they required, because ComTech made changes without telling them and did not provide even rudimentary training, let alone user documentation or on-line help. In this sense, TASS had virtually no context sensitive help.

For benchmarking purposes, it was fortunate that at the time of the research event, ComTech had had a three-year supplier-client relationship with EnergyCorp. It allowed the technical writer to do an informal capability maturity assessment of their development processes. It is stressed that it was not a formal assessment that would be performed during an ISO 15504 (SPICE) assessment (Software Engineering Institute: 2, 2003), or that of the Software Engineering Institute's Capability Maturity Model (CMM) assessment (Software Engineering Institute: 3, 2003). The technical writer was nonetheless at the time a qualified SPICE Assessor with a well-developed understanding of software development process assessment.

In addition to the feedback from TASS users, examination was made of project documentation from earlier projects undertaken by ComTech. In this way, ComTech's performance over the 18 months was assessed and was found to be consistent. It might therefore be reasonable to assume that the outcomes of the Bulk Data Load V2.0 upgrade project would have been approximately the same as ComTech's earlier upgrade projects that had a similar nature and scope. This benchmarking had been done early in the research project by means of informal interviews with a wide range of TASS users and management across the various functional areas.

### 5.6.1. Specific observations relevant to data analysis

As discussed above a large body of data was developed through observations conducted over a 12 month period. Detailed notes were recorded in a research journal during this period, and used when performing the data analysis discussed in the next chapter. Some of the data derives from the researcher's memory of the event and knowledge of the participants, in the way that work-mates come to know each other and the organisation in which they work.

Chapter 6 investigates the nature of the cultural gap is discussed in the literature review. It will consider the gap as constituted by communication difficulties, by the shifting nature of the relationship, by perceptions of us and them, by a misalignment of objectives, and by the consequences of those misaligned objectives. Chapter 6 will also discuss the gap in terms of Johnson and Scholes' model (1999). This will consider the six components outlined in the model, namely organizational structure, stories and myths, symbols, rituals and routines, control systems, and power structures.

**Communication difficulties**. From the outset, James had made it clear that communication difficulties existed between EnergyCorp and ComTech. He indicated that these difficulties were the underlying reason for hiring the technical writer. It was a communication breakdown which

James believed would inhibit the requirements analysis of this critical project. Interestingly, George, the ComTech project manager, commented later in the project that communication difficulties between them and EnergyCorp were a major problem, not only from a ComTech to EnergyCorp point-of-view, but also that departments within EnergyCorp were not communicating with each other, necessitating ComTech to act in the role of facilitator of communication. As the relationship between ComTech and EnergyCorp deteriorated, ComTech was less able to perform this role. George referred repeatedly to themselves (ComTech) as Experts.

**Shifting nature of the relationship**. James saw the nature of EnergyCorp relationship with ComTech as a contractual one, having a basis in law. ComTech, as expressed by George, saw the relationship has been collaborative, one in which there was give and take of the kind not permitted by a legal contract.

**Perceptions of "us and them".** Throughout the project, and from the beginning there were frequent references to what might be described as an "us and them" attitude towards the other. EnergyCorp manifested the attitude that ComTech were cowboys, little better than thieves, making things up as they go along, not listening to their wishes, using them as a meal ticket to develop their own products which they would on-sell to EnergyCorp's competitors. The technical writer was immersed in this outlook for the first six months of project, making it very difficult to empathise with the ComTech, or to understand their point-of-view. During the second six months of the project, at EnergyCorp's direction, the technical writer spent more and more time with ComTech, assisting them. ComTech were happy with this arrangement because they were getting an experienced additional staff member at no extra cost to them. Because ComTech were fairly typical of the kinds of developers the technical writer had worked with in the past, he soon became integrated with the ComTech team, becoming able to see the world through their eyes. It astonished the technical writer (and the researcher) just how far apart the two world views were. Certainly it was expected that there would be some significant differences. The differences were in fact so great that the technical writer came to see it in terms of "same planet, different worlds".

**Misalignment of objectives**. There was a fundamental misalignment of objectives in the sense that EnergyCorp was paying ComTech to develop a solution that would help them be competitive with the other operators in their market. On the other hand, ComTech wanted a generic product that they could sell to the 10 or so competitors of EnergyCorp. From experience, the technical writer had seen this apparently unethical practice before. Some successful software developers made their way in the industry in this way. It was seen as a viable way to get established with a product range. When EnergyCorp became aware of this apparent duplicity they became angry, understandably, and this created the conflict which resulted in the technical writer being brought in.

**The consequences of misalignment objectives**. The consequences of the misalignment objectives as discussed in the previous paragraph was that James saw the need to bring in somebody new from outside who could bring about or facilitate the realignment of objectives. As discussed in the shifting nature of the relationship above, James saw the relationship as a legal agreement; George saw the arrangement more as a collaborative venture, two positions which are apparently far apart. Yet with facilitation, it was possible for these two positions to move towards each other and ultimately find some common ground. Both James and George indicated that after the technical writer facilitated the process they were both satisfied with the stated objectives. James was pleased to be getting what was contractually prescribed. George was happy to have established, or re- established, a better collaborative relationship.

In relation to Johnson and Scholes model (1999) the following observations were made:

**Organisational structure**. EnergyCorp presented itself as a fairly typical government owned enterprise (based on earlier experience). It retained its emphasis on bureaucracy inherited from its earlier days, but with some elements of entrepreneurship grafted uncomfortably on to it. With only 200 people working in the organisation, there was nonetheless four layers of management between workers and chief executive. Higher management was aloof, and in some cases unfriendly towards those lower down. ComTech on the other hand was a small organisation of around 20 people. Everyone appeared to be on the first name basis everyone else including the directors of the company. While EnergyCorp was strongly hierarchical, ComTech were at the opposite end of the spectrum.

**Stories and myths**. EnergyCorp had a rich and varied set of organizational stories dating back many decades, reflecting the length of time the parent organisation had existed. Of relevance was the pervasive nature of the need to become corporatised, competitive in the marketplace. EnergyCorp had never needed to do that before, being a government owned monopoly. With an entrenched organisational culture having its origins in government bureaucracy and monopoly, there was strong resistance to this move towards becoming commercial and competitive. ComTech was more future-focussed, having little in the way of history, and the overwhelming story being that of the struggling software developer aiming to make a big in the future. So there was an emphasis on the past and present in the stories and myths of EnergyCorp, while with ComTech there was an emphasis on the present and future. As with organisational structure, it can be seen that the two organisations were at opposite ends of this particular spectrum.

**Symbols**. EnergyCorp had launched a corporate identity re-branding exercise two or three years prior to the project. This exercise, including logo being widely publicised, must have cost many millions of dollars in advertising and sponsorship of sporting events. ComTech on the other hand had very little in the way of corporate symbols, only their logo, which in the technical writer's opinion looked amateurish. It was doubtful whether they used an advertising agency or graphic designer in the way that EnergyCorp had. Corporate symbols were very much about how much money was available to create and promote them.

**Rituals and routines**. The main ritual at EnergyCorp was the Friday afternoon drinks and address by the chief executive. It involved fatty finger-food, low alcohol drinks, to be followed by a motivational address by the chief executive. There was a certain degree of cynicism amongst the rank and file about what went on at these events. While I was never invited to have Friday lunch with ComTech, they apparently were in the habit (said George) of going down into the local pub near their office and having a substantial lunch complete with plentiful drinks. If they were anything like other such lunches that the technical writer participated in at earlier times, they were quite informal in contrast to the relative formality of the EnergyCorp Friday afternoon events.

**Control systems**. EnergyCorp, in keeping with their organisational structure, had quite rigorous control systems in place. Management expected their orders to be carried out to the letter; not doing so would invite sanction. ComTech's control systems were relatively informal. While it was unlikely that one of the workers would telephone the company directors, with only one level of management separating them, it would not be unfeasible to do so. It would be absolutely unthinkable for a worker at EnergyCorp to phone the chief executive, even supposing they could get past his gatekeeper.

**Power structures**. The power at EnergyCorp was concentrated in the well insulated executive team. This team came from either an accounting or sales background. There was no chief information officer on this team, rather the top I team manager reported to the chief financial officer. At ComTech the power is really concentrated in the hands of the two directors; the company was run as a duopoly.

## *5.7. Conclusions*

To summarise, data was collected using the following four methods:

Questionnaire

Interviews

Documentary evidence

Observation

Having a broad range of objectives has necessitated a diverse selection of collection methods. Analysis of the qualitative data collected by those instruments indicates broad support for the research objectives.

For reference, a reiteration is made of the research objectives and how each instrument relates.

| | **Quest'-ionnaire** | **Inter-views** | **Doc. - Evid.** | **Obser-vation** |
|---|---|---|---|---|
| **Understanding the 'Gap'** | No | Yes | Yes | Yes |
| **Tech Writer / Hirschheim et al** | No | Yes | Yes | Yes |
| **Improve Usability** | Yes | Partially | Partially | Partially |
| **Resist to Integ. Processes** | No | Yes | Yes | Yes |

**Table 11: Reiteration of data collection methods to research objectives**

### *5.7.1.1. Questionnaires*

The questionnaires indicate support for objective 3 that (a) earlier versions of M&M as well as other TASS modules were perceived by its user as being not very usable, and (b) that the revised M&M module developed on the basis of an extended SURAC produced through facilitated communication between the users and the developers was clearly more usable than the earlier module. This is usability in terms of ease of use, ease of learning, degree to which it helps the user do their job.

### *5.7.1.2. Interviews*

The interviews, both formal and informal indicate broad agreement from all-but-one participant (Larry, the ComTech programmer who wrote the original SUR for the updated M&M module) that using the technical writer's SURAC template together with the technical writer's facilitated communication had resulted in improved usability (objective 3).

The interviews revealed much about the 'us and them' gap mindset (objective 1) that EnergyCorp and ComTech clearly had towards each other. This appears to derive from a perceived conflict of interest in which EnergyCorp's priority was the development of an information system that fully supported their range of business activities, but were instead being given an inferior product that neither worked nor had the needed functionality even if it did work. Worse still, EnergyCorp knew (ComTech had explicitly said so in one meeting) that they were in effect funding ComTech to develop a generic product that would be sold to EnergyCorp competitors.

From ComTech's point of view, the gap was constituted by their having a 'battler' mentality in which a small software developer was trying to establish itself as a medium to large developer. They were using the end-justifies-the-means argument that having a big corporation fund this effort was justified in the interests of growth. The gap was further constituted by the off-hand, some might say arrogant way in which EnergyCorp dealt with them. Many instances were seen in meetings in which EnergyCorp staff was openly contemptuous towards ComTech staff.

Ultimately these differences can be observed as expressions of the two quite different cultures. The ideational and sociocultural elements of culture, as discussed by Allaire and Firsirotu (1986), is revealed in stark contrast during the interviews with ComTech and EnergyCorp staff. That these two cultures could co-exist at all within the same physical infrastructure, was surprising.

The technical writer, as discussed in the research event had the opportunity to immerse himself in both cultures (EnergyCorp for the first six months, and ComTech in the second six months when he was assisting them with project work). While the technical writer expected differences to be evident, he was surprised at how wide the gap was, and how very compelling each divergent view was. Compelling is used as a descriptor of how persuasive a view was. The proposition was basically, you are either one of us, or one of them, and if you are one of us, you subscribe to our values and help defend us. If you are one of them, you are the enemy and will be viewed as such.

In terms of objective 2 (technical writer in relation to Hirschheim and Klein's paradigms of system development) the interviews revealed much about ComTech's perception of itself as the experts, and EnergyCorp the unenlightened client. ComTech used the term 'expert' explicitly when describing itself to the technical writer. Their view of themselves fits closely the paradigmatic description of Hirschheim and Klein's Analyst as Systems Expert. The interviews also supported the technical writer's application of the Analyst as Facilitator paradigm in the context of this project.

In terms of objective 4 (resistance to integrative processes) George's (ComTech project manager) comment is revealing: George regarded integrative processes as a worthwhile practice, but that they are usually not performed because 'getting the client to pay for it' is usually a problem. Best practice is often sacrificed for expediency.

#### *5.7.1.3. Documentary Evidence*

The documentary evidence does indicate broad support for all four of the research objectives. The nature of the gap (objective 1) is revealed in emails from George that basically say that doing the SURAC is not their way of doing things, and would EnergyCorp kindly leave them alone to get on with the job. The gap is constituted by there being an existing body of knowledge in ComTech about how to go about the job which could be described as a feature of their organisational culture. The technical writer's SURAC at this time was seen as the other side of ComTech's gap. It is an established fact that ComTech strenuously resisted adopting what it saw as foreign and potentially dangerous to their interests.

The role of technical writer in relation to Hirschheim and Klein's Analyst as Facilitator is evidenced by James's (EnergyCorp manager) email to his manager, describing the technical writer's activities. 'Please note that in the absence of documentation and quality processes by ComTech, the IEEE approach that (the technical writer) has expertise in has been very useful with regards the V2.0 development."

Resistance to integrative processes (objective 4) is seen in George's email to James in which the integrative process represented by the SURAC template and facilitated communication is discussed. 'From (the technical writer's) email, it's clear that you want something different from what had been planned in the costing for the investigation phase and from what we had scoped. Actually the Statement of User Requirements wasn't in the original scope at all, but we had concluded we could fit in the statement of business requirements (already produced), and rely on existing documentation / industry standards / known behaviour of the current system as a base.

#### *5.7.1.4. Observation*

The observations were consistent with the data collected in interviews and documentary evidence. They contribute an understanding of the gap through the many occasions when the technical writer heard and saw people talking about and taking action in relation to the other side. The nature of the gap appears to be founded on a fundamentally adversarial position. This adversarial position seemed to be an extension of the broader business practice of leveraging advantage at the expense of others. That doing business is like waging war, there should be no sympathy for the enemy.

Using Hirschheim and Klein's (1989) Analyst as Facilitator paradigm to inform the actions of the technical writer was productive in the sense that it revealed that by doing so, a discernible benefit to project outcomes (in terms of usability) was derived. This was in terms of observations of the users (Donald and Francis) at work with the updated M&M module. The pattern of Donald's trips outside showed a discernible difference in the sense that with the old module trips outside were more frequent over a longer period. With the updated module, Donald was able to complete the work cycle more quickly and presumably with greater ease since most of the additional six functional requirements came from him. The next chapter will focus on deriving possible findings from the collected data.

# 6. Findings

The findings are discussed in terms of the defined research objectives:

- To better understand the nature of the 'gap' that apparently exists between users and developers of systems, especially in relation to the activity of gathering of user requirements.
- To examine the role of the technical writer in relation to Hirschheim and Klein's (1989) paradigms of the Analyst as Systems Expert and Analyst as Facilitator.
- To examine whether system usability (as defined by the SOLE model, Eriksson and Törn, 1991) can be improved by the technical writer acting as a facilitator between user and developer during requirements gathering.
- To explore factors that influence the problem of developer and user resistance to previously proposed integrative processes.

## *6.1. The cultural gap*

### 6.1.1. Introductory discussion on cultural differences

The findings based on the interviews, observations and documentary evidence indicates the existence of a gap between EnergyCorp and ComTech. Whether we can call this gap a cultural gap will be explored in the following sections where the gap is discussed in terms of Johnson and Scholes's (1999) model of organisational culture. However given the level of dysfunctionality evident in the relationship between EnergyCorp and ComTech, this gap is consistent with Grindley's (1991) findings that nearly half of the IS directors surveyed considered the 'culture' gap between IS professionals and their business counterparts to be their most important challenge.

#### *6.1.1.1. The gap as constituted by communication difficulties*

A consistent theme in discussions with both EnergyCorp and ComTech people was difficulty with communication. When the technical writer first arrived at the research site the two sides could barely manage a civil conversation. Yet as Hornik et al (2003) clearly indicate, good communication between IS professionals, IS staff and IS users is critical to the successful completion of an IS development project. They point out that the ability to interact with all potential stakeholders in an organisation, to clearly document requirements, and to effectively express ideas has long been recognised by researchers and practitioners as critical success factors.

ComTech were acutely aware of the gap between their thinking and that of EnergyCorp, as indicated in the discussion with the ComTech project manager (George). It was an example of what Taylor-Cummings and Feeny (1997) describe as the 'cultural gap' between IS developers and users. Taylor-Cummings and Feeny blamed the gap for the failure of IT projects since such projects first began in the 1950s. James, the EnergyCorp manager clearly recognized it too, having made it clear to the technical writer that he considered it one of the biggest risks facing the successful completion of the M&M V2.0 project.

An interesting slant is placed upon the nature of the gap when the ComTech project manager (George) was asked to discuss his perceptions of ComTech's role at EnergyCorp. He commented that their ongoing role at EnergyCorp had often involved their (ComTech) being a 'facilitator' between different functional areas within EnergyCorp. This was necessary in order to resolve issues relevant to projects but which EnergyCorp seemed reluctant to resolve themselves, despite being 'internal issues'. So not only does George recognise the existence of a gap between ComTech and EnergyCorp, but also a gap between different departments and functional areas in EnergyCorp and that if ComTech was to perform its work it would need to act as a facilitator of communication between these departments and functional areas.

According to George, ComTech adopted the facilitator role because "someone had to get people talking to each other". He described EnergyCorp as having 'a silo mentality' in which knowledge is hoarded and not willingly shared with those within the organisation that need it for upstream or downstream processing. This 'silo mentality' had contributed to their difficulties in obtaining, amongst other things, complete user requirements because in some cases users and management either did not know or would not say what their requirements were. George said that as the relationship between stakeholders degenerated, ComTech were finding it increasingly difficult to perform the facilitator role. So in this sense the nature of the gap is constituted by a kind of siege mentality within the larger EnergyCorp organisation, in which departments jealously guarded their data has a way of defending themselves against elements within their own organisation.

George explicitly commented that ComTech adapted their expert approach to include elements of facilitation out of practical necessity. *From his project managers perspective they became facilitators reluctantly because it added complexity in terms of time and effort to fixed price projects, thus reducing profitability. This is a strong indication as to why existing integrative processes are not used on development projects*, plus an acknowledgement of the need for someone to facilitate, though preferably not them.

In acknowledging the existence of a gap, and the practical necessity to perform some kind of facilitation, George also acknowledged that integrative processes were a worthwhile practice. Interestingly, from his project manager's perspective of many years, is considered opinion about why they were not used more often was that 'getting the client to pay for it' is usually a problem. And so for the sake of expediency, cost cutting, and timesaving best practice is sacrificed.

The role of an effective facilitator might be to help each side adjust their perceptions of reality to include elements of the other. When world-views are very different, one consequence might be a lack of a common language with which to communicate.

It seems obvious to suggest that an interpreter would be required when for example an Australian Aboriginal from the western desert and an Alaskan Inuit from above the Arctic Circle wish to communicate. The need for a facilitator/translator has not been widely recognised in the literature in relation to software development projects where the stakeholders are not communicating effectively. It is *perhaps* assumed that if all parties are English speakers, as in this case, that effective communication will follow as a natural consequence.

The technical writer as facilitator aims to find common ground through facilitated discussion. This discussion allowed the two sides to work towards synchronising their world-views. It would seem that the task would be made easier were the participants to agree on a common goal, that of successfully completing the project. In this case it was implicitly agreed by EnergyCorp and ComTech management early in the M&M V2.0 project that for the sake of the common goal of a successful development project outcome, all parties would agree to be willing to collaborate more constructively.

Brian, the EnergyCorp executive (James' manager) that was responsible three years earlier for establishing what was declared to be a collaborative partnership with ComTech had an interest in retaining ComTech in the sense that to not do so would possibly be in some sense an admission of failure, of having chosen the wrong developer. James hinted this at in a private discussion with the technical writer. It is likely that one of the reasons James was hired by EnergyCorp was to address this problem and send a clear message by bringing more and more pressure to bear on ComTech to comply with EnergyCorp's wishes and not pursue their own agenda. The technical writer is likely to have been part of an overall strategy that would see ComTech either exit or 'toe the line'.

#### *6.1.1.2. The gap as constituted by the shifting nature of the relationship*

When the EnergyCorp Data & Application's Manager (James) uses legalese to express his view that a clearly understood and agreed contract must exist between the developer and the client, that creates a legally binding contract as the 'basis in law', and the contract notwithstanding, all parties should nonetheless be willing to 'negotiate around reasonable commercial outcomes', he seems to be suggesting that that process can't be managed on a friendly informal basis, rather a formal, legal basis. The contract he refers to can be used as a lever to enforce compliance. Implicit in this view is the presence of a gap between EnergyCorp and ComTech. If there was no gap, a legal contract would be unnecessary.

James said that by forcing the use of the technical writer's Statement of User Requirements template, the basis of the developer client relationship had shifted from 'Expert Consultancy' to 'Process Consultancy'. This indicates that the nature of the gap had shifted. Formerly the gap had been constituted by an expert dictating terms to a somewhat ignorant client, now the gap was one of facilitator who helped the client determine their real process requirements, working collaboratively. The term 'Expert' used by James resonates strongly to some extent with Hirschheim and Klein's Analyst as Systems Expert. The term 'Process Consultancy' also resonates to Hirschheim and Klein's Analyst as Facilitator paradigm in the sense that the developers role was now one in which they collaboratively helped EnergyCorp determine their real process requirements for V2.0.

When asked about the need for a facilitator, James agreed that when communication is not good, as it had become in the case at hand, then a facilitator is needed. The facilitator role as defined by Hirschheim and Klein's Analyst as Facilitator might therefore be a key agent in the improvement of communication between stakeholders and thereby helping to bridge the gap.

#### *6.1.1.3. The gap as constituted by perceptions of "us and them"*

The gap between EnergyCorp and ComTech was manifested by a distinct "us and them" perception on both sides. From the interviews and observations there was the sense that "this is how we do things, and we have every right to do things the way we want to do them". In terms of how culture has been discussed and defined earlier in this work, "how we do things" is somewhat synonymous with "culture". Edstrom (1977), Gingras and McLean (1979), and Zmud and Cox (1979) all discuss the distinctive cultural styles of IS professionals in relation to other organisational stakeholders, including management and users. The findings of this project are consistent with Edstrom *et al's* view.

Since the technical writer had been brought in to discipline ComTech, he was initially seen as one of 'them' by ComTech, who were consequently guarded in their outlook towards the technical writer. This meant that the technical writer was getting only one side of the story. So persuasive was EnergyCorp's version of the situation that the technical writer made the mistake during the first six months of the project of believing it was a more valid view than ComTech's. This belief was largely based on being told by EnergyCorp people that ComTech were taking advantage of EnergyCorp (by having them fund the development of TASS, not to EnergyCorp's precise specification, but to their own specification that had been determined by their marketing strategy to sell a generic TASS by another name to EnergyCorp's competitors). EnergyCorp were understandably aggrieved and made this clear to the technical writer, who, for his part perceived a loyalty to EnergyCorp.

But ethical considerations aside, once ComTech came to accept the technical writer as a de facto member of their project team, it became startlingly obvious that they had their own, equally compelling but contrary perception of the situation. The apparently unethical action of having the client fund their own commercial agenda, to the detriment of the client, was justified by it being a widely practised way for small to medium-sized developers to fund the development of a breakthrough product while their own resources were limited. "Everyone else does it, so it must be alright. Or if we're to be condemned for the practice, then you must also condemn the industry as a whole" sums up the general attitude manifested by ComTech staff. ComTech had a "we're little guys now, but we're going to take on the big guys and win!" ethic that was expressed in a variety of ways by different ComTech staff over time during interaction with the technical writer.

At various times, many derogatory remarks were made by EnergyCorp staff about ComTech to the technical writer, particularly in relation to the poor usability of their systems. Later in the development project, when the technical writer had been working more closely with ComTech, they were heard to make some highly critical remarks about EnergyCorp, particularly in relation to the 'high-handedness" and unnecessarily bureaucratic practices of certain EnergyCorp staff. Both sides had apparently created a world-view that over time had become very real to them, but which was at odds with each other.

#### *6.1.1.4. The gap as constituted by a misalignment of objectives*

The general mistrust and ill-feeling, plus the clearly misaligned objectives of EnergyCorp and ComTech is consistent with Wang's (1994, p1) discussion in which he defines the gap as *'a conflict, pervasive yet unnatural, that has misaligned the objectives of executive managers and technologists and that impairs or prevents organisations from obtaining a cost-effective return from their investment in information technology'.* EnergyCorp wanted a system to help them be competitive against their rivals, ComTech wanted someone to fund the development of their own product which would be sold to EnergyCorp's rivals. This represents a very clear misalignment of objectives, and highlights the nature of the gap in terms of a misalignment of objectives.

The misalignment of the strategic objectives of EnergyCorp and ComTech also resonates to the Business-Technology gap discussed by Baster et al (2001). Here the gap is constituted by technology specialists lacking the domain expertise to react rapidly to changes in the business environment, while business users lack the technology skills to maintain the systems. This situation is very reminiscent of the EnergyCorp/ComTech situation. EnergyCorp lacked the technical expertise to react rapidly to changes in their commercial environment. ComTech was brought in to make up the shortfall, yet through a misalignment of objectives the gap was widened.

#### *6.1.1.5. The gap as constituted by the consequences of misaligned objectives*

As James said during discussions in weeks 1 and 2, he had been increasing the pressure on ComTech in the months before the technical writer's arrival - the period since he had started with EnergyCorp. James was an exacting manager who wanted things done "by the book". In discussions, it was apparent that a combination of him becoming aware of the seriousness of the gap/misaligned objectives between EnergyCorp and ComTech (as discussed in the previous section), plus his meticulous management style, caused him to systematically go about the process of placing ComTech under increasing amounts of pressure to deliver what EnergyCorp needed and was paying for.

From discussions, James knew that his actions would increase tensions between EnergyCorp and ComTech, but he believed this was a viable first step to resolve the situation. The pressure being brought to bear on ComTech could well have been counterproductive unless a way could be found to bridge the gap. Though he did not explicitly say so, this would appear to be the underlying reason for hiring the technical writer. James realised there was a widening cultural gap caused by his efforts to have ComTech comply with EnergyCorp's wishes, and it was necessary to bridge it, particularly in relation to the requirements elicitation for the M&M V2.0 project.

So a widening cultural gap in this context was caused by one culture (EnergyCorp) insisting that another culture change theirs to accommodate the first. In the spirit of self-protection this had the effect of ComTech acting to protect their own culture by erecting barriers to communication with EnergyCorp.

#### *6.1.1.6. Summary of gap*

It is necessary to distinguish between the *gap* and the *cultural gap*. The findings in relation to the gap discussed above may or may not be culturally based. There was insufficient literature to determine this.

Johnson and Scholes (1999) on the other hand provide us with a useful model to analyse the cultures of these two organisations, and allow the nature of the cultural gap to emerge. This will be discussed in the sections below.

So, in relation to the gap, it was found that it is constituted by the following factors:

- communication difficulties
- the shifting nature of the relationship
- perceptions of “us and them”
- misalignment of objectives
- the consequences of misaligned objectives

### 6.1.2. The gap in terms of Johnson and Scholes model (1999)

The previous discussion focuses on looking at the various ways that the gap is constituted. Johnson and Scholes (1999) model, with its six cultural elements will be used to analyse the nature of the gap in terms of a cultural gap. It may be recalled that the six elements are *organisation structure, stories and myths, symbols, rituals and routines, control systems and power structures.* This model will be used to analyse the nature of the gap.

#### *6.1.2.1. Organisation Structure*

Formal organisational structure, or the more informal ways in which the organisation works, reflect power structures and delineate important relationships. (Johnson and Scholes, 1999).

**EnergyCorp's** organisational hierarchy was highly developed and rigidly defined. It was a reflection of its government bureaucracy origins. With around 200 personnel, its organisational structure had three and in some cases four layers of management between the chief executive and the workers. It was forbidden or at least strongly discouraged to operate outside of the chain of command. This was why the technical writer was unable to interview Brian, James' manager. Staff were expected to know their place, and stay in it. Lower level staff did not address senior management directly if they were to encounter each other in a hallway or lift. This organisational structure inevitably had the effect of discouraging initiative amongst line-workers, and encouraged the kind of silo mentality that George described so clearly.

**ComTech** on the other hand had about 20 employees, including the two managing partners. Management hierarchy was flat with barely one level of management between line-workers and the directors. Everyone seemed to be on a first name basis with everyone else. The technical writer observed Larry, a line worker address William and Arthur, the directors of ComTech by their first names on several occasions. An air of informality existed, at least among the ComTech personnel who were embedded at the EnergyCorp site. At any given time there would be around five ComTech employees on-site, and they were not always the same five people, yet the general mood of informality was consistent across the 12 months of the research project. The technical writer spent considerable amount of time with the ComTech people during the second six months of the project. ComTech was a fairly typical small to medium software developer based on the experience of the technical writer of the previous 10 years working with a variety of such organisations on a variety of projects.

**Nature of the cultural gap.** The gap in terms of this element of culture can be summed up by there being a strong contrast between the old model of strongly hierarchical organisational structure, which is inherently inflexible and conservative, and the newer model of modern organisations with their flat management structure and focus on flexibility and innovation as a way to gain competitive advantage. These two organisations lie at either ends of a continuum, and the distance between them constitutes the cultural gap in terms of organisational structure and power relationships.

#### *6.1.2.2. Stories and Myths*

Stories, the stories related by individuals that embed historical events in the present and highlight important events and personalities. (Johnson and Scholes, 1999).

**EnergyCorp's** stories were rich and varied. About half of its staff of 200 had been drawn from the parent organisation, the statutory government authority that had provided electricity to Southeast Queensland for the previous 50 years or more. For example Donald, the key user, had been with EnergyCorp for more than 20 years, and was well-known by many, was a rich source of stories. With so many long serving EnergyCorp people, there was a lot of material that constituted EnergyCorp's repository of stories. These formed the backdrop for the more pressing an immediate need for EnergyCorp to become commercialised and competitive, to compete against other energy retailers. As a former government body they had no need to think in such ways. The new commercial order was causing considerable anxiety. So many of the current stories related to its struggle to compete in a newly deregulated environment. The stories related to the valiant efforts to achieve good commercial outcomes, while implicitly suggesting that this would be difficult for a former government monopoly.

**ComTech's** stories were also about waging valiant battles in the marketplace, but with an important difference. They cast themselves as a metaphorical David, in a David and Goliath-like struggle with larger organisations such as EnergyCorp. ComTech appeared to have been in existence for perhaps five or six years at the time the technical writer joined EnergyCorp, so there was very little historical storytelling. The focus was very much on the present and future. History did not appear important, what mattered was the future. The perceived differential between the science and financial resources of EnergyCorp relative to ComTech perhaps helped them to justify in their own minds the clearly unethical practice of using the client to fund their own programmes, to the detriment of the client. The stories that were told focused on achieving successful outcomes in the face of adversity and frustration.

**Nature of the cultural gap.** The gap in this sense is constituted by a focus on the past and coming to terms with a difficult present in the case of EnergyCorp, and a focus on the present and the future in the case of ComTech. The stories that constitute this focus in both cases serve to reinforce what would appear to be the fundamental values of the organisation. By telling stories, the participants reinforce their perception of who they are and what their organisation is.

### *6.1.2.3. Symbols*

Symbols, like logos, offices, cars and titles; or the type of language and terminology commonly used; and which become a short-hand representation of the nature of the organisation. (Johnson and Scholes, 1999).

**EnergyCorp.** When EnergyCorp became a commercial entity three to four years earlier, there had been a major rebranding exercise aimed at changing its somewhat dated image. This involved what appeared to be a full rebranding effort, with new logo, extensive public relations and advertising campaign, new stationery and other material is seen by the public, sponsorship of major sporting events, and a variety of community service initiatives, all in an effort to change its image from a conservative statutory government body into a right-up-to-the-minute, socially responsible commercial entity. The exercise is likely to have cost in the order of millions of dollars. EnergyCorp clearly wanted to create a symbol for itself that conveyed the image it wanted to convey. But while all of this effort had been made, it had not changed the basic nature of the organisation, as discussed in these sections dealing with the elements of culture. EnergyCorp wanted to be seen to be progressive, but there was a shortfall between the perception and the basically conservative nature of the organisation. This caused a certain amount of cynicism, particularly amongst the older EnergyCorp staff like Donald.

**ComTech** with its relatively slender resources could not afford expensive advertising campaigns at taxpayer's expense. Their logo was relatively simple and unsophisticated, and it appeared on all ComTech artefacts. Beyond this there was very little propagation of symbols, at least from what the technical writer could see.

**Nature of the cultural gap.** A wide gap existed with this element of culture. It was constituted by the amount of money and resources that were put into creating and promoting the symbols. At one end of the continuum was EnergyCorp spending millions of dollars creating a new image, at the other end was ComTech with its minimal marketing budget. The effect of this gap was manifested in a somewhat condescending attitude by EnergyCorp towards unsophisticated ComTech, whilst ComTech seemed resentful towards EnergyCorp.

#### *6.1.2.4. Rituals and Routines*

Routines and Rituals. The routine ways that members of the organisation behave towards each other, and that link different parts of the organisation. Rituals include training programmes, promotion and judgments that indicate relative importance in the organisation. (Johnson and Scholes, 1999).

**EnergyCorp**. With its long history, deeply entrenched values, and strongly hierarchical organisational structure, EnergyCorp had many routines and rituals. Due to its hierarchical nature that restricted communication up the hierarchy to the level immediately above any particular employee, the way that people communicated with each other was somewhat restricted. Communication was formalised, characterised by heavy use of the passive voice. While senior management could theoretically communicate with anyone lower down in the hierarchy, in practice this did not usually happen. Senior management would communicate with the next level of management below them, and not beyond. And given that this heavy emphasis on status existed, the routines and rituals of EnergyCorp could be described as rigid, conservative. George noted the silo mentality that existed in EnergyCorp and which created the need for ComTech to act as facilitators of communication between departments. This is an indication that the routine ways that members of the organisation behaved towards each other was limited and perhaps somewhat dysfunctional.

A specific ritual was the Friday afternoon progress updates/motivational talk by the Chief Executive. At four o'clock staff would gather in the boardroom and an adjoining entertainment area opened up with bi-fold doors. Finger food in the form of potato chips and peanuts was provided, as was light beer and wine spritzers. Staff was encouraged to mingle and relax, and theoretically the status barriers would come down, though in practice this did not appear to occur in a widespread way. After half an hour, and the Chief Executive called the room to order, and he delivered a friendly presentation in which EnergyCorp's performance in the competitive market over the previous week was outlined, noteworthy events reported on, and occasionally a preview of a new advertisement. While this weekly event was generally a positive affair, many staff departed as soon as they could after the Chief Executive's address. This is quite likely to be a reflection of people's desire to leave at five o'clock, which was the nominal finish time. It is also possibly a reflection of people's attitude towards this ritual. If people were enjoying themselves, enjoying each other's company, enjoying the food and drink, they would be less inclined to leave.

**ComTech**. Again with its relatively short history, and small size, and flatter organisational structure of ComTech did not appear to have a great many routines and rituals. Certainly not in the way that EnergyCorp did.

While the technical writer had not attended any, he had been told by George that ComTech's weekly staff morale ritual was a Friday lunch at a local pub. This small informal gathering was characterised by people sitting together at a table in the congenial atmosphere of a pub, drinking the drink of their choice, eating a light or full meal according to their preference, and speaking freely with workmates, including management.

**Nature of the cultural gap.** Beyond the obvious gap is seen in the differences between the two Friday morale building exercises, the gap is generally constituted by the degree of formality that characterises the organisation. EnergyCorp's routines and rituals were formal, ComTech's were informal. In discussions with Larry and George it was evident that EnergyCorp's rigid hierarchy and formality was a source of some irritation to them. From discussions with Francis and James, it was clear that ComTech's informality, including its informal way of gathering user requirements, was also a source of considerable irritation.

#### *6.1.2.5. Control Systems*

Control systems, measurement and reward systems that emphasize what is important in the organisation, and which focus attention and activity. (Johnson and Scholes, 1999).

**EnergyCorp.** As previously discussed control was exercised by a formal management structure in which compliance was mandatory. For example in James and Francis were both highly formalised in their activities. James was a meticulous manager who demanded perfection. Francis was also a perfectionist. Measurement of achievement tended to be against prescribed performance goals. Failure to reach these arbitrarily set goals would be the subject of performance evaluation and possible sanction.

In this sense punishment was a primary control mechanism. Staff was made aware that if they "stuffed up" they would "get their bum kicked" (sic). If they successfully carried out their duties, the reward would be an absence of punishment. This system worked to preserve the status quo, as it discouraged initiative and removed the motivation to look for ways to improve. In a formally structured organisation such as EnergyCorp, it seemed important that the control mechanisms work to preserve the existing structure.

**ComTech**, with its flat management structure and its ambition to grow and become a powerful software house appeared to reward initiative that helped it towards its goal. The researcher was not directly involved in that dynamic, but over the 12 months at the research site, evidence of this was during informal discussions with George and Larry.

**Nature of the cultural gap.** This gap is constituted by the punishment versus reward approach to the control of the organisation. Performance measures lead either to punishment or an absence of punishment in the case of EnergyCorp. Initiative and creativity leading to reward in the case of ComTech.

#### *6.1.2.6. Power Structures*

Power structures, the most powerful managerial groupings in the organisation are likely to be ones most associated with core assumptions and beliefs about what is important. (Johnson and Scholes, 1999).

**EnergyCorp**. Again, as discussed in Control Structures above, the power in EnergyCorp (no pun intended) resided solely in the hands of an aloof Chief Executive, and the two or three members of his senior executive team. This team was dominated by members with accounting and finance backgrounds, with sales/marketing also represented. The manager of the IT department was not on this team. The fact that the IT manager reported to the Chief Financial Officer rather than *be* the Chief Information Officer who reports directly to the CEO reflects an attitude that IT is less important. It is possible that had EnergyCorp placed more value and importance on the IT function they would have had the internal resources to perform effectively, and would not have been in the unenviable situation of being dependant on ComTech.

At **ComTech**, the power resided solely in the hands of the two managing partners. One was the technical expert with detailed domain knowledge; the other was the gum-chewing sales and marketing expert. Between them they ran ComTech as a duopoly.

**Nature of the cultural gap.** As observed in the previous elements, power is closely related to hierarchy. In the case of EnergyCorp the hierarchy served to reinforce the power of the Chief Executive and his executive team. All major decisions were made by the Chief Executive and Board of Directors. The executive team acted on the explicit authority of the Chief Executive. The implication of their directives is that non-compliance amounts to disobeying the Chief Executive, the consequences of which could be very unpleasant. In the case of ComTech with its small informal organisational structure, the power simply lies in the hands of the two men who started the company. When George wanted to obtain feedback from Arthur, he was as close as a phone call away. No need for appointments, no "gate-keepers" in the form of personal assistants. James would need to go through three levels of management to reach the Chief Executive. In practice it would have no occasion to approach the Chief Executive directly. Conversely, observing Arthur and William together, it would appear that decisions were made as a result of informal discussion, with no reference to Board of Directors. They constitute the Board of Directors and can be as informal as they like.

#### *6.1.2.7. Summary of analysis using Johnson and Scholes (1999) model*

Based on Johnson and Scholes' model, the differences between the cultures of EnergyCorp and ComTech were analysed. The differences are summarised below:

| Element | EnergyCorp | ComTech |
|---|---|---|
| **Structure** | hierarchical | flat |
| **Stories** | past/present | present/future |
| **Symbols** | affluent | economical |
| **Routines/ Rituals** | formal | informal |
| **Control** | punishment | reward |
| **Power Struc- tures** | paternalistic | entrepreneurial |

**Table 12: Summary of cultural differences using Johnson & Scholes 1999 model**

## *6.2. Role of the technical writer in relation to Hirschheim and Klein's (1989) paradigms of the Analyst as Systems Expert and Analyst as Facilitator*

### 6.2.1. Summary of paradigms

For reference, the four paradigms are summarised below (Hirschheim and Klein (1989):

**Analyst as Systems Expert**. Such a role is that of the expert in technology, tools and methods of system design and project management. From interviews with George, ComTech clearly regarded themselves in this way, and referred to themselves explicitly in those terms. But while their role aims to make systems development more formal and rational, minimising where possible reliance on human intuition, judgement and politics, these human factors are in practice virtually impossible to dispense with. At some point in the requirements gathering process, the users and management need to articulate their needs to the developers in a mutually intelligible form. ComTech was no longer in a position to do this. Human intuition, judgement and politics form an inherent part of the communication between the EnergyCorp and ComTech.

**Analyst as Facilitator** came about because of the problems inherent with the systems expert paradigm. It recognises the fundamental complexity and subjectivity of human interaction. There is no objective reality, only individual perceptions and interpretations of "reality". In particular, system requirements are constructed by a continuing process of an organisation defining its objectives.

Hirschheim and Klein (1989) observe that system requirements emerge as a consequence of that organisation's sense-making activities, their "construction of reality". In the analyst as Facilitator paradigm of systems development, the Analyst should work from within the user's perspective, working with them to derive their real requirements. The differences between the user's and the developer's perspectives are thus merged, alleviating the tension that may develop through there being differing perspectives.

Hirschheim and Klein (1989) recognise the significance of culture as discussed by Johnson and Scholes (1999) in the sense that they describe the developer-as-facilitator as being engaged in complex, on-going social interactions which results in unique experiential knowledge, or in specific terms, the real system requirements (p1205). This view implicitly recognises the existence of differences in perception between individual and group members of an organisation.

**Analyst as Labour Partisan** postulates that there is a fundamental conflict between the owners of the means of production and labour in the sense that labour is exploited by the owners who place their own interests ahead of labour's and do so to the detriment of labour. The developer must side with one or the other, to develop a system that meets the needs of the organisation.

**Analyst as Emancipator**, like the Labour Partisan paradigm is essentially a theoretic position although some work has been done in Scandinavia in this area. The Analyst as Emancipator paradigm sees systems development occurring through a process of rational discourse that results in the emancipation of the organisation.

### 6.2.2. Discussion

Hirschheim and Klein's work in defining archetypal IS development paradigm's offers a useful framework within which the role of technical writer as facilitator might be explored. As discussed in the paragraphs that follow, *the technical writer as facilitator appears to fit the description of Analyst as Facilitator given in the literature review.* Hirschheim and Klein clearly recognised the need for a facilitator in order to overcome the problems inherent in the Analyst as Expert paradigm.

Analyst as Facilitator does indeed seem to be a sensible solution to the problem of developers not listening to the users, and users not knowing how to get their thoughts across to developers who believe they already know the answers. The big limitation on applying the Analyst as Facilitator paradigm in this case is that it requires the deeply entrenched Analyst as Expert culture of ComTech to change. Interestingly, George explicitly mentioned in his interview that ComTech had been forced to adopt a facilitator role in relation to various EnergyCorp departments who he described as having a "silo mentality", and who would not talk to each other constructively, or share information. George recognised from a practical, project management point-of-view that facilitation was required. His manner indicated that he saw this facilitation role as been beyond ComTech's scope of work, but it was necessary in order to get the job done. He did not think it was necessarily their job to get EnergyCorp people talking to each other.

Ironically, it was when the widening gap, or James' perceptions of misaligned business objectives between their two organisations, became so wide that they themselves needed a facilitator of communication in order to communicate with EnergyCorp, the role that the technical writer performed. Clearly, from the evidence of the interviews and observation, a facilitator of communication is a practical requirement for making progress when participants cannot or will not communicate. As Hornik et al (2003) suggests, good communication between IS professionals, IS staff and IS users is critical to the successful completion of an IS development project. The ability to interact with all potential stakeholders in an organisation, to clearly document requirements, and to effectively express ideas has long been recognised by researchers and practitioners as critical success factors (Hornik et al, 2003).

The research objective to explore the role of technical writer in relation to the aforementioned development paradigms can be supported by the findings in the sense that in this case the Analyst as Expert culture was part of the overall problem, and that the problem might be addressed by the developer adopting an Analyst as Facilitator role. Yet given ComTech's initial unwillingness to cooperate, a successful strategy might be to have a technical writer, who would normally be part of the ComTech development team act as a facilitator of communication and to take responsibility for the development of critical project documentation like the statement of user requirements. An apparent weakness in this argument is that ComTech initially refused to cooperate with the technical writer. The technical writer was not joining *their* development team however. Rather he was being imposed on them from outside by an increasingly hostile client, making him a substantial threat. In the second half of the project, the technical writer worked extensively with ComTech, gaining their confidence and acceptance. Had the technical writer joined in that capacity in the first instance, he may well have been as readily accepted. ComTech were happy to have a qualified technical writer working on the project *with* them (not against them as he was initially perceived), it removed the burden of document production from the analyst programmers, who much preferred writing code than documents.

This strategy therefore redefines the role of technical writer to include useful elements of Analyst as Facilitator, and does so in a way that minimises the threat to the developer culture since the technical writer is usually part of the development team, and not employed separately by the client (EnergyCorp). It should be remembered that threat to culture and perceived costliness are major contributing factors to the non-use of integrative processes, as indicated by George in his interview.

The results of the questionnaire, the documentary evidence, the interviews and observations all suggest quite strongly that using a technical writer on the M&M V2.0 upgrade project did bring about a more usable system, and did have the effect of improving the communication between ComTech and EnergyCorp. These results also offer some evidence of the validity of Hirschheim and Klein's paradigms of IS development.

For clarity, the sections that follow outline in some detail Hirschheim and Klein's (1989) position on the IS development paradigms, and how technical writer as facilitator can be related to the Analyst as Facilitator.

### 6.2.3. The Analyst as Systems Expert

#### *6.2.3.1. Technical writer as facilitator*

This approach suggests adapting the technical writer's role to Hirschheim and Klein's (1989) Analyst as Facilitator, or Social Relativist (Hirschheim, Klein and Lyytinen, 1995) paradigm. This seems appropriate since the facilitator paradigm developed as a reaction to the shortcomings of the expert analyst. The technical writer in this role may have much to offer when seeking a solution to the problem of poor communication between developers and users.

Added to the role of facilitator as defined by Hirschheim and Klein is recognition of the merits of the various integrative processes like Participative Design and JAD. The Facilitator fits comfortably with the processes outlined by PD, JAD and others in the sense that they all recognise the requirement for more effective communication.

The technical writer as facilitator also recognises that budgetary pressure and established organisational culture work against the adoption of integrative processes. The technical writer is already a member of the project team, and so is more likely to be accepted by the project team as a facilitator, than an external person might be. The technical writer's involvement is also less likely cause budgetary problems.

#### *6.2.3.2. How it usually is*

The figure below illustrates the process of developing the statement of user requirements in the Analyst as Systems Expert paradigm. The analyst is an expert in technology, tools and methods of system design who translates user requirements into a system.

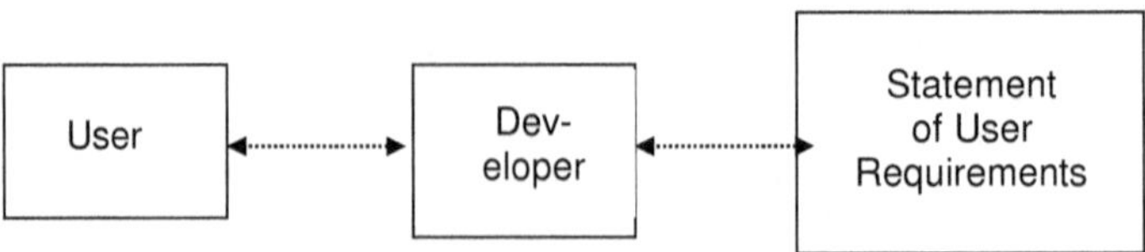

**Figure 4: Developer (Systems Expert) liaises directly with user to produce the statement of user requirements (Tuffley, 1999).**

#### *6.2.3.3. How it could be*

Recognising the complexity and subjectivity of human interaction as outlined in the Analyst as Facilitator, the technical writer is positioned to facilitate communication between developer and user. The technical writer assumes the role of the Analyst as Facilitator because under normal circumstances the Systems Expert is unlikely to make the transition to Facilitator.

System requirements are negotiated in an on-going process of management and users defining their objectives. The technical writer analyses what kind of system will achieve these objectives. They work from the user's perspective to help them arrive at their preferred view of reality. This is a role for which the technical writer might be well-suited.

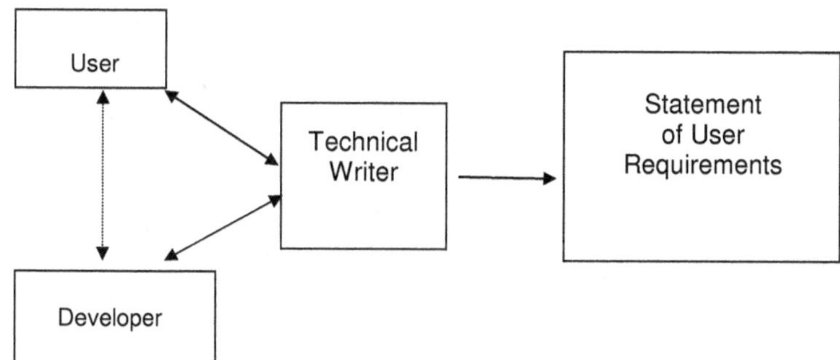


**Figure 5 technical writer as facilitator (Tuffley, 1999).**

### 6.2.4. Technical writer as facilitator

Since Hirschheim and Klein's Analyst as Facilitator paradigm developed as a reaction to the shortcomings of the expert analyst, but is often not practised due to the problems encountered by existing integrative processes, having the technical writer in the facilitator role proved to be a viable solution to these problems.

The technical writer as facilitator acknowledges the pressure that restricted project budgets place on development practices, and overcomes the problem of threatening developer culture by already being a member of the development team.

The technical writer as facilitator develops the system requirements by working with management and users, helping them to define their requirements. They work from the user's and management's perspectives to help them arrive at their preferred view of reality. They can then translate these requirements, preferably using an appropriate template, into a form intelligible to the developer.

### 6.2.5. Modification to Hirschheim & Klein's four paradigms

The approach in a sense extracts the role of facilitator from Analyst as Facilitator paradigm and inserts it into the Analyst as systems Expert paradigm, disguised as a technical writer so as not to alarm project managers keeping a wary eye on budgets, nor others prospect of change or departure from accepted practice. In such a way it is hoped to overcome the problems inherent in other integrative processes that are in practice not used, despite being effective.

### 6.2.6. ComTech regards itself an expert

The results of the interviews, observations and documentary evidence explicitly (from direct statements) and implicitly (from implied statements) show that ComTech consciously regarded themselves as the experts who had been hired to apply their expertise at a client site where the client would use that expert knowledge to solve problems.

The results therefore suggest that ComTech's particular development culture falls within the scope of the Analyst as Expert paradigm in the sense that they adopted the role of being the expert in technology, tools and methods of system design and project management. Therefore in terms of this research project, the modified Analyst as Facilitator (technical writer) was able to be tested against in an appropriate Analyst as Expert environment.

### 6.2.7. IS development is a social system technically implemented

Technical writer as facilitator recognises Hirschheim et al's (1995) position that IS development is a social system, technically implemented, not the other way around. It recognises that it is simplistic to assume that being expert in technology, tools and methods of system design and project management is not enough when the context of the development project is a complex social situation in which perception defines reality and where parties have created widely divergent beliefs about the situation and about each other.

### 6.2.8. Analyst as facilitator works towards user's preferred view of reality

Technical writer as facilitator fits with Hirschheim et al's (1995) paradigm of Analyst as facilitator in that it (a) works from the user's perspective to determine their preferred view of reality, and (b) that Analyst as Facilitator developed as a reaction to Analyst as Expert.

### 6.2.9. Participative processes all work to improve communication

Technical writer as facilitator recognises the value in established integrative processes such as Joint Application Development and Participative Design in the sense that they recognise the importance of, and work towards better communication.

In interviews, both James and George, the two principle protagonists from EnergyCorp and ComTech clearly agreed on this point; that having a technical writer act as a facilitator did improve communication in the sense that it enabled a more complete statement of user requirements to be developed. From this it may be concluded that technical writer as facilitator can be described as a successful integrative process, at least in the context of this project.

## *6.3. Can the technical writer acting as a facilitator improve usability?*

As discussed in the literature review, there are difficulties in developing an all-encompassing model of IS Quality. This is due to an inability to reconcile the diverse perspectives taken by the IS stakeholders (management, developer, user) each with their own idea of quality. To resolve this problem, this research project takes Andersson and von Hellens' (1997) general-purpose definition of IS quality to develop the concept of IS work quality by using the SOLE (SOftware Library Evolution) quality model. In this model usability is a key determinant of IS quality. It concerns itself with answering the questions; how easy was the module to use?, how easy to learn was the module?, and does it do what you need it to do (in terms of doing your job)?

By taking a user oriented approach to IS Quality it is appropriate to speak of a facilitator who works from the user's perspective to determine their preferred view of reality.

**Questionnaire.** The results of the questionnaire, in which the users were asked to assign a numerical value to each of the three dimensions of usability, *clearly indicate that having a technical writer act as facilitator in the development of the SURAC improved usability.* Furthermore, having the technical writer use a facilitation tool like the SURAC template helped to identify a further six functional requirements that were not present in ComTech's original statement of requirements.

The small size of the primary questionnaire (two respondents) was offset by:

- The later survey of all system users. This involved surveying around 35 individuals within various departments of EnergyCorp.

The questionnaire was administered either verbally by the technical writer, or via email.

- The results of interviews and observations of users.

In all cases the M&M V2.0 software was considered more usable. No-one said it was the same as, or less usable than ComTech's earlier work.

Given the range of supporting evidence, and the lack of any contradictory evidence, it is reasonable to conclude that having a technical writer act as a facilitator of communication does result in more usable software.

**Interviews**. While the interviews largely centred on obtaining feedback on the specific research question "did using the Statement of User Requirements template and having a facilitator mediate in the requirements collection result in a more complete set of requirements" there was also discussion on and around the related issue of usability. Discussion and feedback in relation to usability during interviews was universally positive. It was generally felt by Donald and Francis who were the principal users of M&M version 2 that it was simply common sense. Going about the requirements process in this way would benefit the functionality and usability of the resulting system simply because the users requirements were clearly understood.

**Documentary evidence**. James (EnergyCorp manager) took the view that a major contributing factor to poor systems quality was ComTech's lack of documentation and quality processes, and that the application of the IEEE-derived Statement of User Requirements has brought about a discernible improvement in Bulk Data Load V2.0 (the subject of the research project). This is supported by this quote from an e-mail from James to his manager Brian that the technical writer was copied on:

*... please note that in the absence of documentation and quality processes by ComTech, the IEEE approach that (the technical writer) has expertise in has been very useful with regards the V2.0 development."*

## 6.4. Overcoming developer and user resistance to previously proposed integrative processes

### 6.4.1. Integrative processes unlikely to be used when threaten culture

While the various integrative processes that have developed over the past 30 years vary in the precise way in which they work, they all appear to have the goal of improving communication as a prerequisite for obtaining a complete set of user requirements. The technical writer as facilitator also has this as its basic assumption; and so on this basis can be described as an integrative process.

But the problems recognized by Feeny, Earl and Edwards (1996) of integrative processes being avoided because they are seen to be expensive and time-consuming was evident at the research site in terms of the way requirements gathering had been performed up until the M&M V2.0 project. Had the failure of the M&M V2.0 project not had the potential to cost EnergyCorp millions of dollars, it is unlikely they would have spent the money on this particular integrative process, considering their normal practice. This assumption is based on their normal practice of allowing ComTech to perform the requirements analysis.

From ComTech's point of view, George, who had been in the industry for 35 years, was asked whether he thought having someone like a technical writer develop the project documentation was a viable practice, he replied that it undoubtedly could be, but that the pressures of tight budgets and low profit margins usually meant that there was no money for that purpose. These few words from George are a strong indication that it is budget and profit considerations, rather than the culture-threatening issues surrounding some integrative processes that prevents the more developer culture-friendly process of technical writer as Facilitator from being used more often.

But budget and profit considerations notwithstanding, from ComTech's early actions, it was also clearly the case that the formal SURAC template part of the process was indeed a threat to their culture. They resisted strenuously every effort to adopt it. It was only when the technical writer wrote it that ComTech started to co-operate. It would appear that they would tend to resist changing the way they themselves as individuals 'do things', but are far less resistant to a technical writer using whatever means they possess, as long as those means are seen to be effective., and as long as it is taking a perceived burden from the shoulders of the developer. In later, more amicable discussions with George and Larry it became clearly evident that they did indeed consider themselves to have 'our own way of doing things'. There existed a strong sense of team belonging that manifested in times of conflict as an 'them and us' attitude.

A major benefit of having a technical writer as facilitator is that it helps to minimise the perceived problem that integrative processes are too costly by using an established member of the project team to perform the integrative process.

George (ComTech project manager) clearly indicated in an interview with the technical writer that having a technical writer as a facilitator did undoubtedly help, but that budgetary constraints, and slim profit margins

# 7. Conclusions

## *7.1. Research question and method*

The question is "can IS usability be improved by having a technical writer facilitate stakeholder communication during the development of the requirements specification?" To arrive at an answer, this project took an action research approach that allowed the researcher to function as a technical writer involved in a real software development project. Action research was an appropriate research method under these circumstances, as it authorised the technical writer to act in ways not normally open to researchers, namely to oblige the project participants to follow the process that is the subject of this research, and in so doing was able to explore the possibility that a technical writer might improve the quality (in terms of usability) of a developed system by facilitating communication between the developers and the users. The action research approach in this project allowed the careful and deliberate exploration of the research question. The researcher was not constrained by simply observing participants going about their work, though observation to perform a substantial role. The researcher was able to proactively direct proceedings, and then observes the effects, thus providing a richer source of data than from observations alone.

Action research allowed the research question to be explored in a real environment, rather than a contrived research environment that may or may not be an accurate facsimile of a real environment. Thus the credibility of the findings is enhanced. In this way, something of use to the practitioner community might be devised, in addition to the contribution this project makes to the research literature. In something of the same sense that the technical writer is able to bridge the gap between developers and users, this action research project may work to build a bridge across the gap between IS research and practice.

It is the participant's perceptions of reality that is important to the research (Burrell & Morgan, 1979; Orlikowski & Baroudi, 1991). An action research project of the kind undertaken here takes an interpretive approach, one which is appropriate when dealing with the communication occurring between two categories of person (developer and user) with differing perspectives on organisational 'reality'. It is an assumption of the research that these differences exist.

## *7.2. Avoiding the pitfalls of action research*

### 7.2.1. In relation to *Baskerville's* framework for conducting valid action research

Baskerville (1999) distinguishes action research from consultancy in the following ways (quoted in full in italics):

- ***Motivation.*** *Action research is motivated by its scientific prospects, perhaps epitomised in scientific publications. Consulting is motivated by commercial benefits, including profits and additional stocks of proprietary knowledge about solutions to organisational problems.* In terms of this research project, the primary motivation was to explore a longstanding and troublesome problem facing software developers and users. The results of this exploration would be of interest both to an academic audience and the practitioner community, both groups having long recognised and acknowledged the existence of this problem. It is true that the project also furnished the technical writer with 12 months income. This was a practical necessity in order to support his family.

- ***Commitment.*** *Action research makes a commitment to the research community for the production of scientific knowledge, as well as to the client. In a consulting situation, the commitment is to the client alone.* Such a commitment has been made to the research community, in the sense that a significant research project, taking six years from start to finish, involving a full 12 months full-time attendance at the research site, has been performed. The results of this project have been distilled into a work, and will form the basis of several subsequent research journal and conference paper submissions. Any commitment to EnergyCorp ceased at the exit point.

- ***Approach.*** *Collaboration is essential in action research because of its idiographic assumptions. Consulting typically values its 'outsider's,' unbiased viewpoint, providing an objective perspective on the organisational problems.* The technical writer on entry at EnergyCorp became a collaborative member of the EnergyCorp team. This involved working with ComTech and EnergyCorp in the production of a statement of user requirements for a critical software upgrade project. The project is characterised by collaboration. The technical writer did not act like, nor was he perceived as an outsider, with the exception that during the first four to six weeks he was perceived by ComTech to be an outsider brought into EnergyCorp with the task of making them do something they didn't want to do. The technical writer was able to change this perception during the second six months of the project through almost daily contact, working collaboratively on other projects.

- ***Foundation for recommendations.*** *In action research, this foundation is a theoretical framework. Consultants are expected to suggest solutions that, in their experience, proved successful in similar situations.* As has been discussed, the theoretical framework that is the foundation for this project was developed by the technical writer during the five years before the research project, while working on a series of projects that allowed this theory to be developed through a process of trial and error, lessons learned. The recommendations are also solidly based upon a literature review that examined the relevance academic literature in relation to the research question. As will be seen throughout this work, it has been on the foundation of the research question, giving rise to the four research objectives, leading to a literature review dealing explicitly with those four objectives. On this basis the action research project plan was developed after careful review of other research approaches that concluded that action was research was the most appropriate approach in this instance. The data collected from implementation of the plan was analysed, again in direct relation to the research questions, and findings derived from the analysed data. At all stages the project is firmly based on a prescribed foundation.

- ***Essence of the organisational understanding.*** *In action research, organisational understanding is founded on practical success from iterative experimental changes in the organisation. Typical consultation teams develop an understanding through their independent critical analysis of the problem situation.* An understanding of the organisational factors at work in this research project was based on the practical success of the one event. As mentioned previously, it is a limitation of this project that it did not offer the scope to perform a process reiteratively. The single event was however a success, and on reflection and analysis a better understanding of the organisational factors at work was derived.

#### *7.2.1.1. Making it up as we go along*

One of the dangers associated with action research (Baskeville 1996) is "making it up as we go along". In the of the sometimes a rough and tumble, and somewhat chaotic world of commercial software development conditions can be changeable, making it difficult to establish and follow-through a prescribed plan. The researcher is forced to change the plan on-the-fly in order to move forwards in the face of changing conditions.

In this project, this pitfall was avoided by making certain that the plan that was established that the outset was practical, in terms of what is known to work in commercial software development projects. The researcher drew on his knowledge as a practitioner technical writer to devise a simple plan that he would use his template to develop a comprehensive set of user requirements based on facilitated discussion with stakeholders.

And then to assess the effects based on a combination of questionnaire, discussions, observations and documentary evidence. So this pitfall was avoided *by planning at the outset how the action part of the project will be performed, and then executing the plan without variation.* If a plan of action is formulated, and is subsequently implemented in the form that it is originally took, this will go a considerable distance towards avoiding the charge of "making it up as we go along". As events transpired, the plan came close to being derailed when ComTech kept refusing to use the SURAC template, despite EnergyCorp's (James) repeated instruction to do so, and the higher level political activities that ComTech engaged in that initially over-ruled James' instructions. That eventuality had not been foreseen in the original plan, so the solution to the problem was made up "on the fly", but it was sufficient to bring the project back to the plan. The solution had been to have James agree to implement the technical writer's proposition (Research Journal, Friday 9th April, 1999, see section 9.5.7); *"If the SURAC is complete, as ComTech maintain it is, then it would not take long to apply the template, since the detail is mostly there already. If it not complete, it is far better to know about it now, and remedy the situation, than it is to find out about it after the system has been developed".*

### *7.2.1.2. Blurring the distinction between roles*

Due to the inherently split-personality nature of action research, perhaps one of the greatest challenges facing a researcher is to maintain a clear distinction between the various roles played by the participants. As Baskerville (1999) indicates the researcher is also likely to be a consultant who is expected to do commercial consulting work. In the sometimes pressurised environments in which many consultants work, it is sometimes a challenge for him or her to be sufficiently objective to maintain a clear distinction in their own minds between the role of the consultant and that of the researcher. While Baskerville uses the term consultant, a technical writer with particular skills might be substituted for a consultant in this regard.

The blurring of the roles of researcher and technical writer was avoided by the technical writer being the *only persona* that the participants (except James) perceived at the research site over the 12 month period. Even James, after the initial weeks of the project, did not refer to, or act in any way towards the technical writer as anything but a technical writer. It was as if the researcher component of the project was forgotten as more pressing matters were dealt with in bringing the M&M version 2 project to a successful completion. The technical writer acted as the participants expected a technical writer to behave, with the researcher persona being nowhere apparent. This avoided the obvious danger that the participants would perceive and relate to the technical writer as a researcher, possibly giving the answers they thought the researcher wanted to hear.

Being able to present the persona of a normal technical writer represents a distinct strength in this action research project. Not all action researchers would have the opportunity to submerge their researcher persona beneath the consultant persona, therefore they could never be entirely sure about how and why their co-workers were acting towards them. Were they reacting to the researcher?, were they reacting to the consultant?, or a combination of both, which is likely to be somewhat confused. This was avoided to a very large extent in this action research project. The researcher persona emerged off-site when he reflected and wrote up his research notes. In this way, the question "can IS usability be improved by having a technical writer facilitate stakeholder communication during the development of the requirements specification?" could be effectively explored in the context of an action research project.

On the many occasions during the course of the 12 months on-site research event, the benefits of being able to maintain a simple, straightforward professional relationship with his co-workers not only simplified matters, but also helped to quarantine the data and findings from the kind of role confusion mentioned by Baskerville. It would seem this problem has two components. The first being caused by the researcher losing perspective on the distinction between their roles, the second being because of the way people were acting towards them. The first was avoided in this project by consciously leaving the researcher persona out of his day-to-day work, the second was avoided by excluding the whole problem from the event. The first problem was also effectively managed by the technical writer using the same professional persona as he had used as a working technical writer over the previous 15 years.

### 7.2.2. In relation to *Checkland's* criteria for conducting valid action research

Lau (1999), citing earlier work by Checkland outlines a framework for conducting valid action research. This provides a structure for an action research project that will legitimise it as an alternative to positivistic hypothesis testing. These criteria are (in bold):

- **There is a real-world problem relevant to research themes of interest to the researcher.** In relation to this action research project, there was a clear focus on a longstanding real-world problem that had been of great interest to the researcher over the previous 10 years. Indeed it was this specific real-world problem that was a decisive factor in leading the researcher to make the transition from practitioner to academic. During his career as a practitioner, the researcher repeatedly saw instances where systems that had been developed were of poor quality and low usability, despite considerable expertise and resources put into their development. An interest in exploring this puzzling situation developed over time, culminating in this research project.
- **Respective roles of the researcher and participants defined in the problem situation**. The respective roles of the researcher and participants were clearly defined at the outset, as discussed in

the previous section. The researcher would perform in every way as a professional technical writer would be expected to behave at a commercial development site. The only non-standard elements of his behaviour was the application of the IEEE based template, and the facilitation of communication between stakeholders. This is non-standard work for a technical writer, but it is a logical extension of the technical writer role. The researcher would perform his work outside the research environment, where quiet reflection could be performed. The other participants also had their standard roles prescribed by the organisational context.

- Inclusion of an intellectual framework by means of which the nature of research lessons can be defined and the method in which the framework is embodied. The nature of the research lessons could be explored using the framework of this prescribed action research project, in which a plan was developed, implemented, data collected and analysed to produce findings, all within the framework of a rigorously executed research project.

- **Researcher involvement in unfolding the situation with a view to help bring about changes deemed improvements**. At the initial prospective employment interview with James, the EnergyCorp executive charged with making the M&M version 2 upgrade project a success, it was discussed and agreed that the technical writer would use the IEEE derived template, and employ certain facilitation techniques, in order to produce a comprehensive set of requirements for this critical project. This was the explicit proposition that the technical writer could put to James and it was accepted. (It will be noticed that this is the central research question of this research project.) In this way the technical writer received a mandate to explore the research question, whilst providing a solution to EnergyCorp's problem. The technical writer was given an initial six months to perform this process, with an implied six-month extension should his performance be satisfactory. In this way the technical writer was actively involved in an unfolding situation, in a position to influence events in order to bring about changes that are deemed to be improvements.

- **Rethinking of earlier stages by making sense of the accumulating experience through the declared framework and method, and revising changes**. A limitation of this research project was that EnergyCorp hired the technical writer to perform a single specific task. There was not the opportunity to perform multiple reiterations. This is a significant limitation of this research project. The effects of this limitation have been mitigated by having a clearly enunciated plan the outset, and executing the plan without significant variation.

- **Point of exit for the researcher in order to review the experience and to extract lessons for learning in relation to the re-**

**search themes and/or definition of new themes**. As mentioned above, the exit point was identified and the outset to be either at the end of six months, or at the end of 12 months. James from EnergyCorp had built the six-month termination as a contingency plan in the event that the technical writer was not performing to their satisfaction. It was clear from the outset that the technical writer would be engaged for no longer than 12 months.

## *7.3. Summary of research findings*

This research project has sought to find answers in relation to the stated research objectives. This section will indicate how each specific objective has been addressed and supported by the research, and summarises the conclusions that may reasonably be drawn.

The findings have been grouped, as has been done throughout this work, according to how they relate to the research objectives. The objectives themselves being the tools chosen to explore the research question.

| Research Objective | Conclusion |
|---|---|
| 1. To better understand the nature of the 'gap' that apparently exists between users and developers of systems, especially in relation to the activity of gathering of user requirements. | In relation to the gap (not specifically a cultural gap) that is discussed in the literature, it was found that it is constituted by the following specific factors:<br>• communication difficulties<br>• the shifting nature of the relationship<br>• perceptions of "us and them"<br>• misalignment of objectives<br>• the consequences of misaligned objectives<br>Supporting points:<br>• The technical writer acting as an impartial facilitator of communication helped both sides see that the other side's views were valid.<br>• The facilitator helped each side incorporate elements of the other side's view into their own, leading to more constructive collaboration.<br>• The technical writer as facilitator qualifies as an integrative process that assists with communication between sides.<br>• The project managers on both sides both agreed that having the technical writer as a facilitator had brought about a good project outcome. James felt it had created a collaborative environment, while George thought it undoubtedly could be good, but that the pressures of tight budgets and low profit margins usually meant that there was no money for that purpose.<br>• Budget and profit considerations notwithstanding, |

<table>
<tr>
<td></td>
<td>
from ComTech's early actions, it was also clearly the case that the formal SURAC template part of the process was indeed a threat to their culture. They resisted strenuously every effort to adopt it.<br><br>
Using Johnson and Scholes' model of organisational culture, the nature of the cultural gap between EnergyCorp and ComTech were analysed, and summarised as follows:
<table>
<tr><th>Element</th><th>EnergyCorp</th><th>ComTech</th></tr>
<tr><td>Structure</td><td>hierarchical</td><td>flat</td></tr>
<tr><td>Stories</td><td>past/present</td><td>present/future</td></tr>
<tr><td>Symbols</td><td>affluent</td><td>economical</td></tr>
<tr><td>Routines/ Rituals</td><td>formal</td><td>informal</td></tr>
<tr><td>Control</td><td>punishment</td><td>reward</td></tr>
<tr><td>Power Struc-</td><td>paternalistic</td><td>entrepreneurial</td></tr>
</table>
</td>
</tr>
<tr>
<td>2. To examine the role of the technical writer in relation to Hirschheim and Klein's (1989) paradigms of the Analyst as Systems Expert and Analyst as Facilitator.</td>
<td>
• ComTech clearly defined itself as expert in the context of the services provided to EnergyCorp.<br>
• Technical writer as facilitator fits with Hirschheim et al's (1995) paradigm of Analyst as Facilitator in that it (a) works from the user's perspective to determine their preferred view of reality, and (b) that Analyst as Facilitator developed as a reaction to Analyst as Expert.<br>
• Technical writer as facilitator recognises the value in established integrative processes such as Joint Application Development and Participative Design in the sense that they work towards better communication.<br>
• Technical writer as facilitator helps to minimise the perceived problem that integrative processes are too costly by using an established member of the project team to perform the integrative process<br>
• Technical writer as facilitator recognises Hirschheim et al's (1995) position that IS development is a social system, technically implemented, not vice versa.<br>
• Technical writer as facilitator recognises the complexity and subjectivity of human interaction as outlined by Analyst as Facilitator.
</td>
</tr>
<tr>
<td>3. To evaluate whether a system can be made more usable (as defined by the SOLE model) by</td>
<td>
• According to the evidence of the two SUR's, at least six additional requirements were identified that made the V2.0 more useable. The six additional requirements added useful functionality that would not have been otherwise present.<br>
• The results of the questionnaire does reasonably
</td>
</tr>
</table>

| | |
|---|---|
| the technical writer acting as a facilitator between user and developer during requirements gathering. | indicate that the usability (as defined by the SOLE model) of V2.0 relative to V1.0 was improved by the technical writer acting as a facilitator between user and developer during requirements gathering.<br>• In the questionnaire Donald and Francis were asked to compare Version 2.0 with 1.0 in terms of the questions (a) how easy was the module to use?, (b) how easy to learn was the module?, and (c) does it do what you need it to do? returned responses that clearly indicated V2.0 was more usable (V2.0 = 8.5/15, V1.0 = 13.5/15), with lower scores indicating greater usability.<br>• The later technical report into TASS, in which all users (34) were given the same questionnaire some three months after Donald and Francis did the initial questionnaire helps to confirm the improvement.<br>• In interviews, when asked about whether usability had improved from V1.0 to V2.0) by the technical writer acting as a facilitator:<br>• **James** said (the technical writer had) '*undoubtedly improved the outcome'* by forcing the developers to listen to what the users and management wanted, to formally document the requirements, then to feedback what they thought the client wanted in order to confirm their understanding was correct.<br>• **Donald** said 'Yeah, it probably did help'<br>• **Francis** said '*Yes, I'd say so'.* |
| 4. To explore factors which influence the problem of developer and user resistance to previously proposed integrative processes | Given the likely reasons for resistance to integrative processes, it is a viable integrative process to have an existing member of the development team act as project documentation writer, while using a JAD derived facilitation approach to elicit requirements during the preparation of the template-based Statement of User Requirements.<br>This integrative process has the benefit of:<br>• Not threatening developer culture by using an existing project team member,<br>• having a minimal effect on the project budget<br>increasing the likelihood of meeting development schedules because the analyst/programmers are relieved of the task of writing technical documentation, thus saving time while at the same time producing a professionally written SURAC document is produced. |

## *7.4. Significance of the findings in relation to the research question*

*Can IS usability be improved by having a technical writer facilitate stakeholder communication during the development of the requirements specification?*

This work has sought to answer the research question by breaking the question into four elements and transforming these elements into the research objectives. The research objectives are then used as informing principles throughout the work to give it structure, consistency and traceability. Each chapter uses the research objectives as its basic structure, so that each objective can be traced from the beginning through to the end of the work. By rigorously following this approach, an answer to the research question can be developed that has due regard and traceability to the original question.

The findings in general address a long recognised problem in IS development, one which has frustrated project management and stakeholders generally with a persistent over-budget, over-time and defect-ridden product problems. The findings point toward a viable solution to this persistent problem. They recognise that the processes employed by developers, while inadequate, are nonetheless deeply entrenched cultural practices that seem to be highly resistant to change.

Any viable solution to the problem must recognise this and work within its constraints. A technical writer, already a member of the project team, is unlikely to be perceived as a threat to the developer's culture. The technical writer in the context of this project was indeed perceived as a threat at the beginning of the project, because he had quite clearly been brought in by the client, and given a mandate to impose change upon the developer, ComTech. Change that was strenuously resisted until the technical writer later become to some degree accepted by ComTech as a member of their own team. This occurred around six months into the project.

The technical writer, by definition, is someone adept at the development of project documentation, and does not mind doing that job. The programmers on this project did not like preparing documentation, resenting it because it kept them from their real job of writing programmes. A slight cultural change in this context, in which the technical writer gets involved with the project sooner than the testing stage, and takes over the responsibility for handling the requirements specification development, is likely to be welcomed by project staff. It removes an unwanted task from their workload. Hence, there might be minimal resistance to this possible solution to the persistent problem discussed above.

Because the technical writer, using an IEEE-derived template, and acting as a go-between, is able to develop a complete, and well-written specification, the developed product is more likely to do what the user needs it to do. The project is concluded sooner because less time is spent fixing problems that only emerged at the end of the project, but which could have been avoided with a more complete specification. This was evidenced by ComTech's original specification that they insisted was complete. The final specification, the one developed by the technical writer using the IEEE-derived template contained six additional functional requirements, ones which were not present in the original specification, and which would nonetheless need to be included in the finished product, with additional time and expense, later in the project.

The IEEE-derived template can be seen as an element of the "facilitated communication" part of the research question. The template serves as an organised set of questions, or areas that need to be addressed in order for the job to be completed comprehensively. This is in the same way that an interviewer will prepare a set of questions to ask an interviewee in order for the desired information to be gathered. The template serves this purpose, and is an integral part of the "facilitated communication" process.

The findings clearly indicate that using a process of facilitated communication did produce a more complete requirements specification, and did this at the beginning of the project rather than at the end when it would take considerable time and expense to include them.

In addition to there being a more complete set of requirements, the usability of the developed system was recognised by the respondents to the usability questionnaire as being distinctly improved compared with earlier versions developed by ComTech. While it may be an intuitive or common-sense observation to make that approaching the development of the requirements specification is likely to derive better results, the findings of this project indicate the same conclusion by using a formal research methodology to test the question.

### 7.4.1. Significance of the findings in relation to the specific research objectives

The significance of the findings in relation to the specific research objectives are discussed below:

**Objective 1**. To better understand the nature of the 'gap' that apparently exists between users and developers of systems, especially in relation to the activity of gathering of user requirements.

The findings derived from the interviews and observation over the 12 month period indicate the presence of a significant cultural gap existing between the EnergyCorp and ComTech due to differences between their respective organisational cultures. The gap created communication difficulties, and differing agendas created a certain amount of resentment towards each other. Differing agendas in this sense refers to ComTech being an embedded presence at EnergyCorp but who were pursuing their own development agenda. Rather than develop the product that EnergyCorp was paying for, they were using EnergyCorp to fund the development of their own generic product that would then be sold to EnergyCorp's competitors. This was seen by EnergyCorp as an act of betrayal which might well have been enough to end the relationship had EnergyCorp had too much invested, and too much dependence upon ComTech.

So the nature of the cultural gap in this project derived from several sources, as recognised in the findings:

- Different organisational cultures; one a SME (small to medium enterprise), the other a large, government owned enterprise with a culture that has been described as being arrogant towards their suppliers generally (by ComTech)
- Inherent differences in the world-views and communication styles of developers and users/management leading to difficulties in establishing common ground.
- EnergyCorp trusting ComTech, and ComTech betraying that trust in a calculated way, knowing that EnergyCorp was too dependant to look elsewhere.

The first two elements may be applicable more broadly in that they refer to a general trend that has been recognised and discussed in the literature. The third is specific to this project, yet some aspects of the relationship between developer and client in the IT industry may still be in common in the larger world. The client looks to the developer as a consultant whose special expertise is being hired to solve a specific problem that the client recognises it has. If the consultant takes the client's money and knowingly delivers something other than what has been specifically asked for, then this constitutes a breach of trust.

The findings indicate that a technical writer, with their ability to see both technical and non-technical points of view is in a position to act as a facilitator of communication, as a integrator of two different world-views that were in conflict to arrive at a position where the two world-views were still held, but where common ground had been identified and used as the foundation for a more constructive relationship. This finding highlights the assertion by Gallivan and Keil (2003) that power asymmetry between developers and users leads to poor project outcomes, even when the stakeholders are communicating. Asymmetric power relationships, in which the developer is free to disregard the wishes of the user are unlikely to result in users investing their trust in the final system. The technical writer is able to reduce the perceived asymmetry, and include the user in the dialogue more constructively. In this sense, the technical writer acts to reduce the sanctionary power of the developer over users.

The technical writer was also, in this project, in a position to help rebuild the trust that had been lost, by demonstrating to EnergyCorp that Com-

Tech were now willing to develop the product they had specifically asked for. Again, the power asymmetry spoken of by Gallivan and Keil is reduced. There was a change from ComTech's initial response to include certain functionality "I don't know if we can give you that. It doesn't fit with our product development strategy", to a more cooperative "Yes, we can certainly do that".

**Objective 2**. To examine the role of the technical writer in relation to Hirschheim and Klein's (1989) paradigms of the Analyst as Systems Expert and Analyst as Facilitator.

The key finding in relation to this objective was the pervasive reference that ComTech made in relation to itself, that they were the "experts". Their expert status, which was not disputed by EnergyCorp, was perhaps the main reason EnergyCorp engaged them in the first place. They portrayed themselves as experts in developing the kind of software EnergyCorp needed, and EnergyCorp accepted this portrayal and perceived them as experts.

Expert status was the justification for overruling EnergyCorp's requests for certain functionality. ComTech deflected criticism by implying that EnergyCorp did not really know what they wanted. The experts would decide in the way that a consulting doctor used their expert judgment to make decisions about patients. The patient could not be trusted with such decisions.

The findings from the interviews and observations clearly indicate that ComTech cast themselves in the role described by Hirschheim and Klein's (1989) paradigm of the Analyst as Systems Expert. Inherent in the Analyst as Systems Expert paradigm and in ComTech's observed actions was the assumption that the developer knows more about systems development than does the user, therefore spending time, effort and money on liaising with users during requirement gathering is seen as unnecessary, even counterproductive. This is a further indication of the problems caused when there a is a perceived power asymmetry (Gallivan and Keil, 2002).

The findings also indicate that the technical writer can successfully assume the role of Analyst as Facilitator in response to the same perceived problems identified by Hirschheim and Klein that are inherent in the Analyst as Expert paradigm. The technical writer as facilitator works from the user's perspective to determine their preferred view of reality. They recognise the complexity and subjectivity of human interaction as outlined by Hirschheim and Klein's Analyst as Facilitator.

The remaining two paradigms (Analyst as Labour Partisan, and Social Therapist) were not relevant to this project.

**Objective 3**. To examine whether system usability (as defined by the SOLE model, Eriksson and Törn, 1991) can be improved by the technical writer acting as a facilitator between user and developer during requirements gathering.

The findings based on the questionnaire results and interviews show that usability (as defined by Erikkson and Törn and the SOLE model, mentioned above) was clearly improved compared to earlier versions of the same module, and other modules in the same suite, developed by ComTech. While the questionnaire results cannot be said to be quantitative, they do indicate a clear trend.

Poor system usability is a common problem in the world of IT. This research project has identified the possible underlying reasons (poorly defined process, cultural difference, poor communication) and tests a possible solution. The technical writer, based on these findings, can improve usability, and do it in a cost effective manner that is more likely to be embraced by developers as it does not threaten the existing development culture. Rather it grafts an improvement onto that culture that is likely to be welcomed by that culture because it relieves the programmers of the need to write documentation.

**Objective 4**. To explore factors that influence the problem of developer and user resistance to previously proposed integrative processes

There have been quite a number of Integrative processes developed in response to the long-recognised problem of poor user/developer communication (Participative Design, User Participation, Joint Application Development etc.). The findings of this research project support the exploration of the question "Why are they not used, or not used more often?"

Taking the fundamental position that an integrative process must function in the organisational culture that exists at the development site, what factors might contribute to one integrative process being practiced, while another is not? The findings of the interviews in which ComTech were asked directly what reasons exist for using or not using an integrative process such as the SUR template. The replies indicated that they "were not the way we do things" (cultural barrier). They were also cited as being too expensive and too time consuming. Projects have tight schedules and tight budgets, and integrative processes were considered to be niceties that were not practical "in the real world".

From this, it might be concluded that for an integrative process to succeed in being adopted, it must avoid:

- being perceived as a threat to organisational culture,
- adding significant effort to the project,
- costing significantly more than the established ways of doing things.

Having the technical writer act in the manner prescribed in this research project stands a significant chance of overcoming each of these barriers. The first barrier listed above can be overcome by offering to make the job easier for the developer by taking on the development of the specification, a documentation task not enjoyed by the programmer on this project, and perhaps not by other programmers on other projects. So while having the technical writer change their role somewhat could be perceived as a threat, the fact that they are already a member of that culture means that it is an internal matter, with a benefit to all. This might be easier to accept than an external threat.

The second barrier can be mitigated by considering the time saved by having the technical writer act in this capacity. Rework at the end of the project to include functions that need to be there but were not included in the original specification adds significantly to the overall effort. The technical writer might actually save overall time and effort by effectively dealing with this crucial issue of requirements definition.

The third barrier is related to the second. While having the technical writer involved from the beginning of a project may create an additional expense, it is unlikely to be a major expense, and the efficiencies and benefits indicated in the previous paragraph serves as a justification.

## *7.5. Contribution of the work*

In summary, this work establishes or adds to the body of research relating to:

- action research methodologies,
- requirements engineering and the nature of the 'gap' that apparently exists between users and developers of systems, especially in relation to the activity of gathering user requirements,
- the role of the technical writer in relation to Hirschheim and Klein's (1989) paradigms of the Analyst as Systems Expert and Analyst as Facilitator,
- information systems quality,
- developer and user resistance to previously proposed integrative processes.

1. The work explores how the action research methodology can be applied to effectively explore a research question. It identifies a possible danger to an AR project that of the intransigence of certain participants in the face of properly constituted authority. The technical writer had been authorised to have participants perform certain actions (which were central to the AR project), yet those

participants can be unexpectedly difficult and thus pose a threat to the AR project. The lesson to be learned is that such difficulties are foreseeable, and therefore should be planned for at the outset, and contingency plans made.

2. It explores the nature and dynamics of the so-called 'gap' that apparently exists between users and developers of systems and which tends to inhibit communication. While this problem has been widely recognised and discussed, leading to the development over decades of a variety of 'integrative processes' little apparent progress has been made towards a better understanding of why the solutions intended to remedy the 'gap' are not more widely used, despite the apparent need.

3. The work explores the implications of Hirschheim and Klein's (1989) paradigms of the Analyst as Systems Expert and Analyst as Facilitator in order to redefine the role of technical writer. It explores the nature of the Analyst as Facilitator paradigm, and draws parallels between it and a technical writer who facilitates communication and uses a structured SURAC template to perform a role that has much in common with that of the Analyst as Facilitator paradigm. After extensive searching, no evidence could be found in the academic literature that this role connection and comparison has not previously been made.

4. The work builds on earlier work that recognises the existence of a 'culture gap' between developers and users (Feeny, Earl and Edwards, 1996). It extends the idea of integrative processes, which can help bridge, the culture gap between developers and users (Lawrance and Lorsch, 1967, Galbraith, 1977) by proposing and testing a process that can be successful in environments where 'Analyst as Systems Expert' (Hirschheim and Klein, 1989) is the prevailing paradigm. Such environments may be resistant to the use of integrative processes that involve significant investments in time, money and resources. Rightly or wrongly, examples such as the ETHICS model for participative systems development (Mumford, 1983), Joint Application Development (Raghavan, Zelesnik and Ford, 1994) may be seen in such a light. It contributes to the development of a viable integrative process that recognises the inherent problems and mitigates them in ways that are likely to succeed. It forms the basis and starting point for future papers aimed at both academic and practitioner communities.

5. The work contributes to a better understanding of the role of facilitator, whether they are a technical writer or a business analyst or someone else. To be successful the facilitator must merge differing world views in order to build trust, good will and the desire to collaborate. There are potential benefits in increasing our understanding of the role of facilitator of communication, given the clear acknowledgment in the literature that the existence of a gap between stakeholders constitutes a major challenge.

6. The work contributes to the growing body of knowledge in the field of action research. The relevance of the research problem is clear. Decades of IS developers have had to contend with the problem of poor user-developer communication, and the user has been left to deal with the consequences of systems with poor usability. With sufficient rigour applied to the design and execution of an action research project, the results can be useful to the practitioner world, while contributing to the relevant research literature on action research. Rigour in this project was achieved through careful planning based on the accepted literature on action research project design, adherence to the plan throughout the project, as well as using multiple sources of data to provide a dialectic. Interpretation of the data was performed during the data collection.

## *7.6. Limitations & strengths of the research*

**Limitations.**

A limitation mentioned in the action research literature is that of an IS action researcher being unable to maintain a clear distinction between the various roles played by the participants. In the pressurised environments in which many consultants (technical writer in this case) work, it is sometimes a challenge for him or her to be sufficiently objective to maintain a clear distinction in their own minds between the role of the consultant and that of the researcher.

This limitation was clearly recognised in the early planning stages of the research project, and the risk managed by clearly defining the way the research project would be conducted (facilitation techniques, SURAC template, questionnaire, interviews, documentary evidence). Then proceeding according to the plan and following through to its conclusion, all according to the plan established at the beginning. At no time was there any 'making up the plan as I go along'. The only unexpected event was the opportunity to develop a technical report on the whole system of which M&M is one module that enabled the questionnaire to be administered to all users. The results of this questionnaire are not included in the project, but are included for reference in an appendix.

Another limitation was that the research event did not allow for multiple iterations in which there is a rethinking of earlier stages by making sense of the accumulating experience through the declared framework and method, and revising changes (Lau, 1999). EnergyCorp hired the technical writer to perform a single specific task and multiple iterations were not in scope. The effects of this limitation have been minimised by having a clearly defined plan defined at the outset executed without significant variation.

**Strengths.** In addition to the data derived from the questionnaire, and the documentary evidence, the data generated by this project is the result of the researcher interpreting subjective information originating from an on-going, complex human interaction, set in a specific organisational context in which there were at least two quite different cultures present.

This potential limitation is made a strength by ensuring the data was gathered and analysed with sufficient rigor to validate using an interpretivist approach. It does this by (a) not relying solely upon subjective data, but to derive objective data from at least two other sources (questionnaire, documentary evidence), and (b) to have altogether four sources of data with which to triangulate, or in this case quadrangulate.

So it is strength of this work that it is an action research project. Unlike a case study in which the researcher is limited to the role of a passive observer, an action research project can actively create the conditions in which the research question can be answered. The research plan can devise specific activities relevant to the research question. This has the potential to produce results targeted at a particular situation, as outlined in the research question.

Another strength is the relatively long duration of the research event. Twelve months exactly (two by six month contracts). Gathering a considerable amount of data over a long period allowed for data patterns to be identified and compared with earlier or later patterns, thus helping to confirm them. For example ComTech's early attitude towards the EnergyCorp users was consistently dismissive for perhaps the first three months. In the months that followed, their attitude towards the users gradually transformed into one of collaboration. This statement is based on the accumulated data over twelve months and is likely to have more validity than data gained from a one-off snapshot, a glimpse that may or may not be typical or even accurate.

The work also uses orthodox tools (JAD facilitation, IEEE-derived SURAC template) to answer the research question, thus helping to avoid the potential criticism that the tools used are unknown, untried and /or untested. It was recognised in the early planning that it would not be wise to use tools that are not widely recognised and accepted. Unknown or questionable tools would cast doubt on the validity of the results. The SURAC template was based on perhaps the most orthodox software engineering standard of its kind, while JAD had been devised and used for many years by the IBM Corporation, seen by many as a pillar of the IT industry. The work does not try to test the efficacy of a new tool, but rather the efficacy of a set of trusted existing tools that have not been combined and tested in this precise way before. By extension, the technical writer who uses the tools is not a new entity in the development team, he or she still performs their traditional role, but has their role extended in a way that is likely to be accepted by a typical project team (the technical writer is usually employed by the developer, not the user as in this case). While there might always be room for criticism and doubt about the validity of a set of results, this work stays on the safest ground possible when developing those results.

A further strength is that it provides the basis upon which further publications in both the academic and practitioner communities can be developed. In an academic sense, it contributes to the literature of information systems (bridging the cultural gap) and software engineering (requirements engineering. For practitioners it points to a series of articles aimed at project managers and planners that indicate the benefits in terms of on-time, within-budget project outcomes, of having a technical writer perform the functions that are the subject of this work.

## *7.7. Opportunities for future research*

### 7.7.1. Effect of model-based process improvement on organisational culture

A promising area of future research that follows on from this project is the examination of model-based process improvement and the effect it has on the culture of the organisation in which it is performed. In this current research project, the model was the IEEE-based template. Future research might include the longitudinal study of the effect that the Capability Maturity Model (CMMI) has on organisational culture over time.

While there has been extensive work done that examines the financial effects on an organisation of model-based process improvement, there has been little work performed that investigates the effects on organisational culture. Particularly in looking at what cultural effects tend to enhance the benefits of model-based process improvement, and which work against.

An indicative research question is What is the organisational impact of implementing improvement programmes? Can this be expressed in terms beyond economic measures? What factors determine the success of improvement? What factors are central to the failure of improvement programmes?

This question would be addressed in two broad ways. The first by administering a questionnaire that collects quantitative and qualitative data concerning organisational impact of improvement programmes across the participating partner organisations. The data derived will be subject to statistical analysis to produce the range of perspectives, including both non-economic and economic.

The second approach would be to undertake a longitudinal ethnographic or an extended case study of the participating partner's. The anticipated minimum duration is two years, though preliminary findings can be developed after 12 months, with further findings derived at 36 months, 48 months and 60 months. In this way, sufficient data from a sufficiently diverse set of sources can be collected to examine effectively what is the affect on organisational culture of model based process improvement programmes. The study will seek the critical success factors, as well as those factors that increase the likelihood of failure. A combination of quantitative and qualitative methods will assist in the data triangulation of results (Jick, 1979) which will strengthen the validity of those results.

The study described above is the subject of an ARC (Australian Research Council) linkage grant application, pending a decision in the second half of 2004. If successful, the researcher will be a Chief Investigator who will perform the research project as described, assisted by a significant research grant. The grant application includes three other Chief Investigators who will examine other research questions. If the application is not successful, there is nonetheless an opportunity to perform the research, given the agreements currently in place with four industry partners who have agreed to be the research sites.

### 7.7.2. Prototyping tool

A second worthwhile future research project is one that extends on this research by introducing a third tool to the set. In addition to facilitation techniques and a SURAC template, the efficacy could be tested of having the technical writer use a prototyping tool to gather the requirements, and the usability of the resulting system then assessed. User interface design and dynamics can be tested more effectively with a prototype once the requirements have been gathered.

## *7.8. Concluding remarks*

This project set out to conduct research into the nature of the gap that appears to exist between the stakeholders of the M&M upgrade project, and whether usability might be improved by having a technical writer act as a facilitator of communication between stakeholders. The reality of M&M version 1, as with other modules already installed and working in this environment over the previous three years was poor usability, high defect rates, dissatisfied users. ComTech had developed all modules.

Even though the client organisation was at significant financial risk were the M&M project a failure (did not have the required functionality), EnergyCorp nonetheless had enough confidence in the technical writer's proposed approach (as defined in the research plan) at the outset to decide to employ him.

All project participants, with the exception of the ComTech programmer, agreed that the technical writer's approach had resulted in improved usability. The programmer later conceded that the approach worked, but on the proviso that he himself did not have to develop the IEEE-derived SURAC.

The results of the questionnaire that was administered as part of the original action research plan, as well as the results of the same questionnaire administered to all users in the organisation later, when the opportunity fortuitously presented itself, clearly indicate that (a) almost all users right across the EnergyCorp organisation considered the software developed by ComTech to be of poor usability, defect-ridden and difficult to use. This indicates a clear characteristic in ComTech's work, and (b) that in the M&M upgrade project, usability was clearly improved.

The only difference between this and any other project performed by ComTech in the previous three years was that the technical writer facilitated communication between ComTech and EnergyCorp, and based the SURAC on an IEEE-derived template that was comprehensive in the way that it gathered and organised the users requirements, compared with the less comprehensive, more informal SURAC used by ComTech.

This project has explored the nature of the gap, and in particular the cultural gap. The findings of this research might form a fruitful basis for further research into what is a well-recognised but poorly understood problem that has afflicted the IT industry for decades.

# 8. References

Ackoff, R. (1967). Management Misinformation Systems. Management Science, 14(4), 147-156.

Allaire, Y. and Firsirotu, M. (1984) Theories of Organisational Culture, Organization Studies (5:3).

Andersson, T., & von Hellens, L. (1997). Information systems work quality. Information and Software Technology 39(12), 837-844.

Argyris, C., Putnam, R., & McLain-Smith, D. (1982). Action Science: Concepts, Methods and Skills for Research and Intervention. San Francisco: Jossy-Bass.

Avison, D.E., & Myers, M.D. (1995). Information Systems and Anthropology: an anthropological perspective on IT and organisational culture. Information Technology & People, (8:3), 48-49.

Avital, M. & Vandenbosch, B. (2000).The Relationship Between Psychological Ownership and IT-Driven Value. Proceedings of the International Conference of Information Systems, Sydney, Australia, 652-659.

Barki, H., & Hartwick, J. (1994, December). User Participation, Conflict and Conflict Resolution: The Mediating Roles of Influence. Information Systems Research, 422-432.

Baskerville, R. (1992). Three Perils for Action Research in Information Systems Consulting (Management Working Paper 92-1). New York: Binghampton School.

Baskerville, R., & Pries-Heje, J. (1995) Grounding the Theory in Action Research. Proceedings of the 3rd European Conference on Information Systems. Athens, Greece, June 1-3.

Baskerville, R. (1999). Investigating Information Systems with Action Research. Communications of the Association for Information Systems, 2, article 19.

Baster , G., Konana , P., Scott, J., (2001) Business Components: A Case Study of Bankers Trust Australia Limited, Communications of the ACM, 44(5), 92-98.

Blyth A.J.C., Chudge J., Dobson J.E. & Strens, M.R. (1993). ORDIT: A New Methodology to Assist in the Process of Eliciting and Modelling Organisational Requirements. Proceedings of the ACM Conference on Organisational Computing Systems, Milpilas CA: ACM Press.

Boehm, B. (1981). Software Engineering Economics. Prentice Hall, Engelwood Cliffs, New Jersey.

Burrell, G., & Morgan, G. (1979). Sociological Paradigms and Organisational Analysis. Gower: Aldershot, 4-35.

Carmel, E. Whitaker, E, R. D. and George J. F. (1993) PD and joint application design: A transatlantic comparison. Communications of the ACM, 36(4), 40-48.

Champy, J. (1997). IT and Line Managers Need to Close the Gap. Computerworld, Jan. 27, 76.

Checkland, P., Scholes, J. (1990). Soft Systems Methodology in Action. Toronto, John Wiley and Sons.

Checkland, P. (1991). From Framework through Experience to Learning: the essential nature of Action Research. In H. E. Nissen, H.K. Klein, & R. Hirschheim (Eds.), Information Systems Research: Contemporary approaches and Emergent Traditions. Amsterdam: Elsevier.

Christel, M., Wood, D., & Stevens, S. (1993). AMORE: The Advanced Multimedia Organiser for Requirements Elicitation (CMU Technical Report; CMU/EI-93-TR-12), Carnegie Mellon University, Pittsburg.

Chua, W. (1986). Radical developments in accounting thought. The Accounting Review, 61(4), 601-632.

Dahlberg, T., & Jarvinen, J. (1997). Challenges to IS quality. Information and Software Technology, 39(12), 809-818.

Dick, B. (1997) Action learning and action research [On line]. Available at
http://www.scu.edu.au/schools/gcm/ar/arp/actlearn.html

Dobrin, D. N., (1989). What's technical about technical writing? Chapter 3 in Writing and technique. Urbana, IL: National Council of Teachers of English.

Earl, M.J., Skryme, D. Hybrid managers: what do we know about them? Journal of Information Systems, vol. 2, 169-187.

Eason, K., Harker S., & Olphert, W. (1997). Working with Users to Generate Organisational Requirements: The ORDIT Methodology. ICL Systems Journal, 11(2).

Edstrom, A. (1977). User influence and the success of IS projects: a contingency approach. Human Relations, 30(7), 589-607.

Eierman, M. A., Niederman, F., & Adams, C. (1995). DSS Theory: A model of constructs and relationships. Decision Support Systems 14(1), 1-26.

Eriksson, I., Törn, A. (1991). A model for IS quality. Software Engineering Journal, August 1991, 152-158.

Eriksson, I., Törn, A. (1997) Introduction. Information and Software Technology 39(12), 797-799.

Feeny, D.F., Earl, M.J., & Edwards, B. (1996). Organisational arrangements for IS: roles of users and specialists. In M. Earl (Ed.), Information Management: the organisational dimension. Oxford: Oxford University Press. (232-233)

Firesmith, D., (2003) The Business Case for Requirements Engineering, The 11th IEEE International Requirements Engineering Conference, 12 September, Monterey California.

Fisher, J. (1998a). Defining the role of a technical communicator in the development of information systems. IEEE Transactions on Professional Communication, 41(3).

Fisher, J. (1999b). Improving the usability of information systems: the role of the technical communicator. European Journal of Information Systems 8: pp 294-303.

Galbraith J.R. (1977). Designing complex organisations. Reading, Massachusetts: Addison-Wesley.

Gallivan, M.J., Keil, M., (2003). The User-to-Developer Communication Process: A Critical Case Study. Information Systems Journal 13, 37-68.

Galliers, R.D. (1994). Relevance and Rigor in Information Systems Research: Community. In Proceedings of the IFIP TC8 Open Conference on BPR Business Process Reengineering, " Information Systems Opportunities and Challenges". Holland: Elsevier.

Garvin, D. (1984, Fall). What does 'Product Quality' really mean? Sloan Management Review, 25-39.

Garvin, D. (1987, Nov-Dec). Competing on the eight dimensions of quality. Harvard Business Review, 101-109.

Gillies, A. (1992). Modelling software quality in the commercial environment, Software Quality Journal, 1, 175-191.

Gingras, L., & McLean, E.R. (1979). A study of users and designers of information systems (IS working paper 2-79). California: Graduate School of Management, UCLA.

Goguen, J. A. (1994). Requirements Engineering as the reconciliation of social and technical issues. Requirements Engineering. Academic Press. 165-197

Grindley, K. (1991). Managing IT at board level: The hidden agenda exposed. London, Pitman.

Grundy, S. (1982). Three modes of action research. In S. Kemmis & R. McTaggart (Eds.), The Action Research Reader. Geelong: Deakin University Press.

Hayes, F. (1998). IT and the Big Picture. Computerworld, Feb. 23, 8-11.

Herlea, D.E. (1996) Users Involvement in the Requirements Engineering process, Proceedings of KAW'96. Banff, Alberta, Canada.

Hirschheim, R., & Klein, H.K. (1989). Four Paradigms of Information Systems Development, Communications of the ACM, 32(10), 1199-1216.

Hirschheim, R., Klein, H.K., Lyytinen, K. (1995). Information systems development and data modelling: conceptual and philosophical foundations, Melbourne: Cambridge University Press.

Houp, K.W., Pearsall, T.E., Tebeaux, E. (2001). Reporting Technical Information (10th ed.), Oxford University Press, NY.

Hornik, S., Chen, H-G, Klein, G., Jiang, J., (2003). Communication Skills of IS Providers: An Expectation Gap Analysis From Three Stakeholder Perspectives. IEEE Transactions on Professional Communication, Vol 46, No. 1. 17-29.

Iivari, J. (1991). A paradigmatic analysis of contemporary schools of IS development, European Journal of Information Systems, 1(4), 249-272.

Järvinen, P. (1991, June). On Approaches in Information Systems Research, (University of Tampere Dept of Computer Science Series of Publications A, A-1991-3).

Järvinen, P. (1999). On Research Methods. Tampereen Yliopistopaino Oy, Jevenes-Print, Tampere.

Jick, T.D. (1979). Mixing qualitative and quantitative methods: Triangulation in action, Administrative Science Quarterly, 24, December. Cornell University.

Johnson, G., & Scholes, K. (1999). Exploring Corporate Strategy, 5th edition. London, Prentice Hall.

Keen P.G.W. (1991) Relevance and rigor in information systems research: improving quality, confidence, cohesion and impact. In H. E. Nissen, H.K. Klein, & R. Hirschheim (Eds.), Information Systems Research: Contemporary Approaches and Emergent Traditions. Amsterdam, North-Holland.

Kensing, F., Simonsen, J., & Bødker, K. (1996). MUST - a method for Participatory Design, (Datalogiske Skrifter,. No. 64). Roskilde Universitetscenter.

Kitchenham, B., & Pfleeger, S.L. (1996, Jan). Software Quality: The elusive target, IEEE Software, 12-21.

Koltzblatt, K and Beyer, H.R.(1995). Requirements Gathering: The Human Factor, Communications of ACM, Vol. 38 No. 5, p. 30-32

Lau, F., (1999). Towards a framework for action research in information systems studies. Information Technology & People 12 (2).

Lawrance, P., & Lorsch, J.W. (1967). Organisation and environment: managing differentiation and integration. Boston: Division of Research, Graduate School of Business Administration, Harvard University.

Lewis, I.M. (1985) Social Anthropology in Perspective. Cambridge: Cambridge University Press, 380.

Lin, A. & Conford, T. (2000). Framing Implementation Management. Proceedings of the International Conference on Information Systems, Sydney, Australia, 2000, 197-205.

Lindroos, K. (1997). Use Quality and the World Wide Web, Information and Software Technology 39, 827-836.

Lockett, M. (1989) The factors behind successful IT innovation. Oxford: Oxford Institute of Information Management and Templeton College. 6.

Lyytinen, K., & Hirschheim, R. (1987) Information system failures - a survey and classification of the empirical literature. Oxford Surveys in Information Technology, 4, 257-309.

Mann, J., (2002). IT Education's Failure to Deliver Successful Information Systems: Now is the Time to Address the IT-User Gap. Journal of Information Technology Education, Vol 1, No. 4, 255.

Martin, P.Y. & Turner, B.A. (1986). Grounded Theory and Organisational Research, The Journal of Applied Behavioural Science, 22(2), 141-157.

Martinsons, M. G. & Chong, P.K.C. (1999). The influence of human factors and specialist involvement on information systems success. Human Relations, 52, 123-152.

McCann, J.M. (1995). Why Category Management Fails: Look to the MIS/Marketing Gap, Brandweek, 36, 18.

McKeen, James D., Guimaraes, Tor. & Wetherbe; James C. (1994). The Relationship Between User Participation and User Satisfaction: An Investigation of Four Contingency Factors; MIS Quarterly 18(4), 427-451.

Melymuka, K. (1998). IT Managers Face Understanding Gap. Computerworld, 32, 54.

Miller, Carolyn R. (1989). What's practical about technical writing. In Technical writing: Theory and practice, ed. Bertie E. Fearing and W. Keats Sparrow. New York, NY: Modern Language Association, 14–24.

Mottl, J.N. (1999). Respect, Training Top IT Wish List. Internetweek, Feb 1, 22-24.

Morgan, G. (1986). Images of organisation. London: Sage Publications.

Mumford, E., Hirschheim, R., Fitzgerald, G., & Wood-Harper, T. (1984). Research Methods in Information Systems, Proceedings of the IFIP WG 8.2 Colloquium. Manchester: Manchester Business School, 1-3 September.

Mumford, K., & Henshall, D. (1991). Participative Approach to Computer system Design. London: Associated Business Press.

Myers, M. (1999) Qualitative Research in Information Systems, [online] ISWorld website, Available at http://www.auckland.ac.nz/msis/isworld/index.html, Accessed 10 November 1999.

New Group Will Bridge the Gap to Business. (1999). Computer Weekly, Oct. 7, 79-80.

Nurminen, M. I. (1997). Paradigms for sale: Information Systems in the process of radical change. Scandinavian Journal of Information Systems, 9(1), 25-42.

Orlikowski, W, & Baroudi, J (1991) Studying Information Technology in Organisations: Research Approaches and Assumptions. Information Systems Research, March, 1-28.

Ouellette, T. (1999). Living with the Pain, Computerworld, Apr. 19, 50-53.

Pender, L. (2000/2001). How to Communicate Value. CIO Magazine Online, published Dec. 15/Jan. 1. Retrieved from the World Wide Web, http://www.cio.com.

Rainer, R. Kelly Jr., & Carr, H.H. (1992) Are Information Centers Responsive to End User Needs? Information and Management, 22, 113-121.

Raghavan, S., Zelesnik, G. and Ford G. (1994): Lecture notes on Requirements Elicitation, SEI Curriculum Research Project, (Doc. No. CMU/SEI-95-EM-10) Carnegie-Mellon University, Pittsburg.

Rapoport, R.N. (1970). Three Dilemmas in Action Research, Human Relations, 23(4), 499-513.

Reich, Y., Konda, S. L., Levy, S. N., Monarch, I. A., & Subrahmanian, E. (1996). Varieties and Issues of Participation and Design, Design Studies, 17(2), 165-180.

Sackman, H. (1983). Problems and promise of Participative Information Systems design, Systems Design for, with, and by the Users. Amsterdam, North-Holland, IFIP, 339- 348.

Scalet, S.D. (2000/2001). The View from the Top. CIO Magazine Online, published Dec. 15/Jan. 1. Retrieved from the World Wide Web, http://www.cio.com.

Shackel, B. (1991). Usability - context, framework, definition, design and framework. In B. Shackel & S. Richardson (Eds.), Human factors for Informatics in Usability. Cambridge University Press, 21-38

Shah, H.U., Dingley, S. & Golder, P. (1994). Bridging the Culture Gap between Users and Developers. Journal of Systems Management, 45, 18-21.

Shore, B. (1998). Managing End-User Challenges. Information Systems Management, 15, 79-83.

Standish Group. (1995). Most Programming Projects Are Late. West Yarmouth, MA.

Slack, J. D., Miller, D.J. Doak, J. (1993). The technical communicator as author: Meaning, power, authority. Journal of business and technical communication 7, no. 1:12–36

Smircich, L., (1983). Concepts of Culture and Organisational Analysis, Administrative Science Quarterly, 28, 339-358.

Software Engineering Institute: 1, SEI Independent Research and Development Projects: Learning from Software Development and Acquisition Failures, Carnegie-Mellon University, Pittsburgh, CMU/SEI-2002-TR-023, 61-69.

Software Engineering Institute: 2, An International Collaboration to Develop a Standard on Software Process Assessment [online] Carnegie-Mellon University, Pittsburgh, Available http://www.sei.cmu.edu/iso-15504/ Accessed 5 July 2003.

Software Engineering Institute: 3, Capability Maturity Model® for Software (SW-CMM®) [online] Carnegie-Mellon University, Pittsburgh, Available http://www.sei.cmu.edu/cmmi/ http://www.sei.cmu.edu/cmm/, Accessed 5 July 2003.

Stiemerling, O., Kahler, H., and Wulf, V., (1997). How to Make Software Softer – Designing Tailorable Applications, in: Proceedings of DIS '97, G. v. d. Veer, A. Henderson, and S. Coles, Eds., Amsterdam, ACM Press, pp. 365-376.

The Standish Group. The CHAOS Report (1995). <http://www.pm2go.com/sample_research/chaos_1994_1.asp>

Swanson, E., B. (1997). Maintaining IS quality. Information and Software Technology 39, 845-850.

Taylor-Cummings, A., & Feeny, D.F., (1997). Managing IT as a strategic resource, London: McGraw Hill, 171-198.

Torkzadeh, G., & Doll, W.J. (1993). The place and value of documentation in end user computing, Information and Management, 24, 147-158.

Tuffley, D. (1999). Enhancing IS Quality through design-based documentation production. In E. Coakes, R. Lloyd-Jones, and D. Willis, (Eds.), The New Sociotech: Graffiti on the Long Wall. London, Springer-Verlag, 126-133

U.S. Bureau of Labor Statistics, (2003), Occupational Outlook Handbook 2002-2003, U.S. Department of Labor.

Vidgen, R., Wood-Harper, A.T., & Wood, R. (1993). A soft systems approach to Information Systems Quality, Scandinavian Journal of Information Systems 5, 97-112.

von Hellens, L.A. (1995, Sept). Quality management systems in Australian software houses: some problems of sustaining creativity in the software process. AJIS, 14 -24.

von Hellens, L.A. (1997). Information systems quality versus software quality: a discussion from a managerial, an organisational and an engineering viewpoint, Information and Software Technology 39, 801-808.

von Hellens, L.A. (2001) CIT 6116 Advanced Topics in Information Systems, Preliminary Research Design for the PhD Work: Enterprise Reference Architectures and Modelling Frameworks. Retrieved from the World Wide Web: http://www.cit.gu.edu.au/~noran/Docs/Prel_Res_Des.pdf

Walsham, G. (1993). Interpreting Information Systems in Organisations. Chichester: Wiley.

Wallace, B. (1998). Frustrated Networking Pros Say Efforts Not Appreciated. Computerworld, Mar. 2, 12-14.

Wang, C.B. (1994). Techno Vision, New York, McGraw-Hill.

Whiting, R. (1998). Dangerous Liaisons. Software Magazine, April, 20-26.

Williams, M.G., & Begg, V. (1993). Translation between software designers and users. Communication of the ACM, 36(4), 102-103.

Winograd, T.(Ed.) (1996). Bringing Design to Software, Stanford University and Interval Research Corporation, Reading MA, Addison-Wesley.

Wood, J., Silver, D., (1995). Joint Application Development, John Wiley and Sons, Inc., 2nd Edition,

Wood-Harper, T., Research Methods in Information Systems: Using Action Research, Procedings of the IFIP WG8.2 Colloquium, Manchester Business School, 1-3 September, 1984, 169-191.

Wood-Harper, T. (1991). Multiview: Action Research Learning in Context?, Action Research Seminar, Turku 8/3/91.

Zmud, R.W. & Cox, J.F. (1979). The implementation process: a change approach. MIS Quarterly, 3(2), 35-43.

# 9. Appendixes

The Appendixes include the following:

9.1 APPENDIX A: Statement Of User Requirements (Statement Of User Requirements)

9.2 APPENDIX B: Elements Of Joint Application Development

9.3 APPENDIX C: Technical Report On TASS

9.4 APPENDIX D: Questionnaire

9.5 APPENDIX E, Examples From Work/Research Diary

9.6 APPENDIX F, The Role of Software Project Documentation

9.7 APPENDIX G, The Nature and Scope of Requirements Engineering

9.8 APPENDIX H, What do we Mean by Software quality and IS quality?

9.9 APPENDIX I, Defining the role of the technical writer

APPENDIX J, Culture as two systems

APPENDIX K, Critical review of other research approaches (besides action research)

APPENDIX L, Comparison between EnergyCorp and one of its competitors

## *9.1. Appendix A: Statement Of User Requirements (SUR) Developed by ComTech and Technical Writer*

The appendix contrasts the two SURs developed by ComTech and the Technical Writer. ComTech had insisted for weeks that their SUR was complete and accurate, a suitable basis upon which to perform design work.

### 9.1.1. SUR Developed by ComTech

22. M&M Version 2 Requirements

Document Overview and Purpose

The purpose of this document is to define the requirements for the M&M Version 2 system.

Document Scope

This document covers requirements for the first phase of enhancements for M&M Version 2. It does not detail functional requirements for the overall M&M system (which are taken as being defined by the version 1 system) except where there is a particular need to emphasise retention of functionality.

Project Background

History

PCMS Metering and Modelling Data Management System (M&M DMS) was developed in response to the need to have a core validating storage of consumption data and other critical data (Pool, Customer History).

The system was developed from the initial work carried out in developing a MDA-MS system for the market. During this development, the MV90 Data loader and the metering data storage were used as a basis for M&M ver. 1. This was to meet the urgent demand for a robust data management system for PCMS (TASS and RTS) to deal with the meter data supply issues in order to cope with the immaturity of the market processes at that time.

Development of MDA-MS Ver 1.0 continued in order to meet the changing market design requirements. Research and architectural considerations (moving to stream centric major storage) resulted schema and validation changes, which created a divergence in the base design of the system from the original M&M ver 1.0 system and the components installed as part of TASS.

The released MDA-MS front-end components (MV90 Loader and Storage schema) were used to create the RTS02 Ver 2.0 Loader (In Unify).

Driven by market requirements and based on the experience of the retail data loaders and in preparation for the final development and release of an upgraded system, the MDF data loader was developed to incorporate a number of important productivity and management capabilities.

The development and release priorities of sub-modules was and is driven by the tactical needs of our customers. However the conception and evolution of M&M has been engineered around an architectural vision which will scale to meet the increasing needs of the marketplace.

All these functions are brought together in the proposed M&M MKII system.

Project Scope

1.) The functional changes to M&M are focussed on improvements in scalability, operational effectiveness and automation of data load. The new and reworked modules will be where this is the case.

2.) The project will be split into 2 phases. The first of these (and the scope of this document) will deal with the data-loading segment of M&M. The second phase deals with the packaging sub-system.

3.) The project will re-use modules and designs from ComTech's more recent meter loading systems and from the existing M&M Version 1 system wherever possible.

User Requirements

- Legend

The requirements are scaled on the following legend:

M – mandatory

O – optional

A – attribute

- Operational Effectiveness

1. Minimise manual interventions.

1.1. Mappings requirements reduced. (M)

1.1.1. Supply-point configurations entered only once and used throughout the system.

1.1.2. Meter-level configurations entered once and used throughout the system.

1.2. Improve handling of unrecognised data. (M)

1.2.1. Unrecognised data retained for future recovery.

1.2.2. Unrecognised data loaded as soon as supply-point and other details are correctly configured.

1.2.3. Unrecognised data deleted if selected for deletion (manual or aging process).

2. Decrease storage requirements. (O)

2.1. Primary metering data table design modified.

2.2. Automatic deletion of data from raw data tables following successful load.

3. Improve data reporting. (M)

3.1. Report the mapping status of all incoming data.

3.2. Report the data quality.

3.3. Report gaps in daily data feeds.

3.4. Automate error reporting for missing mapping and incorrect data.

3.4.1. Use of e-mail to alert operator of missing configurations.

3.4.2. Automatic e-mail re missing data and data quality problems to interested parties.

4. Improve throughput performance. (A)

4.1. Loading of data without human interaction.

4.1.1. Supply-point level data passed through without additional manual mapping or other intervention for correctly configured supply-points.

4.2. Move data load and aggregation processing to database server.

· Functionality

5. Basic functionality of current M&M system retained. (M)

5.1. Packaging system maintained in current form.

5.1.1. Current package formats maintained.

5.1.1.1. CSV

5.1.1.2. DM3

5.1.1.3. DirectLoad

5.1.2. DM3 Writer will support all markets

5.2. Data Feeds maintained to all data stores as defined in Appendix 1.

6. Provide SERC with the ability to load data from different market sources. (M)

6.1. Ability to load 'Market Data File' (MDF) format files.

6.2. Ability to process data from different types of MV90.

6.2.1. Standard MV90 file.

6.2.2. TOHT system MV90 file.

7. ELSIS Integration. (M)

7.1. The current ELSIS meter-level data feed will be retained.

8. Position SERC to take advantage of future ComTech developments of its data management products. (O)

8.1. Table designs

8.2. Use of standard ComTech modules.

9. Minimise development effort. (M)

9.1. Re-use existing ComTech modules where possible.

9.2. Use existing ComTech MDF Loader code.

9.3. Retain modules from existing M&M where no requirement for future change.

Improve integration with TASS. (M)

9.4. Shared configuration for supply-points.

Automated load of TASS aggregated supply-point data.

| Requirements | | **Billing** | Settle-ments | Forecast-ing | Wholesale Pricing |
|---|---|---|---|---|---|
| UOM | 1 | Yes | Yes | Yes | Yes |
| | 3 | Yes | Yes | Yes | Yes |
| | Other... | No | No | No | No |

| Substituted | | No | Yes | Yes | Yes |
|---|---|---|---|---|---|
| Incomplete | | No | Yes | Yes | Yes |
| Aggregation Level | | Supply Point | Supply Point | Supply Point | Supply Point |
| Date Range | | Contract Start to Finish | Contract Start to Finish | As much as Possible | As much as Possible |
| Losses Applied | | No | No | No | No |
| Contestables | Won | Yes | Yes | Yes | Yes |
| | Lost | No | Yes | Yes | Yes |
| Internal | Won | Yes | Yes | Yes | Yes |
| | Lost | No | Yes | Yes | Yes |
| Pre-contestable | | No | No | Yes | Yes |
| Boundary | | No | Yes | Yes | No |
| Embedded Generators | | No | Yes | Yes | No |
| Output | | TASS-ELSIS interface tables. | TASS_TSPREADING | DM3 File | DM3 File |
| Frequency | | Every Day/On Demand | Every Day/On Demand | On Demand | On Demand |
| Quantity | | 1 Day | 1 Day | Entire History | Entire History |

### 9.1.2. SUR Developed by Technical Writer based on IEEE

Statement of M&M V2.0 User Requirements

Purpose & scope of document

To define a statement of user requirements and acceptance criteria for the M&M V2.0 system.

M&M V2.0 project background

Circumstances surrounding project

On the 1st July 1999, Tranche 3 energy consumers shift from being franchise customers to being contestable customers, meaning they will be free to purchase their energy from the lowest retail bidder.

Until July, EnergyCorp's total number of customers will be around 500. It is estimated that on 1 July 1999, the numbers will increase to around 900, and on 1 October EnergyCorp expects to have around 2000 customers.

The Metering and Modelling Data Management System (M&M DMS) system was developed to address the need for a core validating storage of consumption and demand data and other critical data (Customer History) for Tranche 1 and 2 customers,

M&M DMS) built upon initial work to develop a MDA-MS system. The MV90 loader and the metering data storage of the MDA-MS system formed the basis for M&M V1.0, which was developed in response to the need for a robust data management system for TASS (Trading And Settlements System). This was to deal with the meter data supply issues.

Development of MDA-MS Ver 1.0 continued in order to meet the changing market design requirements. Architectural considerations (stream centric major storage) resulted in schema and validation changes, which created a divergence in the base design of the system from the original M&M ver 1.0 system and the components installed as part of TASS.

Why M&M V2.0 project was requested

The released MDA-MS front-end components (MV90 Loader and Storage schema) creates the RTS02 Ver 2.0 Loader (In Unify). The MDF data loader was developed to incorporate a number of important productivity and management capabilities.

The conception and evolution of M&M has been engineered around an architectural vision which will scale to meet the increasing needs of the marketplace. All of these functions are combined in the proposed M&M V2.0 system.

M&M V2.0 system & business scope

What is covered in M&M V2.0

M&M V2.0 will include functional changes to improve:

- scalability
- operational effectiveness
- automation of data load

The project will be split into 2 phases.

- the data-loading sub-system of M&M
- the packaging sub-system

The project will re-use modules and designs from ComTech's more recent meter loading systems and from the existing M&M Version 1 system wherever possible.

What is not covered in M&M V2.0

- What business advantage is likely to be derived

M&M V2.0 will enable:

- Improved system performance
- Lower operating costs by automating some currently manual processes
- Improved business flexibility by enabling the loading of both meter data file formats
- A standard platform on which to deliver enhancements to the co-operating processes of accumulations and forecasting, TASS and ELSIS.
- Daily meter data processing will be on the basis of 'operator intervention on exception' only
- M&M V2.0 system overview

M&M V2.0 is a critical link in the flow of meter data. It replaces V1.0 in relation to the following pre-existing systems:

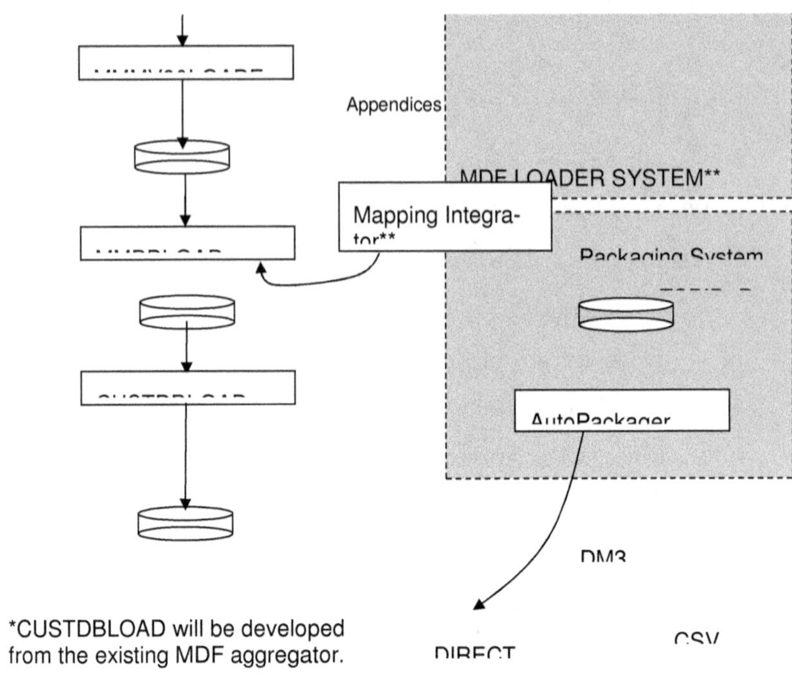
Appendices
Mapping Integra-
*CUSTDBLOAD will be developed from the existing MDF aggregator.

**The MMDBLOAD ice to EnergyCorp's business

M&M V2.0 is very important to EnergyCorp's business in that it is a key enabler of EnergyCorp's ability to forecast (daily) undertake weekly settlement with market operators and bill its customers accurately and on-time given V1.0 inability to process the expected rise in customer numbers.

M&M V2.0 will decrease the number of manual interventions in the system, hence, improving data loading efficiency.

M&M V2.0 system constraints

- Mappings are still required for standard MV90 feeds where no mapping currently exists between the MV90 recorder id and the NMI. This feed could be requested through a MDA or the MAS system.
- No user-specific security is imposed on the M&M system apart from physical access.
- TOHT and MV90 only to handle UOM codes of 1 and 3.
- TOHT data assumed already aggregated to supply point-level.
- Quality flags for the entire day and not for a particular period.
- 15 minute data
- Significant risks of M&M V2.0

Overview. The principal risk associated with M&M V2.0 is that it will not be finished in time to relieve the version 1.0 system from being overwhelmed by the processing load, resulting in a period in which EnergyCorp's ability to issue bills will be curtailed, leading to a loss of customer confidence and a cash flow problems.

Specific risks include:

· Time available for implementation. Implementation and release is required for the beginning of tranche 3 (1 July).

· Conversion of the pre-existing data. The TMETERINGDATA table has over a million rows. This presents problems for processing the SQL query that converts the table.

· EnergyCorp's business processes for managing and configuring supply points are not fully defined.

· No service-level agreement with the MDA.

Other risks include:

· Key staff leave or are absent through illness

· Risk of having insufficient resources to train staff

The'window' of opportunity

The window of opportunity is the period leading up to 1 July 1999.

· M&M V2.0 security considerations

There are no special security considerations beyond those which apply to other TASS processes.

· M&M V2.0 data protection

Safeguards are needed to ensure the integrity of the data.

· M&M V2.0 system accessibility factors

User access is required on the same basis as version 1.0 users.

· M&M V2.0 operator constraints

· M&M V2.0 operators will be working under extreme pressure during the period EOM-2 to EOM+5 to process the meter data into a form suitable for billing and settlements.

· Needs someone implicitly familiar with metering data and TASS operational processes.

· M&M V2.0 Interfaces

- Human interface(s)

Additional mapping components are required for standard MV90 data. There will need to be screens created or edited to handle the mapping of a meter to a supply point.

The data re-run function also requires a screen.

- Hardware interface(s)

None

- Software interface(s)

- Packaging Routines

M&M V2.0 system will feed the packaging routines. Supply point level data is placed in a row per day structure in the TSPIDREADINGS table. The Forecasting division uses the data, hence, it can be for all contestable and franchise customers, as well as boundary meters.

The data that is provided to the TSPIDREADINGS table must have UOM codes of 1 and 3.

Also, the M&M system has a number of routines to create a DM3 file and thus interface with the Katestone forecasting package.

These routines can be called as a package. They do not use the metering data loaded by the front-end of the M&M system. However, they do use the market data loaded by other TASS data scripts.

- Elsis

M&M interfaces with the ELSIS system. This interface is a group of UNIX scripts which loads the relevant M&M data into interface tables. This existing process will be maintained.

If the ELSIS interface is included as part of the M&M Version 2 project the:

- the interface will be changed to cater for supply point level data

- the interface will provide data for only customers found in the M&M mapping tables and not the TASS meter setup tables.

- using the STATUS column, the TASS_TSUPPLYPOINT will further reduce the number of supply points that are loaded.

- Communications interface(s)

None.

- M&M V2.0 outputs

- Business events
- Reports

Reporting is required on the mapping status of all incoming data, data quality, gaps in the daily data feed, error notification.

- Data for export to other system(s)
- Data Requirements for Billing & Settlements

| Requirements | | **Billing** | | Settlements |
|---|---|---|---|---|
| UOM | | 1 | Yes | Yes |
| | | 3 | Yes | Yes |
| | | Other … | No | No |
| Substituted | | No | | Yes |
| Incomplete | | No | | Yes |
| Aggregation Level | | Supply Point | | Supply Point |
| Date Range | | Contract Start to Finish | | Contract Start to Finish |
| Losses Applied | | No | | No |
| Contestables | Won | Yes | | Yes |
| | Lost | No | | Yes |
| Internal | Won | Yes | | Yes |
| | Lost | No | | Yes |
| Pre-contestable | | No | | No |
| Boundary | | No | | Yes |
| Embedded Generators | | No | | Yes |
| Output | | TASS-ELSIS interface tables. | | TASS_TSPREADING |
| Frequency | | Every Day/On Demand | | Every Day/On Demand |
| Quantity | | 1 Day | | 1 Day |

Data Requirements for Forecasting & Wholesale Pricing

| Requirements | | Forecasting | | Wholesale Pricing |
|---|---|---|---|---|
| UOM | | Yes | Yes | Yes |
| | | Yes | Yes | Yes |
| | | No | No | No |
| Substituted | | Yes | | Yes |
| Incomplete | | Yes | | Yes |
| Aggregation Level | | Supply Point | | Supply Point |
| Date Range | | As much as Possible | | As much as Possible |
| Losses Applied | | No | | No |
| Contestables | Yes | Yes | | Yes |
| | Yes | Yes | | Yes |
| Internal | Yes | Yes | | Yes |
| | Yes | Yes | | Yes |
| Pre-contestable | | Yes | | Yes |
| Boundary | | Yes | | No |
| Embedded Generators | | Yes | | No |
| Output | | DM3 File | | DM3 File |
| Frequency | | On Demand | | On Demand |
| Quantity | | Entire History | | Entire History |

- M&M V2.0 inputs
- Business events

MV1 meter data received daily by 0800 on Day 1.

MV2 meter data received daily by 1300 (Day 4 data).

MV3 meter data received monthly by 1500 on EOM-2 (end of month minus 2 days).

MV4 meter data to be delivered to EnergyCorp (Q drive) no more than 2 days after the final NEMMCO settlements run (week 3 data).

- Input screens

All screen formats will conform to the system specification.

Two screens are required:

- Supply point and meter data configuration screens
- Re-run screens
- Data imported from other system(s)

| Data Format | Current Volume (supply points) | Expected Volume at 1 Jan 2000 (supply points) | Time Margin (complete cycle) |
|---|---|---|---|
| MDF | 30 | ? | 6am – 7am |
| TOHT MV90 | 420 | 2800 (?) | |
| Standard MV90 | 700 | 1000 (?) | |
| Total | 1150 | 3800 | |

- M&M V2.0 Processing

From a business point of view, describe the following.

- Special processing to be applied

The system needs to be able to:

- Handle 15 minute data streams (data fed into the system as a 'stream')
- Convert MV90 data into TOHT system data.
- Perform supply point maintenance.
- Load meter data file formats other than the currently required formats.
- Resolve SPID mappings.
- Parse the meter data.

- Validate the meter data.
- Store the meter data.
- Data for supply points over a noncontiguous date range must not result in zeroes being stored for the in-between dates. Currently if an mv90 file contains data for a supply point over a noncontiguous date range (eg. 29/5/99, and 31/5/99) M&M processes for the overall date range, resulting in zeros being stored for the in between dates (ie 30/5/99).
- Formulae
- Calculations
- Any applicable standards

M&M V2.0 must conform to existing TASS interface and processing standards.

- Performance issues

M&M V2.0 must offer substantial performance improvements over V1.0.

- M&M V2.0 data storage
- Name and description
- Data storage will be on the M&M Server.
- The M&M V2.0 application code will be on hardware managed and deployed by IT&T.
- The M&M V2.0 application code should run in a Unix environment.
- Name of database?
- Physical location

The M&M server is located in the secured area occupied by the Energy-Corp's Energy Trading Department.

- Storage capability
- Current requirement
- Predictions for future requirements

?

21. M&M V2.0 Acceptance criteria

FR = Functional Requirement

Can we think of any other criteria relating to either Appearance, Functionality, Capacity and Performance??

| Ref | Brief Description | Status |
|---|---|---|
| FR-1.1.1 | Supply point configuration entered once only | Will be included in V2.0 |
| FR-1.1.2 | Stream level configurations entered once only. | Will be included in V2.0 |
| FR-1.2.1 | Unrecognised data retained for future recovery | Will be included in V2.0 |
| FR-1.2.2 | Unrecognised data loaded when supply point & other details data are correctly configured | Will be included in V2.0 |
| FR-1.2.3 | Unrecognised data deleted if selected for deletion (manual or aging process). | Will be included in V2.0 |
| FR-3.1 | Report on mapping status of incoming data stream | Will be included in V2.0 |
| FR-3.2 | Report on data quality | Will be included in V2.0 |
| FR-3.3. | Report on gaps in daily data feed | Will be included in V2.0 |
| FR-3.4 | Automate error reporting using email | Will be included in V2.0 |
| FR-5.1.1 | Current package formats retained (CSV, DM3, DirectLoad) | Will be included in V2.0 |
| FR-5.1.2 | Dm3 Writer to support all markets | Will be included in V2.0 |
| FR-5.2 | Datafeeds maintained to all data stores | Will be included in V2.0 |
| FR-6.1 | Ability to load 'Market Data File' format. | Will be included in V2.0 |
| FR-6.2 | Ability to load standard and TOHT system MV90 file formats. | Will be included in V2.0 |
| FR-7.1 | ELSIS meter-level data feed retained. | Will be included in V2.0 |
| FR-10.1 | Improve integration with TASS by sharing supply point configurations. | Will be included in V2.0 |
| FR-10.2 | Automate load of TASS aggregated supply-point data | Will be included in V2.0 |

| | | |
|---|---|---|
| FR-11.1 | Non-contiguous data stream storage. Data for supply points over a noncontiguous date range must not result in zeroes being stored for the in-between dates. | Possible to include in V2.0, however further investigation and discussion is needed to establish whether the benefits of inclusion in V2.0 justify the cost of the redevelopment work.<br><br>May be more appropriate to include in V2.X. |
| FR-12 | Able to handle 15 minute data handling through to RTS | Will be included in V2.0 |
| FR-13 | M&M V2.0 application code should run in a Unix environment. | Two modules (MV90 & TOHT Loaders) would need to be redeveloped in C for the M&M V2.0 application code to run entirely in a Unix environment.<br><br>Further investigation and discussion is needed to establish whether the cost and time required to redevelop the two VBA modules in C is justified for V2.0.<br><br>May be more appropriate to include in V2.X. |
| FR-14 | System must be able to process meter data for 5000 daily customers in ≤ 1 hour | Will be included in V2.0. Ways of testing the achievement of this requirement is yet to be determined. |
| FR-15 | History records to be updated only if daily data is different. | Possible to include in V2.0, but further investigation and discussion is needed to establish whether the cost and time required to redevelop the two VBA modules in C is justified for V2.0.<br><br>May be more appropriate to include in V2.X. |
| FR-16 | Revisions / Data Versioning Summary Report. An exception report on data revisions/changes. It should summarise information on new versions of data subsequent to the initial version received/loaded.<br><br>This report would identify/confirm edits/changed supplied by Banyo and also a summary audit trail. | |

| | | |
|---|---|---|
| FR-17 | For mv90 data files, the normal data stream should be of either E-type or P-type data. If the normal stream changes from E-type to P-type M&M must produce an exception report of this occurrence. The data type is included in the channel header for the data stream | To include in V2.X. |

## *9.2. Appendix B: Elements Of Joint Application Development*

The following describes the elements of JAD that were used in this research project. It is acknowledged that the elements used represent a small portion of the overall JAD approach.

Overview of JAD

JAD is a structured approach consisting of five phases:

Phase 1: JAD Project Definition

Phase 2: Research

Phase 3: Preparation

Phase 4: The Session

Phase 5: The Final Documents

The goal of the overall process is to build a final document that captures project requirements that is accepted by all users and the client organisation. The resulting document can be very large, so for practical reasons, the only phase to contribute elements to this research project is phase 4, the session.

Phase 4: The Session

The opening session of the workshop will start with the agenda prepared in the second phase to overview each session. JAD sessions usually contain the following activities (Wood and Silver, 1995):

Discuss Assumptions

Define Data Requirement

Design Business Processes

Design Screens

Design Reports

Resolve Open Issues

In the context of this research project, the formal sessions (or meetings, as they were called) were repeated on a weekly basis for a period of a month. Not all activities were performed in every meeting. Subsets of the defined activities were performed as appropriate to the group and available time.

Facilitation Techniques

The following are the facilitation techniques derived from JAD that the technical writer applied during meetings with the user and the developer. They were adapted from the widely publicised and available sources on Joint Application Development approach (JAD):

1. **Keep to the point**. Remain focussed on the matter at hand. Be clear and concise.

2. **Active Listening**. Listen actively to the other person, asking questions to clarify, then interpret, dissect, and integrate it with the whole picture. Be able to recognise diversions from the real issue(s), and change the subject back to the real issue(s). Be able to recognise when consensus has been reached, to restate the consensus and capture it. Active listening also includes using one's eyes to interpret the body language of participants.

3. **Treat ideas impartially**. Recognise the person's ideas as ideas in their own right, and not interpret the idea based on who is presenting them.

4. **Retain control**. Remain in control of the meeting but do so discretely, not overtly. Control in this context means staying on track, while allowing participants to explore ideas and options, and recognises that the more the participant s are allowed to do this, the more the final product will meet their needs.

5. **Be aware of the organisational context**. Recognise and make the connection between the matter at hand and the organisation context in which they are discussed. Also to decisions already made, to previous discussions or to future discussions.

6. **Business, not Systems**. Remain focussed on solving business, not technical problems.

## *9.3. Appendix C: Technical Report On TASS*

The following report was prepared by the technical writer in February 2000 as part of EnergyCorp's preparation for contract review with Com-Tech. **It was not related to either the research project or the M&M upgrade project, but is nonetheless highly relevant in that it surveyed every user of every module of TASS** seeking their response to the same usability questionnaire that Donald and Francis completed in relation to the M&M Upgrade project.

Its purpose was to benchmark the actual state of TASS against what was agreed would be delivered by then under the terms of the contract.

The following list summarises the usability rating results for the six TASS modules.

Note: the usability questionnaire involved the user assigning a numerical value from a five point scale, with Very Easy/Well at 1, through to Very Difficult/Badly at 5. A higher cumulative score indicates poor usability.

- Forecasting: 6/15
- Whole Sale Portfolio Management: 0/15 (no result)
- Energy Trading: 0/15 (no result)
- Wholesale Pricing: 0/15
- Meter Data: 10/15
- Wholesale Hedge Contract Settlements: 6.25/15

| Forecasting: | S | | Usability |
|---|---|---|---|
| 1. Forecast customer load profile | C | Not at all | 6 / 15 |
| 2. Identify customer segment | S | Not at all | Min 3 = very |
| 3. Develop customer calendar | C | Not at all | easy, Max 15 = very |
| 4. Develop customer segment load profiles | C | Not at all | hard |
| 5. Select standard forecast customer load profile | C | Not at all | |
| 6. Develop forecast customer load profile from the customer info and segment | C | Not at all | |

| | | |
|---|---|---|
| 7. Forecast aggregate customer load | S | Not at all |
| 8. Short term load forecasting | S | Largely |
| 9. Medium term load forecasting | S | Partially |
| 10. Total system load forecasting | S | Largely |
| 11. Short term total system load forecasting | S | Partially |
| 12. Medium total system load forecasting | S | Partially |
| 13. Long term total system load forecasting | S | Partially |
| 14. Medium term pool price forecasting | S | Largely |
| 15. Historical market analysis | S | Not at all |
| 16. Collect and store market management company published information | S | Not at all |
| 17. Analysis of market information | S | Not at all |

| | | | |
|---|---|---|---|
| Whole sale portfolio management | S | | **0/15** Indeterminate |
| Measurement and monitoring of exposure | S | Largely | |
| Optimization of wholesale portfolio | C | ? | |
| Short term cost minimization (0-24hr) | S | ? | |
| Short term cost optimization (1-7 days) | S | ? | |
| Medium term cost optimization | S | ? | |
| Evaluate external wholesale contract offers | S | ? | |
| Develop wholesale contract bids | S | ? | |
| Perform trading | S | ? | |
| Trading decision | S | ? | |
| Management approval | S | ? | |

| | | | |
|---|---|---|---|
| Maintain status of bid/offer | S | ? | |
| Telephone, fax, email, mail | S | ? | |
| Screen trade through third party market | C | ? | |
| Interface with market management company | C | ? | |
| Short term forward market | C | ? | |
| Hedge contract administration | S | ? | |
| Develop cost matrix for each market class | C | Not at all | |
| Allocate wholesale costs | S | ? | |
| Monitor position | S | ? | |
| Develop matrix | C | ? | |

| | | | |
|---|---|---|---|
| Energy Trading | C | | |
| IPP contract bidding Estimate pool revenues<br>- Develop bid strategy<br>- Evaluate bid strategy<br>- Submit bids to market management company | C | Not at all | 15/15<br>Min 3 = very easy, Max 15 = very hard |
| Demand side bidding<br>- Develop bid strategy<br>- Evaluate bid strategy<br>- Submit bids to market management company | C | Not at all | |
| IPP contract administration | C | Largely | |
| IPP operational management | C | Not at all | |

| | | | |
|---|---|---|---|
| Wholesale pricing | C | | |
| Develop and manage market class load profiles | S | Not at all | **0 / 15**<br>Indeterminate |
| Calculate wholesale energy costs | C | Largely | |

| Calculate network and market costs | C | Largely |
|---|---|---|
| Assign risk margin | C | Not at all |
| Develop standard pricing product | C | Not at all |
| Pricing and retail portfolio management | S | Not at all |
| Develop customer energy price | S | Not at all |
| Apply standard price product | S | Not at all |
| Customize price profile | S | Not at all |
| Assign customer credit risk premium | C | Not at all |
| Add retail margin | S | Not at all |
| Assign site network charges | S | Not at all |
| Assign VPX/NEM charges | S | Not at all |
| Create price book | S | Not at all |
| Add prices of products and services | S | Not at all |
| Assemble and dispatch quote | S | Not at all |
| Quoting to contract | S | Not at all |
| Contract initiation | S | Not at all |
| Administer retail contracts | S | Not at all |
| Monitor performance of retail portfolio | C | Not at all |
| Optimize retail contract portfolio | C | Not at all |

| Meter data | S | | 9 / 15 |
|---|---|---|---|
| Metering data | C | Largely | Min 3 = very |
| Market data | S | Largely | easy, Max 15 = very hard |
| | | | |
| | | | |
| | | | |

| | | | |
|---|---|---|---|
| Settlements | S | | |
| Wholesale hedge contract settlements (buying and selling) | S | Largely | 6.25 / 15<br>Min 3 = very easy, Max 15 = very hard |
| Customer settlements (selling) | S | Not used | |
| Power purchase agreement settlements | C | Not at all | |
| Pool settlements | C | Partially | |
| Network and metering service settlements | S | Partially | |
| EnergyCorp network settlement statements for network usage. | S | Partially | |

## *9.4. Appendix D: Questionnaire*

The EnergyCorp users (Donald and Francis) were asked to complete the following questionnaire, once for M&M V1.0, and once for V2.0. This was done after they had been using V2.0 to perform live work (not testing) for a period of two weeks (ie two weeks after V2.0 went live).

A numerical value is assigned by applying a five point scale, with Very Easy/Well at 1, through to Very Difficult/Badly at 5.

| Question | Very Easy | Easy | Neu-tral | Diffi-cult | Very Diffi-cult |
|---|---|---|---|---|---|
| Ease-of-use: how easy was the module to use? | | | | | |
| Ease-of-learning: how easy to learn was the module? | | | | | |
| | Very Well | Well | Neu-tral | Badly | Very Badly |
| How well the module meets your needs: does it do what you need it to do? | | | | | |
| Comments: | | | | | |

# 9.5. Appendix E: Examples From Work/Research Diary

This appendix is a transcription of significant research journal entries. It is indicative of the kind of notes that were made. The journal entries are somewhat illegible due to the researcher's individual hand-writing.

All italicised text is quoted from research journal.

### 9.5.1. Tuesday 23 March 1999

In both formal and informal meetings with TASS users, they are clearly unhappy with the performance of TASS and that of ComTech.

Users say the software is very likely, that changes are made with no notification, the documentation and training is mostly nonexistent.

There is quite some cool evening in the. They are seen as incompetent and greedy, but there is no alternative so they are somewhat resigned to the relationship.

### 9.5.2. Wednesday 24 March 1999

EnergyCorp consider they are being ripped off by ComTech. Despite promises to do the a custom design solution, after 18 months they have a defect ridden generic solution that shows every likelihood of being a solution to sell to EnergCorp's competitors.

James sees me as a stick the to belt them, to give them a richly deserved belting. I am uncomfortable in this toecutter role.

Have yet to speak to ComTech, this is developing into a highly charged situation. We could see some real fireworks because there is so much barely repressed anger towards ComTech. Will need careful handling

### 9.5.3. Tuesday 30 March 1999

Phew! Talk about tension:

went in with gameplan as discussed last week

emphasised the need for EnergyCorp to have more control of the development process in light of the past failure. Tranche three makes it imperative.

I am perceived as the enemy

Arthur and William gave assurances of cooperation but George's face said no way

said they had a well-developed functional quality management system that would handle every thing

there is going to be in a battle to get ComTech to accept the statement of user requirements, but I feel we have made a start

### 9.5.4. Wednesday 31March 1999

James has said he is somewhat pleased with progress

ComTech given the statement of user requirements template from yesterday's meeting we are waiting to hear from them

had a visit from William, they seem to be trying to figure out how much of a threat I might be to them

I have adopted a pleasant yet assertive approach in which I reiterate what we want, gently reminding that we are paying them

### 9.5.5. Monday 5 April 1999

ComTech meet with George

he insisted on them using the statement of user requirements template

meeting ended civilly

Brian has told James to forget the statement of user requirements template. Apparently George got Arthur to do a job on them. This is looking bad for my project

James has said to me the old story 'it would be nice to have, but in the real world was not practical as it would cost too much and take too long'

going to have to think hard about what I do next. Not ready to give up. James appears spineless.

### 9.5.6. Thursday 8 April 1999

Spoke to George today, he seemed to be gloating over his victory. The buggers really aren't are doing the right thing.

I feel quite angry towards them. They connive to avoid doing the right thing. They are ripping EnergyCorp off.

To me that George maintains a veneer of civility Larry can barely conceal his contempt.

James seems to lack conviction to see it through. He hired me and now he went back me up. I feel like I've been hung out to dry.

### 9.5.7. Friday 9 April 1999

Went and sat in Anzac Square to contemplate my situation and how to save it.

It is very peaceful there, there's a certain energy that may be comes from its solemn ceremonial function

A simple solution presents itself: basically, Basically if ComTech already have all of the requirements like they say they do, then to do my statement of user requirements template should not take long. It will assure us that they have all, but if they don't have all, and we strongly believe that they don't, then now is the time to find out, not later when it is more difficult. It will have to be done some time and now the best time.

Will think of this over during the weekend run it by Ange

### 9.5.8. Thursday 23 September 1999

Talked to Donald: 'yeah it probably did'. He was in no doubt that my template had been beneficial. Big improvement over version 1 (of M&M)

Talked to Francis: 'Yes, I'd say so'. He was also sure that will stop expressed great dislike towards ComTech even maybe not healthy. A usability boost, seems relieved.

### 9.5.9. Friday 24 September 1999

James responded to the research question that it ' undoubtedly improved the outcome' by making ComTech listened to what we wanted

Enforced formal documenting of requirements and feedback

basis in law, binding contract

negotiable

a process of negotiation, no fixed outcome

expert consultancy transforming into process consultancy

usability, yes obviously follows

### 9.5.10. Tuesday 28 September 1999

Talked to George:

ComTech's role was to facilitate communication between internal elements of EnergyCorp

silo mentality

silo mentality inhibited in getting complete user requirements, amongst other things

their relationship with EnergyCorp had degenerated, making it hard

he specifically commented on how their expert status had to be adapted to facilitate, as a necessity, they didn't like it, ate to their margin

EnergyCorp is a ' house divided"

asked about integrative processes, agreed was worthwhile but client doesn't usually want to pay for it

Talked to Larry:

wouldn't say much. Get the impression he really dislike to me for having forced him to do stuff, and made him look bad.

Saw no value in SUR.

about the six additional requirements, conceded it was okay as long as ' someone else did it'.

## *9.6. Appendix F: The Role of Software Project Documentation*

This section is included as background discussion relating to the role of documentation in software development projects. The SUR template that was used in this project is an example of documentation in software development projects. It is not directly related to the research project.

Software project documentation can be categorised as being either system or user documentation. The requirements specification document that is a product of the research event is an example of system documentation (see Appendix A) . The Institute of Electrical and Electronic Engineers (IEEE) Computer Society also recognise Project Plans, Quality Plans, Design Documents, Test Plans and others that fall into the system documentation category. It is that documentation that is used by the developer during the project in support of the project objectives. A technical writer in the context of this project is defined as a person experienced at effectively producing any of the above mentioned documentation. Further clarification of this definition is necessary because the widely accepted definition of a technical writer is someone who put scientific and technical information into easily understandable language (U.S. Dept of Labour, 2003). In the context of this research project, the technical writer is someone skilled at producing the kinds of project documentation recognised by the IEEE, listed above. This clarification is specifically made in the next section dealing with defining what a technical writer is in relation to this project.

### 9.6.1. The place of software project documentation in ISD methodologies

In their paradigmatic analysis of ISD methodologies, Hirschheim, Klein and Lyytinen (1995, p99-139) examined the strengths and weaknesses of four IS development methodologies. It is interesting to note that despite document production underpinning every IS development approach, there is little explicit mention made about how it serves the ISD methodologies.

In relation to the structured approach, Hirschheim et al (1995) observe that early implementations of this approach had severely deficient documentation practices, leading to quite considerable problems. This approach lacked a standard format for researching and documenting system requirements, thus making it impossible to create adequate requirements specifications. In the absence of a standard format and commonly agreed interpretation of the terminology used, the same specification would be interpreted differently by different audiences (users, developers, and programmers). Obtaining meaningful user input was difficult due to the large amount of unstructured documentation. Furthermore, the specifications document became immediately out-of-date because it is very difficult to find all of the places in the documentation where a change in the specification needed to be indicated. Later implementations of this approach have made great progress in developing well-defined formats of systems analysis and specifications.

One way to overcome the problem of deficient documentation practices when developing user requirements is discussed by Hirschheim et al (1995) in the prototyping approach. This was to develop a complete and fully formalised specification by using an executable specification language. The specification document can then be compiled to make a prototype. The user can evaluate the specification by examining the compiled result. Recognising the problems of developing an adequate document-based specification, this approach develops a complete and fully formalised specification which traditional prototyping tried to avoid and which the structured approaches find difficult to achieve.

One of the weaknesses of the professional work practices approach to IS development, according to Hirschheim et al (1995), is a lack of clear communication. Documentation which is supposed to systematically record the activities of project teams is then likely to be deficient.

In considering Hirschheim et al's (1995) findings, it is apparent that while little explicit reference is made to documentation practices, it might be inferred that since each of the four IS development methodologies places some reliance on producing documentation to support the development process, that documentation can be considered a quite significant part of the overall ISD process.

Iivari (1991) concludes in his paradigmatic analysis of contemporary schools of IS development that all of the schools analysed share similar assumptions; an important one of which is that information/data are 'descriptive facts' (p267). By implication then, it is important to the outcome of an ISD project that those descriptive facts are recorded and organised by an efficient documentation process in a way that supports the ISD effort.

### 9.6.2. User documentation and IS quality

As a category of project documentation, for completeness it is useful to examine the role of user documentation in relation to the quality of the developed system.

User-related documentation includes user manuals, training guides, reference documents – any documentation that the user comes into contact with. Taking the view that IS Quality corresponds to the user-based view of product quality discussed in the IS research literature, as well as by Garvin (1984), in which the quality of an artefact lies in the eyes of the beholder, the user-related documentation which supports a system may be assumed to make a significant contribution to IS Quality. Torkzadeh and Doll (1993) indicate that user documentation does have the potential to be an important determinant of the success of an Information System in the end-user environment. High user satisfaction can be implied as an important contributor to IS Quality.

Torkzadeh and Doll (1993) further point out that many organisations have made considerable investments in IS, and the user documentation which supports those systems play an important role in maintaining user satisfaction. Users need to be able to understand how the system works, and how to use it (Ackoff, 1967) High quality user documentation enhances the value of the system to the user. Yet Torkzadeh and Doll (1993) determined that organisations have, on the whole, failed to provide even adequate, much less high quality, user documentation. Their study revealed that in a traditional data processing environment, only about a half of the operational applications had good documentation. This has led to considerable user dissatisfaction.

The contribution of user documentation to IS Quality is further explored by Fisher (1998a) in her survey of Australian technical writers. She found that in their role as developer of user documentation, the technical writer contributes to the usability of the end product. Fisher (1998a) found that the technical writers' role has been extended beyond their traditional role of simply writing the user manual. These extended activities include acting as a user advocate, writing on-line help, error messages, and by helping to design user interfaces. Such extended documentation activities, with the exception of user advocacy, might nonetheless still be considered 'user documentation' in the sense that Torkzadeh and Doll (1993) discuss. To define the user manual as the only form of user documentation is too narrow a definition.

## *9.7. Appendix G: The Nature and Scope of Requirements Engineering*

This section is included as background discussion only. It is not directly related to the research project but is included in order to place the activity of requirements analysis, as performed in the project, in its larger context.

Leading on from the previous section that considered definitions of software quality, and how IS quality may be viewed in relation to it, this section continues with the exploration of requirements engineering in general with a view to gaining a better understanding of the causes of poor requirements analysis.

In the broadest sense, the literature discusses requirements engineering, as the process of determining what a software system must do in order to meet the user's requirements. While conceptually simple in terms of needing to arrive at a true understanding of the user's requirements, the literature widely discusses the problematic nature of effectively performing this process.

Brooks (1987) indicates that the most difficult part of developing an information system is in deciding what exactly to build. No other part of the development process is as problematic as establishing the detailed technical requirements, including all the interfaces to people, machines, and other software systems. Brooks observes that no part of the work so cripples the resulting systems if it is not done correctly, and no other part is more difficult to later rectify.

Siddiqi (1994) points to requirements analysis as a critical issue of the '90s, questioning the conventional notion that "requirements describe (only) the 'what' of a system, not the 'how'". Siddiqi (1994) recognises the problem that it is often difficult to specify the 'what' level of a system because one person's 'what' may be another person's 'how' and vice versa. This is therefore the challenge that faces the requirements analyst -- to meet the needs of the user while at the same time meeting the needs of the developer.

The conventional view discussed by Siddiqi (1994) that requirements should describe only the 'what' of a system, avoiding dealing with the 'how' as a later design-related matter, relates to this research project in the sense that clear, unambiguous communication between project stakeholders is likely to be a critical success factor in effective requirements analysis.

The view expressed by Siddiqi (1994) can also be related to a review of to Hirschheim and Klein's (1989) paradigmatic analysis of ISD methodologies in which one paradigm Analyst as System's Expert, emerges as the dominant paradigm. The Analyst as System's Expert in general assumes responsibility for determining system requirements. In this paradigm, the analyst's expert knowledge of the user's domain is the source from which the requirements are derived. The Analyst as System's Expert is therefore inclined to take the view that requirements describe (only) the 'what' of a system, not the 'how'.

### 9.7.1. What is Requirements Engineering?

Requirements engineering and analysis is a general term describing all those activities relating to system requirements. The process can be broken down into four interrelated steps (Herlea, 1996):

Requirements elicitation -- deriving system requirements through direct (verbal) and indirect (inspection of artefacts) communication.

Requirements analysis -- processing the elicited data.

Requirements specification -- formalising the requirements into a structured specification document.

Requirements validation -- ensuring that the requirements contained in the specification meets the needs of the users.

Herlea (1996) suggests that while these four processes might appear to be separate and performed sequentially, each of them is likely to be performed repeatedly due to the inherent ambiguity of determining system requirements. Initial requirements may change as the project proceeds, thus necessitating process reiteration.

This highlights Herlea's (1996) point that effectively performed requirements engineering involves multiple iterations of the four stages seen above. It is understandable that this would be the case with a complex and often ambiguous process. By contrast, if a developer does not perform the requirements engineering process reiteratively, then the process is likely to be incomplete.

### 9.7.2. Survey of requirements engineering methodologies

Herlea (1996) discusses in detail the following representative group of requirements engineering methodologies.

Inquiry Cycle Model

Soft Systems Methodology (SSM) and Organisational Requirements Definition of Information Technology Systems (ORDIT)

Joint Application Development

Participatory Design

Advanced Multimedia Organiser for Requirements Engineering (AMORE)

Each methodology recognises that the process of defining system requirements must include significant user involvement. They also each recognise that the requirements process it is also is a cyclic one in which the information derived by the on-going dialogue between the stakeholders builds upon and reinforces the integrity of that information. As a consequence there is no assumption that the process is a quick linear one that must be disposed of before the system design and implementation begins.

Each methodology, with the exception of the Inquiry Cycle Model, extend their activities into the design stage that follows requirements definition. By assuming as a basic assumption that the requirements definition process is cyclic, the practice of proceeding onto design after only one attempt at determining the requirements is avoided.

#### *9.7.2.1. The Inquiry Cycle Model*

The Inquiry Cycle Model proceeds from the basic assumption that the analysis process is a series of questions and answers that form the basis of an understanding of the information needs of a proposed system (Potts, Takahashi and Anton, 1994). This approach has been used in mass-market product development for which there may be no stereotypical clearly recognisable customer. The Inquiry Cycle Model uses the term 'stakeholder', a generic term for anyone who shares information about the system, its implementation constraints or its problem domain.

The Inquiry Cycle Model is an integration of three phases; requirements documentation, requirements discussion and requirements evolution. The 'stakeholders' document their perceived requirements that are then discussed and refined, eventually reaching an acceptable degree of consensus.

Potts et al.(1994) suggest a scenario-based approach to the Inquiry Cycle Model in which the end-to-end process is mapped showing its component parts in relation to the environment in which it operates. The advantage of this approach is that it can give stakeholders insights into the overall process and its organisational context that helps in the refinement of the requirements.

#### *9.7.2.2. Soft Systems Methodology (SSM) and Organisational Requirements Definition of Information Technology Systems (ORDIT)*

Soft System Methodology (Checkland, 1981) is a methodology for analysing the so-called 'soft' problems of systems engineering, including requirements. This category of problem has been described as that which deals with the what of the problem situation as distinct from those how problems addressed by the 'hard' approach to systems engineering. In the SSM methodology, groups of participants negotiate requirements as well as such matters as contractual issues between customers and suppliers.

Checkland (1981) indicates that conventional systems analysis focuses on defining information-processing requirements, yet in order to capture a more complete set of requirements, the broader organisational context in which the proposed system exists must be understood. The soft systems approach recognises the need to consider these broader implications, as does a later development upon SSM called the Organisational Requirements Definition of Information Technology Systems (ORDIT). (Eason, Harker and Olphert, 1997) They do this by adopting a socio-technical approach (Mumford, 1983). Here the system is viewed as a whole, placing it in its organisational context and viewing the user is an integral part of the overall system (Goguen, 1994). System requirements are not separated from their social context. They can only become clear when the system is successfully operating in its social and organisational context (Blyth, Chudge, Dobson and Strens, 1993).

ORDIT recognises also the requirements of the collective organisation as well as those of the individual user. It emphasises the importance of social context in the requirements definition process. ORDIT's underlying rationale is that design methods appropriate to technical systems cannot be successfully applied to socio-technical systems. Equal consideration must be given to both human and technical issues. Successful outcomes of the ORDIT method is the construction of a relevant socio-technical system that meets the 'real' requirements of the organisation (Blyth, Chudge, Dobson and Strens, 1993). ORDIT defines the human requirements of socio-technical systems, and links them to the technical aspects of system design. Christel (1993) suggests that the software development life cycle in which requirements capture is completed before the design stage is no longer satisfactory. Requirements capture and design are now seen to be symbiotic, reiterative in the sense that system requirements evolve with the project. The initial set of requirements may change as a result of later design work leading to perceived improvements to the system. The improvements then need to be fed into the requirements specification.

In contrast to the traditional sequential models of systems development (for example the 'waterfall' method) in which the output from one stage forms the input to the next stage, ORDIT modelling may be started early and continue throughout the development process as a way of exploring system boundaries and in identifying stakeholders.

ORDIT is comprised of four interactive component sub-processes:

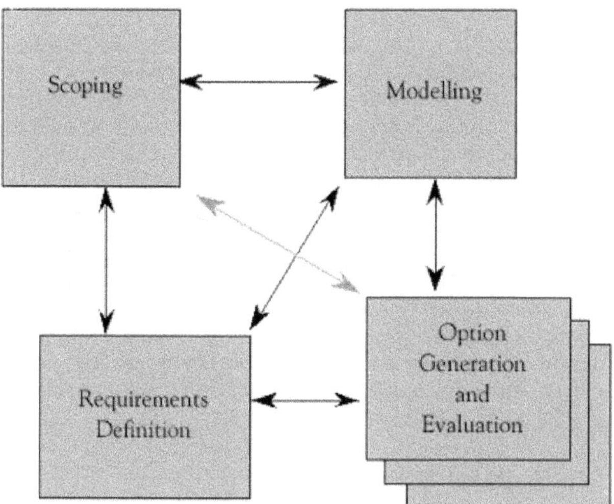


**Figure 6: Activities of the Organisational Requirements Definition of Information Technology Systems (ORDIT) Methodology (Eason, Harker and Olphert, 1997)**

**Scoping** - establishes territory and determines the participants

**Modeling** - represent the current understanding of the socio-technical system by producing a set of models

**Requirements definition** - the reiterative process of participant interaction.

**Option generation and evaluation** - elicited requirements used to generate a possible design into a socio-technical space.

All four phases are typically visited and revisited several times, as shown in the ORDIT diagram above. Policy makers and problem owners are encouraged to participate throughout the design of the system. Problem solvers help the problem owners understand the problem, and the problem owners help the problem solvers understand the implications of possible solutions (Christel, 1993).

#### *9.7.2.3. Joint Application Design (JAD)*

Joint Application Design (JAD) was developed by the IBM Corporation beginning in 1977. JAD is a collaborative approach to system design that became widely practised in North America since the 1970's. The impetus to use JAD derived in part from the recognition by organisations that a high degree of user involvement during development would often lead to higher quality systems (Carmel, 1993).

The JAD methodology involves a structured, controlled session led by a facilitator. In it purest form JAD is intended to support the entire System Development Life Cycle (SDLC), however in practice it appears that it is largely confined to the requirements definition process. JAD sessions tend to be highly structured, supporting involvement by all interested parties. The JAD venue is set up with whiteboards, overhead projectors and flip charts, and participants are encouraged by the facilitator to write their ideas on the various media in the room to stimulate discussion.

In the 2000's, JAD sessions are conducted using Computer Aided Software Engineering (CASE) tools to easily facilitate the production of dataflow diagrams, entity-relationship diagrams, state transitions as well as other diagramming techniques and screen painters. Another technology in the JAD community is Groupware (Mumford, 1979). JAD was conceived as collaborative practice whose object is to enhance the viability of given technical goals (Carmel et al 1993).

#### *9.7.2.4. Participatory Design (PD)*

Participatory Design is sharply distinguished from traditional design methods in which designers have an Analyst as Systems Expert (as discussed by Hirschheim and Klein 1989) mindset. PD began in 1970s Norway. For the first time, software developers worked directly with trade unionists (Winograd, 1996). Its purpose and rationale was to allow the workers to have more influence on the design and introduction of computer systems into the workplace. Kristen Nygaard, who was a well known developer of object-oriented languages, worked with union leaders and members to create a national codetermination agreement, that codified the rights of unions to participate in the design and deployment of workplace systems (Winograd, 1996). But the right to participate in design is frequently ignored and even when it is accepted, obstacles including perceived pragmatic/economic deficiencies and organisational concerns, inhibit the participation process (Reich et al, 1996).

PD is distinguished from JAD placing more emphasis on greater user involvement. This involvement is meant to foster a mutual learning process between users and designers, and to synworke joint experiences into a simulated use case.

Checkland (1981) observes that it is direct action not indirect reflection upon earlier actions that constitutes our fundamental way of being. Developers and users are not subject to the same experiences which has the consequence that they cannot easily understand each other's experience. PD focuses on lower-level end users who are introduced to the developers workplace and who learn about technical possibilities through 'joint applications'. In the same way, during requirements analysis the developers try to collaborate with users in their place of work and both have the potential to be transformed by learning from one another. The developer in PD act both as facilitators and technical advisors to the user, and this can encourage creativity and free thinking among the participants.

Not having a clearly defined structure that must be adhered to, as in JAD, allows PD to have greater flexibility. Users and developers have a shared responsibility for the quality of the requirements.

#### *9.7.2.5. Advanced Multimedia Organiser for Requirements Elicitation (AMORE)*

Advanced Multimedia Organiser for Requirements Elicitation as discussed by Christel, Wood and Stevens (1993) is a requirements elicitation prototype modelling environment developed by the Software Engineering Institute in Pittsburgh. This approach recognises that software systems typically contain large numbers of requirements that are derived from a wide variety of sources and which exist in many formats. This complexity results in a large and unwieldy body of raw data that comprises the basic source material for a given system. AMORE models this raw data into requirements and provides access to certain knowledge about the problem domain. Essentially it is a tool for the capture, modelling, analysis and manipulation of raw requirements data.

Users include such categories as customers, requirements analysts, system analysts, designers, testers, maintenance staff and managers. With AMORE each user and user-type is thought to perceive the raw requirements in different ways. AMORE organises the 'information space' into hierarchical organisational structures, enabling requirements analysis through browsing, navigating and searching from different angles. Multimedia in the form of video and/or audio is stored as segments attached to specific requirements.

AMORE is well-adapted for organising the large and diverse range of requirements for large-scale systems. Requirements are grouped into multi-levelled data flow/control and object hierarchy diagrams. The requirements analyst (or 'elicitor') navigates through the organisational structure in which requirements are located at primitive nodes. Where necessary the hierarchy can be modified by moving, adding or deleting branches as required.

### 9.7.3. Requirements engineering is a process of negotiation

The literature recognises three basic categories of participant: developer, user and customer. Where major projects are concerned there may also be legal and government regulatory people involved. The interactive process that occurs between the participants can be seen as a form of negotiation where users of the system express and explore their perceived requirements for the system to the developer who as the process continues try to validate that they are solving the right problem.

As Koltzblatt and Beyer (1995) suggest, a successful requirements definition is contingent on effective communication between the parties. Those partys' ability to collaborate and negotiate an agreed set of requirements is seen as a critical success factor. This implies that where communication difficulties exist between the parties, the process will not be performed effectively.

The developer's task is to work with the user and customer to determine the structure of the work domain in question. In this sense requirements are regarded as 'emergent' (they did not previously exist), arising out of interactions between the analyst and the client organisation (Goguen, 1992). In a requirements elicitation process no one person has the complete picture (Checkland, 1981); with participants having a limited view of the prospective system. Users may have different needs or priorities that need to be understood by the design team. From this montage of perspectives the developer documents possible solutions to the problem at hand. It is the effectiveness of the relationship, and by implication the clarity of the communication between the developer and customer that determines how effectively the developer performs the requirements engineering process.

Ideally, clear communication and overall good relations between the interested parties makes for a well-performed requirement engineering process, yet the reality of many such situations is that communication is not as clear as it needs to be, nor is there a spirit of collaborative endeavour motivating the participants to perform the process well. Macaulay (1996) recognises that that there is a failure amongst the participants to understand that appropriate human communication mechanisms need to be established as part of the requirements process. If different interest groups do not communicate effectively with each other, each will seek to exert power and influence over the others. (Gasson, 1995; Markus and Bjorn-Anderson, 1987)

## *9.8. Appendix H: What do we mean by software quality and IS quality?*

This section is included to provide background for the notion of usability and how it is constituted. While it is not directly related to the research project it helps to clarify the definition of quality and usability.

This section considers the various models that have been proposed. It begins by considering definitions of software quality, and how IS quality may be viewed in relation to it.

This project is motivated primarily by the need to explore why systems fail. To understand this, we need to start by by exploring what is meant by systems success, interpreted here as software quality.

### 9.8.1. Garvin's high level quality framework

In an effort to arrive at a clearer understanding of the multiple ways in which quality had been defined, Garvin (1984) developed a high-level quality framework that identifies five basic approaches to defining quality.

The first, the transcendent approach, takes the view that quality is an indefinable characteristic that can only be indirectly perceived. The product-based approach on the other hand is highly measurable. Quality is measured by the precise amount of an ingredient or attribute. The highly subjective user-based approach is defined by the user's perception of how well it functions or meets their needs and expectations. The manufacturing-based approach considers conformance to specification and absence of defects to be the measure of quality. The fifth and final approach, value-based, defines quality in terms a product offering performance and features at an acceptable price.

### 9.8.2. What is IS Quality & how is it different from Software Quality?

#### *9.8.2.1. Towards defining IS quality*

In Information and Software Technology's Special Issue on Information System Quality, Dahlberg and Jarvinen (1997) discuss a number of approaches developed during the 1990's for the achievement of IS quality. They argue that no approach yet provides a solution that is detailed enough in either a scientific or practical sense. The existing approaches are limited in that they concentrate too much on the technical and control-oriented aspects of IS Quality management.

Dahlberg and Jarvinen (1997) discuss how the movement that began as Quality Control, which refers to the maintenance of a predetermined level of quality, has developed into the notion of continuous Quality Improvement. It can be seen that most software developers have ISO 9001 certification, yet this alone does not necessarily mean better value for the customer. Dahlberg and Jarvinen (1997) point to the need for a multi-perspective quality model that includes both scientific and practical IS/IT purposes.

The Total Quality Management (TQM) view of quality, according to Dahlberg and Jarvinen (1997), derives from Deming & Juran. The TQM approach sees quality in multi-dimensional terms where quality is defined by gradual improvements (Kaizen in Japanese), involving all levels of an organisation, and leading to greater productivity and profits, increased customer satisfaction and decreased production costs.

Dahlberg and Jarvinen (1997) therefore conclude that IS Quality needs to be multiperspective and linked directly to IS practice. The concepts, models and measures that work in other fields might be usefully applied to the IS field. Furthermore, IS Quality research should be done at real user organisations, so that the results will be both useful and accepted by IS developers. Dahlberg and Jarvinen suggest that when developing IS Quality tools, the important questions are; 'is IS/IT being used to solve organisational problems?', 'can the problem be solved with improved IS quality?', and 'are we trying to improve obsolete processes that should be got rid of?'.

In her 1997 paper, von Hellens seeks to define the concept of Information Systems quality and place it into its organisational context. To this end, an analysis of the distinction and dependence between IS Quality and Software Quality is made. The views of three senior researchers (Professors Niv Ahituv, Burt Swanson and Aimo Törn) are discussed in relation to the three main perspectives - management, user, and developer. In particular it examines how management devises strategies for enhancing both IS Quality and Software Quality. von Hellens (1997) explores the differences between the ontological and epistemological bases of these three perspectives in relation to the way IS and Software Quality improvement is brought about as a dynamic interaction between the IS developer and the user.

Swanson (1997) observes that IS Quality was once thought to have derived from a system's original design and development. It is now recognised that IS Quality is substantially due to how it is maintained after entering production. Swanson suggests that quality can be defined in terms of four dimensions; excellence, value, conformance to specification and meeting and/or exceeding the customer's expectations. IS maintenance is basic to achieving quality in each dimension.

Gillies (1992) indicates the relative nature of quality, that quality is not absolute, it is perceived in relation to its organisational context. Different users within an organisational context will have different perceptions of the same software artefact. The factors which influence the way a user perceives an artefact depends on their level of training and the quality of the supporting documentation (Torkzadeh & Doll, 1993), as well as other factors like how responsive is the IS to their needs (Rainer & Carr, 1992), as well as the user's personality, learning preference and cultural background (Lindroos, 1997).

Torkzadeh and Doll (1993) indicate that user documentation is potentially important to IS Quality because in many IS environments there is a wide variety of applications and the emphasis placed on role of self-training with those application. Furthermore, Torkzadeh and Doll (1993) found that intermittent usage patterns and the emphasis on point-of-need support further increases the potential of documentation to influence IS Quality.

#### *9.8.2.2. IS Quality in the organisational context*

von Hellen's (1997) emphasises that the developer needs to recognise that they are primarily engaged in a service-oriented business, rather than being in the business of producing high-quality software. It observes that in many IS development organisations there is either a covert or overt reluctance to participate with the user in the requirements elicitation, development or implementation of a new system. The absence of user input into this process leads to a decline in use quality (as defined by Garvin 1984) in which users are assumed to have differing needs, and the degree to which a product satisfies those needs determines the quality of the product. The reluctance on the part of the developer to have sufficient user input is often due to the developer having a different view (i.e. manufacturing-based view) of product quality in which quality is defined in terms of engineering and manufacturing practice - usually 'conformance to specification'.

von Hellens (1997) concludes by emphasising the need for more flexible ways of enhancing IS Quality through quality improvement programs.

The differences between the three perspectives and the presence of effective processes which facilitate developer/user collaboration are significant factors in the success or failure of IS projects, as discussed in later sections of this literature review 'differences between IS developer and user' and 'Integrative processes: participative design et al'.

#### *9.8.2.3. Software quality versus IS quality*

Learning to view quality from different perspectives has led to a distinction being made between Software Quality and IS Quality. Software Quality takes a manufacturing-based approach, and IS Quality, which takes a user-based approach (Garvin, 1984).

von Hellens (1997) makes this distinction in terms of Software Quality emphasising the production of the software artefact, while IS Quality stresses the use of the artefact in an organisational context. IS Quality corresponds to the user-based view of product quality discussed by Garvin (1984), in which the quality of an artefact lies in the eyes of the beholder. Quality in this sense is highly subjective and depends on how well the artefact meets the user's particular needs. Vidgen, Wood-Harper and Wood (1993) point to the differences between the production view of IS Quality and the use view by highlighting the importance and validity of user perceptions: 'quality is contingent and resides in the user's perception of the product'.

#### *9.8.2.4. Garvin's dimensions of quality*

While Garvin (1984) does not specifically say so, the dimensions of quality discussed by Garvin (1984) appears useful when considering Information Systems quality in that they help to define the various factors contributing to, for example, the use-quality of a system. From the user's point of view, a system which performs well, has the features they like, is reliable, robust, and well-supported, plus looks and feels like a quality product would be considered a high quality system from use-quality point of view. Garvin's (1984) dimensions of quality are also useful as a strategic tool that IS development organisations can use to gain competitive advantage.

## *9.9. Appendix I: Defining the role of Technical Writer*

This section is included in order to clarify what is meant by a 'technical writer', a term and job function that is not always clearly understood. It is not directly related to the research project.

If the role of the 'technical writer' is so central to the whole research project, it is important to clearly define what a technical writer is and does. As discussed in the previous section a technical writer in the context of this project is defined as a person who produces software development project documentation such as requirements specifications. Examples of other software development project documentation include, but is not limited to, project plans, quality plans, design documents, test plans.
In terms of this research project it is the above specific definition of a technical writer that is used. What follows here is a discussion of some issues that tend to confuse the clear definition of 'technical writer'.

In the IT industry, technical writers are also often called upon to develop non-technical material such as user manuals, on-line help and training materials. Examination of the newspaper and on-line job lists of advertised positions for technical writers shows that this is the kind of technical writing that is most in demand. The expected output of this kind of writer is language that is understandable to the non-technical user. As such it would be more accurate to call such a writer a user documenter, or user documentation writer.

To add to the confusion, the two roles (writing both technical and non-technical material) undertaken by the generically termed 'technical writer' might very well be incompatible. A true technical writer has a sound understanding of technical and engineering matters, and is able to write technical language for a solely technical audience. Such writers have existed for decades in the older, established engineering disciplines such as civil, electrical, aeronautical and metallurgical engineering.

The user documenter-type technical writer may or may not have highly developed technical skills. They may well have a limited knowledge of technical matter, sufficient knowledge to understand the basic issues so that they may be rendered into everyday language for a non-technical audience. A true technical writer may find it difficult to write in common, everyday language. Fisher (1998b) suggests this kind of writer be described as a technical communicator.

## *9.10.Appendix J: Culture as two systems*

This section is included to provide background on the whole, complex topic of culture. It is not directly related to the research project and is provided for background reference only.

Allaire and Firsirotu (1986) who discuss culture in two broad categories; as an ideational system in which culture and societal realms are distinct but interrelated, and as a sociocultural system in which culture is seen as a component of the larger social system, and that are manifested by certain behaviour and the products of that behaviour.

Allaire and Firsirotu, (1986) discuss culture as two systems that can be elaborated as follows:

Ideational system

Culture resides in the minds of the culture bearers. Includes these schools of thought:

**Cognitive**. Culture is constituted by the forms and processes people have in their minds. Their model for perceiving, relating and interpreting external events. That which gives structure to a phenomenal world of forms.

**Structuralist**. Culture is a shared symbolic system that is formed cumulatively by the creative minds of the participants. Universal but unconscious mental processes that generate cultural elaborations and artefacts.

**Mutual equivalence.** Culture is a set of standardised processes that creates the framework that enables predictability of outcomes and mutually dependant behaviour.

Culture resides in the products of minds (shared meaning and symbols). Includes this school of thought:

**Symbolic**. Culture is the mosaic of meaning by which people interpret their experiences and guide their behaviour. An ordered system of shared public symbols giving definition, direction and particularity to people's experiences.

Sociocultural system

Synchronic view, includes these schools of thought:

**Functionalist**. Culture is the problem-solving apparatus for people engaged in need satisfaction. Manifestations of culture explained by basic human needs.

**Functionalist/structuralist**. Culture comprised of those mechanisms by which people acquire mental characteristics (values, beliefs) and behavioural habits that enable those people to participate in a social life.

Diachronic view, include these schools of thought:

**Historical diffusionist**. Culture constituted by temporal, interactive autonomous forms that were produced by historical events.

**Ecological adaptionist**. Culture is a system of socially transmitted behaviour patterns that relate human communities to their ecological context. A dialectic interplay between people and environment.

This typology of schools of thought are derived from cultural anthropology, and is useful in appreciating the breadth and complexity of theoretical thought emerging from this field. They make a useful starting point by which ideas of culture can be applied to organisations to develop a better understanding of the field of organisational culture.

Organisations can be characterised by varying degrees of shared values, norms, roles and expectations, all of which contribute to the organisation's unique 'meaning-structure'. These structures are derived from the organisation's past, the definitions of situation as defined by the dominant actors, and the participant's collective interpretations of on-going events. Allaire and Firsirotu (1986). If organisational culture can be characterised by varying degrees of shared values, norms, roles and expectations, it follows that each organisation will have a unique culture. This implies that there will always be a cultural gap between different organisations.

### 9.10.1. A definition of culture appropriate to IS research

Because the bulk of IS development is undertaken by organisations, as is the case with the research event in this work, and because that development is performed within the context of the culture of that organisation, it seems reasonable to focus on a definition of organisational culture specifically rather than use a more general definition.

Avison and Myers (1995) quote an earlier positivist definition by Schein that they suggest has had the most influence on IS Research, and which in some sense can therefore be described as an orthodox definition:

"Organisational culture is the pattern of basic assumptions that a given group has invented, discovered, or developed in learning to cope with its problems of external adaptation and internal integration, and that have worked well-enough to be considered valid, and, therefore to be taught to new members as the correct way to perceive, think and feel in relation to those problems.'

According to Avison and Myers (1995) this definition is in line with its roots in social psychology, taking the position that culture identifies and differentiates social groups, suggesting that at least some of the time, culture can be actively influenced and changed. Interestingly. they go on to note that this definition is not significantly different from an earlier definition by Anthropologist Ruth Benedict in her seminal work Patterns of Culture, published in 1934.

### 9.10.2. Culture and the Hirschheim and Klein's Analyst as Facilitator

A further, more detailed examination of the Analyst as Facilitator (Hirschheim and Klein, 1989) is carried out in a later section of this literature review. It is notable that Hirschheim and Klein discuss the role of the Analyst as Facilitator to be in effect a "a sense-making" activity. There is no single reality, only different perceptions of reality. What people within an organisation subjectively experience is induced by its culture, or "induced by enculturated habits" (Hirschheim and Klein, 1989, p1204).

Hirschheim and Klein (1989) observe that system requirements emerge as a consequence of that organisation's sense-making activities, their "construction of reality". In the analyst as Facilitator paradigm of systems development, the Analyst should work from within the user's perspective, working with them to derive their real requirements. The differences between the user's and the developer's perspectives are thus merged, alleviating the tension that may develop through there being differing perspectives.

Hirschheim and Klein (1989) recognise the significance of organisational culture as defined by Schein in the sense that they describe the developer-as-facilitator as being engaged in complex, on-going social interactions which results in unique experiential knowledge, or in specific terms, the real system requirements (p1205). This view implicitly recognises the existence of differences perception between individual and group members of an organisation.

## *9.11. Appendix K: Critical review of other research approaches*

This section is included solely to indicate that a comprehensive survey of qualitative research epistemologies has been performed. Action research has not been selected arbitrarily, but on the basis of its suitability in relation to the other methods.

Besides action research, two other qualitative research epistemologies, positivist and critical research, are seen as being less appropriate than action research to this project. They do not lend themselves to the interpretation of subjective data as well as an interpretive approach (Myers, ISWorld website).

Orlikowski & Baroudi (1991) suggest that IS research is positivist if formal propositions, quantifiable variables, hypothesis testing and inferential reasoning based on the results are performed. A positivist research approach is not seen as appropriate to this project since it makes a fundamental assumption that 'reality' can be objectively defined, and that this objectively defined reality possesses measurable properties that exist independently of the researcher.

Positivist studies apply well to the testing of theories as a way of increasing their predictive value, but not as well to an exploration of social phenomena where 'reality' is defined by the perceptions of the participants. And there are as many realities as there are participants. Subjective realities can not therefore be objectively defined.

A review of the following research approaches is made, with discussion relating to their suitability or otherwise to the proposed research project:

Critical research

Case studies

Ethnographic

Grounded theory

A conceptual-analytical study

Mathematical modelling

Critical research takes the view that (social) reality is constructed by a historically constituted process in which it (reality) is produced and reproduced by generations of people. Critical research sees the participants in this social reality as having a degree of autonomy, but are nonetheless constrained by a range of social, cultural and political forces. Critical research has as its goal the identification of the causes of conflict, which inhibit a social system with a view to finding a remedy. Critical research is not seen as appropriate to this research project since it emphasises conflict at the expense of the positive aspects of consensus and collaboration.

Case studies examine contemporary phenomena in its real context when the boundaries between the phenomena and the context can not be clearly defined. A case study would therefore be appropriate to this research question had not the opportunity to test the question directly, as leading change agent, presented itself. Such an opportunity clearly favours the action research method. A case study could also have been completed in the allowable timeframe, unlike an ethnographic study.

Ethnographic research has its origins in work done earlier this century by cultural anthropologists in which the researcher immerses him or herself for an extended period in the milieu of the organisation (or ethnic group) being studied (Lewis, 1985). In ethnography, a distinction must be made between so-called first-order and second-order concepts. First order concepts are the 'facts' of an ethnographic investigation, and the second – order concepts are the 'theories' constructed by the analyst to explain the first-order concepts (Järvinen 1999). One difficulty with ethnography is that the derivation of first-order concepts relies on the contextually and biographically mediated interpretations of the actors to explain the first-order 'fact' (Järvinen 1999). While it is well suited to IS research in organisational contexts, and in particular to the design of information systems, the constraints and timeframe of the research event do not permit an ethnographic study. A suitably complete treatment of the research question would not be possible.

Grounded theory develops theory based on data that has been systematically gathered and analysed. Grounded theory allows the development of a theoretical account of the general features of a topic based on empirical data (Martin and Turner, 1986). In this sense, it is an inductive, theory discovery methodology. As with the ethnographic approach, there is insufficient time to develop grounded theory. The researcher simultaneously develops a theoretical account of the general features of a topic while grounding the account in empirical observations or data. A well-constructed grounded theory meets four criteria; fit, understanding, generality, and control. If the theory accords with 'everyday reality' and has been induced from sufficiently diverse data, then it should fit the substantive area and be abstract enough to be able to generalise it to a variety of contexts (Järvinen 1999). Such a research approach would, in common with ethnography and conceptual-analytical study, take too long with respect to the proposed project. It may be worthwhile approach where a series of action research projects performed that built a body of theory were performed. A grounded theory approach might be applied to this situation over time.

The object of theory-testing research is to try to establish causal relationships that can explain, predict and control the phenomena being studied (Järvinen, 1999). A difficulty with this approach is that it is not always possible to clearly distinguish between what factors contribute to cause and which to effect (Järvinen, 1999). Such a difficulty might well apply to the proposed research project in which the distinction between cause and effect in complex social situations becomes blurred, particularly when in an on-going situation, one effect becomes a cause in itself, which creates another effect and so on.

A conceptual-analytical study is concerned with the collection, integration and systematisation of theory derived from previous research (Järvinen, 1999). A typical form taken by the conceptual-analytical study is the formation of an axiom(s). The propositions of the theory are distilled to a set of basic principles from which the other propositions of the theory may be logically derived (Järvinen, 1999). Ideas arrived at by the application of these axiom(s) can be said to have been derived deductively. Järvinen (1999), citing earlier work by Eierman et al (1995) indicate that a theory is comprised of; a boundary that describes the domain of interest, key constructs within that domain, the values that these constructs may take, and some kind of relationship between the constructs. A conceptual-analytical study would take too long to complete, given the volume of material that would need to be read and taken into consideration. In terms of IS research, a conceptual study might include a broad-ranging literature review in the area of primary interest, as well as surrounding, related areas. From this large amount of information, deductions might be made. It is doubtful whether this approach could be successfully applied to the proposed research event.

Under different circumstances, were more time and resources available, it might be a desirable research approach in that it would allow the large quantity of research in this and related fields, as well as the large number of methodologies (PD, JAD, User Participation, IEEE standards etc.) to be synworked into a potentially useful set of findings.

Mathematical modelling is not an appropriate approach in the social context of this project since one of the conditions of mathematical modelling is that no human subjects are needed (Wood-Harper, 1984). Another condition is that all independent and dependant variables are known, which is not possible in this research context. This approach fits into the third category or 'family' of research approach discussed by Järvinen (1991). As Järvinen (1999) observes, mathematical modelling uses notations that have no direct connection with reality. It seeks to establish a mathematical argument that is 'watertight' and difficult to refute. This is clearly going to be difficult when dealing with people in a dynamically changing and ambiguous social setting, one in which it may very well be impossible to arrive at a set of absolutely correct presuppositions upon which to base the mathematical reasoning.

## *9.12. Appendix L: Comparison between EnergyCorp and one of its competitors*

This section is included as a background reference to illustrate more clearly the organisational culture of EnergyCorp. It is not directly related to the research project.

The technical writer had spent the two months immediately before joining EnergyCorp at a competing energy retailer, doing similar work – that is enhancing existing systems to manage greater volumes of data. The competitor was facing the same challenges as EnergyCorp. It is therefore possible to make a comparison of the organisational cultures of the two organisations, which may serve to indicate what they had in common, and what was different. It is likely that the technical writer's prior experience with the competitor improved his chances of employment with EnergyCorp.

The essential difference between the two organisations was that EnergyCorp had been derived from the electricity board that covered metropolitan Brisbane. The other organisation was an amalgamation of all regional Queensland electricity boards. City versus country basically. Staff move readily from one to the other, such that one might expect a greater degree of homogeneity between the two organisational cultures.

The technical writer noticed many differences between the two organisations. These differences appear to derive from the management styles of their chief executives. The EnergyCorp CEO's management style is modern, similar to that taught by the Harvard Business School. This is characterised by management structures kept flat, project teams empowered to make decisions on their own behalf and having access to the resources they need to do the job. The dress code is casual, and the CEO and his executives are accessible and relatively friendly.

The other organisation's CEO remained aloof. Management structures were more hierarchical. Obtaining approvals was more formal and time-consuming. The dress code was full business attire. Staff morale here was noticeably lower than EnergyCorp's, as evidenced by the number of staff going to EnergyCorp outweighing the number moving in the other direction. The difference in organisational culture, in business terms, can also be seen in the 'bottom line' – EnergyCorp was more profitable than the other.

www.ingramcontent.com/pod-product-compliance
Lightning Source LLC
La Vergne TN
LVHW022312060326
832902LV00020B/3425

* 9 7 8 3 6 3 9 0 0 7 8 3 1 *